AN INTRODUCTION TO
JEWISH–CHRISTIAN RELATIONS

Relations between Christians and Jews over the past 2,000 years have been characterised to a great extent by mutual distrust and by Christian discrimination and violence against Jews. In recent decades, however, a new spirit of dialogue has been emerging, beginning with an awakening among Christians to the Jewish origins of Christianity, and encouraging scholars of both traditions to work together.

An Introduction to Jewish–Christian Relations sheds fresh light on this ongoing interfaith encounter, exploring key writings and themes in Jewish–Christian history, from the Jewish context of the New Testament to major events of modern times, including the rise of ecumenism, the horrors of the Holocaust and the creation of the state of Israel. This accessible theological and historical study also touches on numerous related areas such as Jewish and interfaith studies, philosophy, sociology, cultural studies, international relations and the political sciences.

EDWARD KESSLER is Founder and Executive Director of the Woolf Institute of Abrahamic Faiths and Fellow of St Edmund's College, Cambridge. His books include *A Dictionary of Jewish–Christian Relations* (Cambridge, 2005) and *Bound by the Bible* (Cambridge, 2004).

AN INTRODUCTION TO JEWISH–CHRISTIAN RELATIONS

EDWARD KESSLER

CAMBRIDGE
UNIVERSITY PRESS

CAMBRIDGE UNIVERSITY PRESS
Cambridge, New York, Melbourne, Madrid, Cape Town, Singapore, São Paulo,
Delhi, Dubai, Tokyo, Mexico City

Cambridge University Press
The Edinburgh Building, Cambridge CB2 8RU, UK

Published in the United States of America by Cambridge University Press, New York

www.cambridge.org
Information on this title: www.cambridge.org/9780521705622

First published 2010
Reprinted 2011

Printed in the United Kingdom at the University Press, Cambridge

A catalogue record for this publication is available from the British Library

Library of Congress Cataloguing in Publication data
Kessler, Edward, Dr.
An introduction to Jewish–Christian relations / Edward Kessler.
p.   cm.
Includes bibliographical references and index.
ISBN 978-0-521-87976-7 (hardback)
1. Judaism – Relations – Christianity – History.   2. Christianity and other
religions – Judaism – History.   I. Title.
BM535.K45   2010
296.3′96 – dc22   2009038171

ISBN 978-0-521-87976-7 hardback
ISBN 978-0-521-70562-2 paperback

Contents

Illustrations

Timeline

NEW TESTAMENT

BCE

200	LXX Translation of Hebrew Bible
63	Judea becomes Roman province
37	Herod becomes King of Judea
c. 6–4	Jesus born
4	Herod dies and Antipas becomes Tetrarch of Galilee

CE

c. 10	Hillel dies (*c.* 60 BCE–10 CE)
18	Caiphas appointed High Priest (dismissed in 37)
19	Jews expelled from Rome
26	Pontius Pilate becomes Roman Governor of Judea (dismissed in 36)
28	John the Baptist begins ministry
30	Shammai dies (*c.* 50 BCE–30 CE)
30–3	Ministry of Jesus
33	Crucifixion of Jesus
35	Conversion of Paul
44	James, brother of Jesus, dies
	Herod Agrippa dies
48	First Jerusalem Council
49	Jews and Christians expelled from Rome
50	Philo dies (*c.* 25 BCE–*c.* 50 CE)
	Rabban Gamaliel dies
58	Paul writes his final letter to Romans
64	Persecution of Christians under Nero
66–70	Jewish Revolt against Rome
70	Destruction of Jerusalem Temple by Titus
	Gospels of Mark composed

73	Masada conquered
80–90	Gospels of Matthew and Luke composed
81	Persecution of Christians and Jews initiated under Domitian
90	Council of Jamnia (Yavneh) meets
90–100	Gospel of John and Epistle to Hebrews composed
	Birkat Ha-Minim ('curse of heretics') composed
100	Flavius Josephus dies (37/38 – *c.* 100)

CHURCH FATHERS

70	Destruction of Temple by Titus
100	Flavius Josephus dies (37/38–?100)
c. 125	Aquila's translation of Bible
	Peshitta translation of Bible
	Oldest extant NT fragment, in Rylands library, parts of John 18
c. 130	Hadrian builds *Aelia Capitolina* on site of Jerusalem Temple
132	Epistle of Barnabas, first *Adversus Iudaeos* text, composed
132–5	Bar Kokhba revolt
144	Marcion (*c.* 90–155 CE) excommunicated
160	Justin Martyr (*c.* 100–65 CE) composes *Dialogue with Trypho*
	Death of Valentinus, Gnostic teacher
c. 180	Celsus writes *The True Word*
	Melito (*c.* 140–85 CE) composes *Peri Pascha*
c. 190	Pope Victor I (r. 189–198 CE) excommunicates Eastern churches observing Easter on Nisan 14
c. 200	Theodotion's translation of Bible
	Mishnah compiled
245	Origen (185–253) completes Hexapla
256	Dura-Europos synagogue destroyed by Persians
303–12	Persecution of Christians under Diocletian
306	Council of Elvira
312	Constantine (r. 306–37) converts to Christianity
313	Edict of Milan marks Roman tolerance of Christianity
325	Helena (*c.* 250–330) begins building campaign in Land of Israel
	First Council of Nicaea
330	Constantine moves capital of Roman Empire to Constantinople
335	Church of Holy Sepulchre completed

361–3	Reign of Julian, last pagan emperor
380	Christianity becomes official religion of Roman Empire
c. 381	Egeria makes pilgrimage to Israel
	Nicene creed agreed
382	Jerome (c. 342–420) starts Vulgate Translation
386	John Chrysostom (c. 350–407) writes *Adversus Iudaeos*
373	Ephrem the Syrian dies
c. 400	Jerusalem Talmud redacted
412	Rome sacked by Visigoths
416	Cyril (c. 375/80–444) expels Jews from Alexandria
429	Augustine of Hippo (354–430) writes *Adversus Iudaeos*
438	Theodosian Code
c. 500	Babylonian Talmud redacted
535–53	Justinian Code composed
c. 555	Romanos Melodos dies
598	Pope Gregory I (540–604) issues *Sicut Iudaeis*

RABBINIC WRITINGS

c. 10	Hillel dies (c. 60 BCE–10 CE)
30	Shammai dies (c. 50 BCE–30 CE)
c. 50	Philo dies (c. 25 BCE–c. 50 CE)
	Rabban Gamaliel dies
66–70	Jewish Revolt against Rome
70	Destruction of Jerusalem Temple by Titus
70–200	Period of the *tannaim* and compilations of Mishnah, Tosefta, and various midrashim (e.g., *Mekhilta*)
73	Masada conquered
90	Council of Jamnia (Yavneh) meets
c. 100	*Birkat Ha-Minim* ('curse of heretics') composed
c. 125	Aquila's translation of Bible
c. 130	Hadrian builds *Aelia Capitolina* on site of Jerusalem Temple
132–5	Bar Kochba Revolt
c. 200	Mishnah compiled by Judah ha-Nasi (late 2nd–early 3rd centuries CE)
220–500	Period of the *amoraim* and emergence of rabbinic academies in Babylon
	Compilation of Talmud, and various midrashim (e.g., Genesis, Lamentations and Leviticus Rabbah, *Pesikta de-Rav Kahana*, *Tanhuma*)

1222	Council of Oxford. Jews forbidden to build synagogues and mix with Christians
1232	Henry III (r. 1216–72) establishes *Domus Conversorum* in London
1235	Emperor Frederick II (r. 1215–50) and Pope Innocent IV (*c.* 1200–54) denounce accusations of ritual murder
1236	Crusaders attack Jewish communities of Anjou and Poitou
1240	Paris Disputation. Gregory IX (r. 1227–41) puts Talmud on trial
	24 cart-loads of Talmud manuscripts burned in Paris
	James I (1204–76) of Aragon orders Jews to attend conversionist sermons
1255	Jews of Lincoln accused of killing 'Little St Hugh'
1260	Thomas Aquinas (*c.* 1225–74), whose writings are influenced by Maimonides (1135–1204), publishes *Summa Contra Gentiles*
1263	Barcelona Disputation
1280	Raymond Martini (*c.* 1220–85) writes *Pugio Fidei*
1290	Edward I (r. 1272–1307) expels Jews from England
1306	Jews expelled from France
1348	Jews blamed for Black Death
1349	Death of Nicholas Lyra (*c.* 1270–1349), who compiled biblical commentary, *Postillae*, explicitly quoting Rashi
c. 1375	Geoffrey Chaucer (*c.* 1342–1400) writes *The Prioress's Tale*
1391	Attacks on Jews throughout Spain
1413	Tortosa Disputation
1421	Jews expelled from Austria
1447	Casimir IV (r. 1447–92) renews the rights of Jews of Poland
1478	Pope Sixtus IV (1471–84) establishes the Inquisition
1492	Ferdinand (1452–1516) and Isabella expel Jews from Spain
1496	Jews expelled from Portugal
1516	First ghetto established in Venice
1523	Luther (1483–1546) writes *That Jesus Christ Was Born a Jew*
1543	Luther writes *On the Jews and Their Lies*
1559	Dominicans burn all copies of Talmud in Italy
1567	Jews allowed to return to France
1648–55	Chmielnicki Massacres by Ukrainian Cossacks
1656	Oliver Cromwell readmits Jews to England
1665	Shabbetai Zvi (1626–76) declared Messiah

ANTISEMITISM AND HOLOCAUST

1780s	Anti-Jewish laws begin to be repealed after French Revolution, granting Jews citizenship as individuals while depriving rights as a community
1791	Catherine II of Russia (1729–96) confines Jews to the Pale of Settlement
1827	Law enacted requiring 25 years' military service for Russian Jews
1840	Damascus Blood Libel Affair
1858	Mortara Affair
1879	Wilhelm Marr (1819–1904) coins the term *antisemitism*
1881–4	Pogroms in Russia lead to mass Jewish emigration from Pale
1886	Edouard Drumont (1844–1917) publishes *La France juive*
1893–1903	Dreyfus Affair
1903	Kishinev pogrom
	Publication of *The Protocols of the Elders of Zion*
1904	Aliens Immigration Bill restricts immigration to UK
1921–5	Outbreak of antisemitism in USA, led by Ku Klux Klan
1924	US Immigration Act halts immigration from Eastern Europe and Russia
1925	Adolf Hitler's (1889–1945) *Mein Kampf* published
1933	Hitler appointed Chancellor and legislation enacted to strip Jews of their rights
	Boycott of Jewish businesses
	Concordat between Vatican and Third Reich
	Protestant Reich Church (*Reichskirche*) formed
1934	*Der Stürmer* revives blood libel accusations
1935	Nuremberg Laws introduced.
1937	Pius XI issues encyclical *Mit brennender Sorge* condemning Nazi ideology
1938	Anschluss (unification of Germany and Austria)
	Deportations (of Polish Jews in Germany) to first concentration camps
	Kristallnacht (Night of the Broken Glass, 9–10 November)
	Jewish children expelled from German schools
	Evian Conference, July (6–15): 31 countries refuse to accept Jews trying to leave Germany (only the Dominican Republic will receive them)

1939	Germany invades Poland. Outbreak of World War II
	SS *St. Louis*, carrying 907 Jewish refugees, turned back by Cuba and the USA
1941	Tests for gassing undertaken at Auschwitz (23 September)
	T4 euthanasia programme abandoned
1942	Wannsee Conference and 'Final Solution' agreed (20 January)
	First trains from Paris to Auschwitz (29 March)
	First gassings at Auschwitz (23 June)
	Allies receive details of about 'Final Solution'
1943	New crematorium opens at Auschwitz (13 March)
	Arrest of Dietrich Bonhoeffer
	First Deportation of Roman Jews (18 October)
1944	First Deportation of Athenian Jews (14 April)
	Warsaw Ghetto uprising (1 August–2 October)
	Himmler orders destruction of crematoria at Auschwitz (26 November)
1945	Auschwitz liberated by Red Army (27 January)
	Buchenwald liberated by US Army (10 April)
	Bergen Belsen liberated by British Army (15 April)
	Hitler commits suicide (30 April)
	Germany surrenders (8 May)

ZIONISM

1862	Moses Hess (1812–75) writes *Rome and Jerusalem*
1870	*Hovevei-Zion* (Lovers of Zion) promotes agricultural settlement
	First Aliyah of immigrants, mainly from Russia, begins
1874–6	George Eliot (1819–80) publishes *Daniel Deronda*
1885	Nathan Birnbaum (1864–1937) coins the term 'Zionism'
1896	Theodor Herzl (1860–1904) writes *The Jewish State*
1897	First Zionist Congress. Herzl elected president
1902	Sixth Zionist Congress initially accepts British government's offer of Uganda
1904	Pope Pius X (1903–14) meets Herzl
1917	400 years of Ottoman rule ended by British; General Allenby enters Jerusalem
	Balfour Declaration issued

1921	Chief Rabbinate instituted in Palestine, modelled on Archbishop of Canterbury
1922	White Paper published, restricting Jewish immigration
1937	Peel Commission recommends partition of Palestine into two states, one Jewish and one Arab
1939	White Paper published, restricting immigration and the sale of land to Jews
1942	SS *Struma* not allowed to dock in Palestine, sinks in Black Sea and 770 perish
1946	King David Hotel, the seat of the Mandate and British Army, is blown up
1947	UN establishes Jewish and Arab states, by 33 to 13 with 10 abstentions
1948	State of Israel proclaimed (14 May) by David Ben-Gurion, first Prime Minister War of Independence begins
1949	Armistice agreements are signed with Egypt, Jordan, Syria and Lebanon Jordan controls Old City of Jerusalem
1956	Sinai Campaign launched by Israel, Britain and France
1961	Adolf Eichmann captured, stands trial in Jerusalem and is sentenced to death
1962	Brother Daniel Affair
1964	Pope Paul VI visits Israel
1967	Six-Day War (6–11 June). Jerusalem, Golan Heights, West Bank and Sinai come under Israeli control
1972	*Neve Shalom* ('Oasis of Peace') founded by Fr. Bruno Hussar (1911–96)
1973	Yom Kippur War Tantur Ecumenical Institute founded
1977	Egyptian President Sadat (1918–81) visits Jerusalem
1978–9	Camp David Accords and signing of Peace Treaty with Egypt
1980	Synod of Protestant Churches of the Rhineland
1981	Anwar Sadat assassinated
1982	Israeli invasion of southern Lebanon
1987	First Intifada (Palestinian uprising)
1993	Vatican–Israel accords
1994	Peace Agreement between Israel and the PLO and Israel and Jordan
1995	Yitzhak Rabin assassinated

2000	Pope John Paul II (r. 1978–2005) visits Israel
	Second Intifada
2002	Alexandria Declaration of the Religious Leaders of the Holy Land
2005	Israel leaves Gaza
2009	Pope Benedict XVI (r. 2005–) visits Israel

MAJOR INSTITUTIONAL STATEMENTS SINCE 1945 RELEVANT TO MISSION, COVENANT AND DIALOGUE

1947	*The Ten Points of Seelisberg* (International Council of Christians and Jews)
1948	*Report on the Christian Approach to the Jews* (World Council of Churches (WCC))
1959	Pope John XXIII removes the word 'perfidious' from the 'Good Friday Prayer for the Perfidious Jews'
1965	*Nostra Aetate* (Vatican II, published 28 October)
1967	*The Church and the Jewish People* (Commission on Faith and Order, WCC)
1970	English Catholic missal revises Good Friday Prayer into a prayer that Jews be deepened in the faith given to them by God
1975	*Guidelines and Suggestions for Implementing the Conciliar Declaration Nostra Aetate* (Pontifical Commission for Religious Relations with the Jews)
1979	*Guidelines on Dialogue with People of Living Faiths and Ideologies* (WCC)
1980	*Towards a Renewal of the Relationship of Christians and Jews* (Synod of the Evangelical Church of the Rhineland, Germany)
1982	*Ecumenical Considerations on Jewish–Christian Dialogue* (WCC)
1985	*Notes on the Correct Way to Present the Jews and Judaism in Preaching and Catechesis* (Pontifical Commission for Religious Relations with the Jews)
1988	*Jews, Christians and Muslims: The Way of Dialogue* (Anglican Communion)
	Criteria for the Evaluation of Dramatizations of the Passion (National Conference of Catholic Bishops, USA)
1996	*Building New Bridges in Hope* (United Methodist Church, USA)
	Resolution on Jewish Evangelism (Southern Baptist Convention)
1997	*Declaration of Repentance* (The Roman Catholic Bishops of France)

1998   *We Remember: A Reflection on the Shoah* (Pontifical Commission
        for Religious Relations with the Jews)

2000   *Dabru Emet: A Jewish Statement on Christians and Christianity*
        Universal prayer: confession of sins and asking for forgiveness
        (millennium prayer of Pope John Paul II (r. 1978–2005))
        Central Conference of American Rabbis and Rabbinical
        Assembly Statement

2001   *The Jewish People and Their Sacred Scriptures in the Christian*
        Bible (Pontifical Biblical Commission)
        Church and Israel: A Contribution from the Reformation Churches
        in Europe to the Relationship between Christians and Jews
        (Leuenberg Church Fellowship)

2002   *A Sacred Obligation: Rethinking Christian Faith in Relation to*
        Judaism and the Jewish People (Christian Scholars Group on
        Christian–Jewish Relations)
        Alexandria Declaration of the Religious Leaders of the Holy Land
        Reflections on Covenant and Mission (Consultation of the
        National Council of Synagogues and Bishops Committee for
        Ecumenical and Interreligious Affairs)

2003   Declaration of Joint Commission of the Chief Rabbinate of
        Israel with the Holy See's Commission for Religious Relations
        with the Jews
        Bearing Faithful Witness: Statement on United Church–Jewish
        Relations Today

2006   Joint Declaration by the Archbishop of Canterbury and the
        Chief Rabbis of Israel
        Ecumenical Considerations for Dialogue and Relations with People
        of Other Religions (WCC)

2008   *Revision to Tridentine Rite Good Friday Prayer*, Pope Benedict
        XVI (r. 2005–)

2009   *Revision of 10 Points of Seelisberg* (International Council of
        Christians and Jews)

Acknowledgements

It will be no surprise that writing a book recounting 2000 years of relations between Christians and Jews has been hard work. That it has also turned out to be so rewarding is due to a significant number of people.

I would like to acknowledge the staff of the Centre for the Study of Jewish–Christian Relations (part of the Woolf Institute of Abrahamic Faiths). Many thanks to my colleagues Dr James Aitken, Dan Avasili-chioaie, the Revd Andrew Brown, Lucia Faltin, Dr Emmanouela Grypeou, Jasmine Hou, Debbie Patterson Jones, Trisha Oakley Kessler, Dr Maty Matyczak, Esther Haworth, Dr Helen Spurling, Tina Steiner and Dr Melanie Wright who have encouraged me since 1998. The Centre provides a wonderful forum to engage in the study of Jewish–Christian relations.

I would also like to thank my editors, Kate Brett and Laura Morris, who kept me focused on the task in hand and showed patience throughout. I am also grateful to the publishers, Cambridge University Press, and Gillian Dadd and Aline Guillermet, both of whom have taken a great deal of care in seeing the project to completion.

I would like to acknowledge the support of other colleagues who have been kind enough to offer constructive comments. They include the Revd Guy Wilkinson, who co-founded the Lambeth–Jewish forum; Professor John Pawlikowski, who read through the manuscript at a draft stage and offered wise advice; Andrej Gorazd and Miriam Arkush, whose ready and efficient help in the final stages of the project, not least with preparing the index, was invaluable; my fellow Trustees of the Woolf Institute of Abrahamic Faiths who have given constant support over ten years: the Revd Dominic Fenton, the Revd Professor Martin Forward, Robert Glatter, Lord Leslie Griffiths, Peter Halban, Lord Khalid Hameed CBE, David Leibowitz, Professor Julius Lipner FBA, Clemens Nathan, Martin Paisner CBE and John Pickering.

This book would not have been written without the support of my family: my parents, my wife Trisha, and my children Shoshana, Asher and

Eliana. Together they remind me daily of the priorities in my life and I am deeply grateful for their love and affection.

Finally, whilst many factors have made this work worthwhile, perhaps most important have been my students, who were both the source and recipients of my learning. Much of the material in this book originated in classes and conversations and emerged from teaching at the Centre for the Study of Jewish–Christian Relations, at the University of Cambridge and at the Cambridge Theological Federation.

My students represent the next generation of the encounter between Jews and Christians: they are the scholars and activists of tomorrow – lay and clerical, religious and secular – upon whose shoulders sit 2000 years of traumatic but vibrant history. May they remember that the past only provides a vote, not a veto on our future!

Since teaching is the greatest source of learning, I dedicate this book to all my students.

Much Torah have I learnt from my teachers, more from my colleagues, but from my students most of all. BT. Ta'anit 7a

Abbreviations

BT.	Babylonian Talmud
ENA	Elkan Nathan Adler Collection
JT.	Jerusalem Talmud
LXX	Septuagint
M.	Mishnah
Q.	Qur'an
Tos.	Toseftah

CHAPTER I

Introduction

Since the beginning of the twentieth century, the relationship between Judaism and Christianity has changed dramatically and is one of the few pieces of encouraging news that can be reported today about the encounter between religions. The rapprochement in relations and the development of a new way of thinking were pioneered by a small number of scholars and religious leaders in the first half of the century. However, it was the impact of the Holocaust, the creation of the state of Israel, the development of the ecumenical movement and the work of the Second Vatican Council (1962–5) which in combination made the changes more widespread. As a result, Christianity, so long an instigator of violence against Jews, rediscovered a respect and admiration for Judaism, and the once close relationship, which had become a distant memory, has been to a large extent restored. For Jews, the traditional view that they were on their own and that Christianity was an enemy has been replaced by a realisation that partnership with Christianity is possible.

At the same time as gaining a new appreciation of Judaism, Christians now acknowledge their contribution to antisemitism and the detrimental impact of the legacy of the *Adversus Iudaeos* (anti-Jewish) literature. Christianity no longer holds that Jewish interpretation of Scripture was false or had been replaced by Christian interpretation. This is illustrated by the contemporary teaching of the Roman Catholic Church, which states: 'The Jewish reading of the Bible is a possible one, in continuity with the Jewish Sacred Scriptures [. . .] a reading analogous to the Christian reading which developed in parallel fashion' (*The Jewish People and Their Sacred Scriptures in the Christian Bible*, 2002). The churches are also aware of the intrinsic need to learn about developments in post-biblical Judaism, as demonstrated by the World Lutheran Federation's assertion that 'Christians also need to learn of the rich and varied history of Judaism since New Testament times, and of the Jewish people as a diverse, living community of faith today. Such an encounter with living and faithful Judaism can be profoundly enriching for Christian self-understanding' (*Guidelines for Lutheran–Jewish Relations*, 1998). Consequently, there is today recognition within Christianity that the formation of Christian identity is dependent upon a right relationship with Judaism. Each bishop is now commended to 'promote among Christians an attitude of respect towards their "elder brothers" so as to combat the risk of anti-semitism, and he should be vigilant that sacred ministers receive an adequate formation regarding the Jewish religion and its relation to Christianity' (*Congregation for Roman Catholic Bishops, Directory for the Pastoral Ministry of Bishops*, 2004). Although these are the official teachings of the Church, there remains a great deal to be done before they will have filtered to the pulpit and pew.

For their part, Jews initially responded to the modern changes in Christian teaching about Judaism with distrust; others engaged in dialogue with Christians for defensive reasons, in other words in order to tackle prejudice and antisemitism. There were of course individual Jewish figures who offered a different approach, such as Martin Buber (1878–1965) who reminded Jews that Jesus was a fellow Jew, their 'great brother'. But in recent years there have been stirrings of a new and much more widespread interest in Christianity among Jews, illustrated by the publication in 2000 of *Dabru Emet* (Speak Truth), which consists of a cross-denominational Jewish statement on relations with Christianity and asserts, for example, that 'Jews and Christians seek authority from the same book – the Bible (what Jews call "Tanakh" and Christians call the "Old Testament").' The eight-paragraph statement demonstrates an awareness of a common purpose with Christianity, although there were a number of Jews who were critical of the document. The positive impact of the papal visit to Israel, also in 2000, made an indelible mark on the Jewish psyche.

Of course, the new situation is not one of complete agreement, for there continue to be divisions and quarrels over, for example, attitudes towards the state of Israel and its relationship with the Palestinians as well as its other Arab neighbours. Evidence of increasing antisemitism, particularly in Europe and the Middle East, has also led to a corresponding increase in Jewish sensitivity to criticism, particularly Christian criticism. In addition, the consequences of 9/11 and the upsurge of violence in the Middle East are causing a strain on relations. Nevertheless, it seems clear that many of the main divisive issues have been either eliminated or taken to the furthest point at which agreement is possible. The efforts of Catholics and Protestants towards respect of Judaism project attitudes that would have been unthinkable a few decades ago. Christian theology has been profoundly revised at the official level: all churches are committed to the fight against antisemitism and to teaching about the Jewishness of Jesus, and the problem of mission to Jews has been significantly reduced.

It might be assumed therefore that, because the history of the encounter between Judaism and Christianity stretches over two millennia, it is a well-worn path of study. Yet, although the distinctiveness, even uniqueness, of the relationship between the two faiths has long been noted by Jews and Christians alike, there still exist few works for the interested lay person which explore the variety of aspects that go to make up this relationship. My *Dictionary of Jewish–Christian Relations* (edited with Neil Wenborn and published by Cambridge University Press in 2005) was one of the first works to define the field of study, and this *Introduction* intends to provide an accessible and readable textbook of the long and continuing Jewish–Christian encounter.

It should not be assumed that theology alone provides the basis for relations between Jews and Christians today. Other topics, such as cultural relations, interact and overlap. Take for example Mel Gibson's film *The Passion of the Christ*, which generated great controversy when it was released in 2004. It was not produced within an ecclesiastical context but was the artistic creation of an individual practising Christian. For a number of reasons, including insensitivity to Judaism and the film's graphic and unrelenting violence (90 of the 126 minutes' running time were devoted to bodily mutilation), it raised tensions in the Jewish–Christian encounter. The film was criticised because anti-Jewish features were added to the sketchy New Testament accounts of the Passion, or were grossly exaggerated. Statements in the film, such as that the Pharisees 'hate' Jesus, contradicted official Roman Catholic teaching as well as mainstream biblical scholarship, which depicts Jesus as being closer to the Pharisees than to any other Jewish group. Pilate (governed 26–36 CE) is portrayed not as the cruel Roman ruler that we come across in the Gospels and in other contemporary first-century accounts, but as a weakling.

Gibson indicated that he was not interested in scholarly commentaries on the Gospels to support his own visualisation of the final hours of the death of Jesus. His task, as he explained to the *New Yorker*, was to narrate the story as his devotional reflections revealed it to him. The unusual combination of a cinema blockbuster and personal theology generated controversy. For many of the film's critics, Gibson represented a conscious attempt to turn the clock back to a world before 1965, before Vatican II, to a time before the Roman Catholic Church entered the modern world of interfaith dialogue, and began to engage in reconciliation with Judaism. The film seemed to return to an era when visions of Christ centred wholly on his suffering, to an eighteenth-century period when Christians took it for granted that Jews were collectively cursed for the crucifixion, when narratives emphasised Jewish evil and wickedness.

In Gibson's film, culture and theology came together and demonstrated that it is not only questions of faith that provide the basis for a contemporary conversation about Jewish–Christian relations today. Jews and Christians do not exist only in religious communities – they also live in the world and the Jewish–Christian encounter is consequently influenced by a wide range of factors. The *Introduction to Jewish–Christian Relations* therefore does not only address the theological context, but also explores cultural, philosophical, historical, sociological and political dimensions of the ongoing encounter between Judaism and Christianity. Just as war is too serious a matter to entrust solely to generals, so the encounter between Jews and Christians is too important to leave to theologians.

By its very nature, the study of Jewish–Christian relations is interdisciplinary, and this book features a wide range of subjects. So, for example, it is the author's view that it is essential to include literary studies because a reading of *The Merchant of Venice* or *Daniel Deronda* sheds light on the Christian perception of Jews and Judaism in sixteenth- and nineteenth-century England. It is similarly essential to include biblical studies because a proper understanding of Christian exegesis requires familiarity with Jewish interpretations of Scripture (and vice versa). Likewise, it is important to include the discipline of history since historians are the professional remembrancers of what Jews, Christians and others are tempted to forget.

SETTING THE SCENE: A BRIEF HISTORY OF
JEWISH–CHRISTIAN RELATIONS

In its original form, Christianity consisted of some Jewish followers of Jesus declaring him as the Messiah, claiming to represent the true path during what was to be seen as the last era of world history, and demanding conversion to their interpretation of Judaism. Christianity was one Jewish group amongst many, including the Sadducees, Zealots, Essenes and Pharisees (and we should not ignore the influence of Hellenisers), but only the Jewish followers of Jesus (the Christians) and the Jewish descendants of the Pharisees (the rabbis) survived the destruction of the Temple by the Romans in 70 CE.

The Apostle Paul's missionary work helped spread the Christian movement, while the Roman destruction of Jerusalem and periodic persecution of Christian groups influenced the Gospels' downplaying of Pilate's role in the death of Jesus. Gradually the Church came to view the Jewish people as the preliminary and outdated people of God, replaced by the newly covenanted people of the *ecclesia* (Church). This view deeply influenced the Christian understanding of the Gospels' anti-Jewish passages from the second century onwards, and movement towards separation became considerable. The separation between Christianity and Judaism consisted of a series of 'partings of the ways' (cf. James Dunn), beginning perhaps when the Jewish followers of Jesus started to attract large numbers of Gentiles. Arguments over the abolition of Jewish customs such as circumcision and *kashrut* (food laws) contributed to the rejection of Christianity by most Jews. The main argument over theology concerned Christian claims about the divinity of Jesus. Bitterness between Jews (as well as Gentiles) over the significance of Jesus can be seen in the early Christian writings, and a similar theme can be noticed in rabbinic literature.

Jewish opposition increased when Christians failed to support Jewish revolts against Rome in the first century and the messianic claims of Bar Kokhba in the second. This did not prevent many Christians in the early centuries attending synagogue services, especially at the autumn High Holy Days and at Passover. In response, church leaders such as Chrysostom and even Jerome delivered derogatory sermons and interpretations, which insisted that Jews did not understand that the Old Testament was a prefiguring of Christ and the Church. In the second century, Melito of Sardis produced the first unambiguous accusation of deicide, and later Augustine portrayed Jews as children of Cain whose dispersion and woes were God's punishment. They simply served as witnesses to their own evil and to Christian truth. By the time of the completion of the Talmud (*c.* 500) Judaism and Christianity had fully diverged. It is not coincidental that around the same time Jewish Christianity also ceased to exist.

Once Christianity was established as the religion of the Roman Empire in the fourth century, the situation for Jews became more difficult, though this was a gradual process because the energy of Christian Europe was directed towards defeating pagans and Christian heretics. During this time Christian anti-Jewish writings (*Adversus Iudaeos* literature) resulted in little violence against Jews; nor did it stir much of a Jewish response, possibly because until then Christianity was viewed with little interest. The sixth-century rabbinic anti-Christian text *Toledot Yeshu* seems to be an exception.

As the Church spread outside Palestine it increasingly denied the significance of that land despite the presence of indigenous Christian communities. The Emperor Constantine (*c.* 285–337), however, supported the building of large churches on significant sites of Jesus' life and death.

Monastic orders followed suit and by the sixth century more than 500 churches had been built and attracted each year thousands of Christian pilgrims. Residents claimed that the grace of God was more abundant in Jerusalem than elsewhere and increasingly the term 'holy land' was used. The church fathers opposed Jewish hopes of restoration, and the Emperor Julian's late fourth-century plan to rebuild the Temple worried several generations of Christians, even after his early death in 363.

In the Eastern-Byzantine Empire, the Justinian Code (535–53) removed many Jewish rights granted by previous emperors (such as the Theodosian Code, 438). Severe restrictions on synagogue practices enabled local authorities to outlaw Judaism, close synagogues and enforce baptisms despite some church opposition (e.g., Nicaea, 787). In the West, Pope Gregory the Great (540–604) insisted that Jewish legal rights be respected and their internal affairs not disturbed, but official church protection through the later Middle Ages was more often ignored than observed.

Interestingly, as far as scriptural interpretation is concerned, there is evidence that Jewish and Christian commentators were aware of and sometimes even admired each other's interpretations. This was a two-way process and both Jews and Christians occasionally adopted each other's interpretations. The willingness of some Jewish exegetes to appropriate Christian interpretation, wrap it in Jewish garb and include it in Jewish biblical commentary suggests a closer relationship than might have been anticipated.

From approximately 1100 onwards, as Christendom became more homogeneous, Jews were seen as one of the last 'different' groups, and by the sixteenth century they had been expelled from most of Western Europe, beginning with England in 1290. Jews were liable to mass assaults, as witnessed in the Crusades from the eleventh century and the response to the Black Death in the fourteenth. During this period, Christians were becoming increasingly aware of the existence of post-biblical Jewish writings such as the Talmud and denounced them. This was the time of the Inquisition, the burning of thousands of Jewish books, including the Talmud, the preaching of conversionist sermons at which Jewish attendance was compelled, blood libel accusations and the wearing of a distinctive badge.

Since Judaism was a minority in both the Islamic world and Christendom, Jews were prompted to consider why God allowed these faiths to flourish. One view was that Christianity was a form of idolatry, perhaps not in the full biblical sense but through inherited patterns of idolatrous worship. Another approach categorised Christianity in terms of the Noachide laws, which formulated moral standards without demand for conversion to Judaism. According to Rabbi Johanan, whoever denied idolatry was deemed a Jew (BT. Megillah 13a, a concept revived in the nineteenth century by Elia Benamozegh). Another view, propagated by Judah ha-Levi (*c.* 1070/5–1141) and Maimonides (1135–1204), was that Christianity prepared the way for nations to worship the God of Israel and for redemption. Menachem Ha-Me'iri (1249–1316) put forward the most positive view in the Middle Ages when he argued that Christianity should be understood as a form of monotheism and coined the phrase 'nations bound by the ways of religion' to relax certain rabbinic laws and facilitate a more fruitful interaction between Jews and Christians.

Jews viewed the Reformation as a positive development, partly because of its challenge to the unity of the Church, which at first diverted Christian attention away from Judaism. This was reinforced by the Protestant return to the Hebrew Bible (*sola scriptura*) and some Reformers' awareness of Jewish biblical commentaries (which may also have contributed to a rise in messianic fervour among Jews). The early writings of Martin Luther (1483–1546), such as *That Jesus Christ Was Born a Jew* (1523), suggested a dramatic change in Christian perceptions of Judaism, but expectations were short-lived and the bitter anti-Jewish treatises written towards the end of his life served to reinforce Jewish loyalty to the Catholic emperor. Despite its early promise, most Jews saw the Christian 'teaching of contempt' continue unabated in the Reformation, although John Calvin (1509–64) and Calvinist churches were generally less antagonistic and held a more positive view of Judaism. Calvinism produced tolerance for Jews in the Netherlands and later in the American colonies, where the separation of church and state and an emphasis on the rights of man helped create a more tolerant society.

In Europe, during the dramatic changes of the Enlightenment a small number of Jews, such as Moses Mendelssohn (1729–86), reflected more positively on the Jewish relationship with Christianity. Although Mendelssohn himself remained Jewish, there was significant Jewish assimilation into either secularism or Christianity. Heinrich Heine (1797–1856) famously called his conversion a 'ticket of admission to European culture'. The dramatic increase in assimilation in the nineteenth century was foreshadowed by the French Revolution, which offered Jews equality on condition of abandoning their faith.

A more widespread shift in attitudes to Christianity among some Jewish religious leaders can be noted in the years following the Enlightenment and consequent Jewish emancipation. Reform figures such as Abraham

Geiger (1810–74) and Stephen Wise (1874–1949) embraced the Jewishness of Jesus, and even S. R. Hirsch (1808–88), one of the founders of Modern Orthodox Judaism, argued that Jesus embodied the essence of Judaism. Jewish philosophers such as Hermann Cohen (1842–1918) and Franz Rosenzweig (1886–1929) also made contributions to the Jewish understanding of Christianity, the former arguing that Jewish ethics were superior to Christian (heavily influencing Leo Baeck (1873–1956)), and the latter that Christianity was a pathway to God for Gentiles. As liberal culture spread throughout Europe, East European thinkers also wrote on Christianity: for example, Abraham Isaac Kook (1865–1935), later Chief Rabbi of Palestine, praised Jesus but criticised Christianity for moving far from Judaism.

Jewish views of Christianity were also affected by an increasing anti-Jewish prejudice and the rise of racial antisemitism. The Enlightenment doctrine that, whilst society could be remade, certain people were beyond redemption provided the basis for modern racism and reached a climax in the rise of Nazism and ultimately in the Holocaust. The failure of the churches during 1933–45 resulted in anger towards and distrust of Christianity, epitomised by the radical views of Eliezer Berkovits (1908–92), who argued that the roots of Nazism can be traced back to the New Testament: 'Without Christianity's New Testament, Hitler's *Mein Kampf* could never have been written,' he wrote in 1974.

During the years of the Third Reich, while most German churches accepted the state's 'race, soil, and blood' stance, some churches, such as the Dutch Reformed Churches, began to question traditional *Adversus Iudaeos* theology about Judaism as well as the assumed necessity of Jewish conversion. In 1947 a small group of leading Christians and Jews meeting at Seelisberg, Switzerland called on the churches to revise their thinking and preaching about Judaism and its people. This remained a minority position and in 1948, while acknowledging and regretting the churches' contribution to antisemitism, both the Evangelical Church in Germany and the World Council of Churches insisted that Christians were still obligated to include Jews in their evangelistic work, since Israel's election had passed to the Church.

Deep-seated theological transformation began two to three decades after the Holocaust. Even the term 'Holocaust' was questioned and began to be replaced by the word 'Shoah', which is also biblical in origin. 'Holocaust' is the Greek translation of the Hebrew *olah*, meaning 'whole burnt offering', and its sacrificial overtones, implying an appeasement of God, was offensive to many. 'Shoah' is Hebrew for 'catastrophe' and its connotations of rupture and doubt are often preferred.

Consideration of the Church's 'teaching of contempt' for the Jewish people was put on the Second Vatican Council's agenda by Pope John XXIII (1881–1963) at the urging of Abraham Joshua Heschel (1907–72) and Jules Isaac (1877–1963). This resulted in the publication of *Nostra Aetate* (1965). Both men encouraged church leaders to condemn antisemitism, to eliminate anti-Judaism from church teachings and to acknowledge the permanent value of Judaism. *Nostra Aetate*'s insistence that 'Jews should not be presented as rejected [. . .] by God' was a significant turning point for the Roman Catholic Church and has been further amplified and developed by later pontifical documents. When Pope John Paul II (1920–2005) led the Vatican to recognise the state of Israel in 1994, he overturned centuries of teaching that tied Jewish eviction from their land to their sinful rejection of Christ. Yet at the same time the Church, as representative of God and Christ on earth, is not seen as guilty of any error or wrong. This continues to be a cause of tension when antisemitism and the Holocaust are subjects of discussion, exemplified by contemporary controversies over the role of the wartime Pope, Pius XII (1876–1958).

The Protestant churches in the last sixty years have also come to the recognition that the Holocaust made for ever unacceptable the view of Christianity as the successor religion to Judaism, as though Judaism had no legitimate place or vocation in the world once Christianity had come. Most of the Protestant church bodies have now produced statements, such as the 2001 *Church and Israel* published by the Leuenberg Church Fellowship, that seek to clarify the present-day relationship of their communities with the Jewish people and Judaism, and speak of God's eternal covenant with both Israel and the Church – either one covenant in two modes or two inseparable but distinct covenants.

The Orthodox Church, however, along with fundamentalist and biblically conservative churches generally, did not participate in these theological revisions, and still have not done so. Some churches retain an insistence on active missionary obligation, and both Jewish and Christian liturgy remains, for the most part, unchanged in the light of the modern Jewish–Christian encounter.

Mission remains a problematic topic for the churches, particularly the Protestant branches. The Evangelical Church of the Rhineland's 1980 document was a major turning point with its assertion that Jews were permanently elected as God's people, and that the Church was taken into this covenant with God through Jesus Christ the Jew. It insisted that the Church has no mission to the Jews, and the United Church of Canada has also repudiated efforts to convert Jews since God's covenant with Israel is irrevocable (2002). An ecumenical American scholars' group repeated these assertions and affirmed the redemptive power of God's enduring covenant with the Jewish people (*A Sacred Obligation*, 2002).

As the post-Second World War reassessment of Christian attitudes towards Judaism accelerated and became more widespread, it began to have an impact on Jewish attitudes and contributed to a reassessment of Christianity among Jews. This eventually resulted in the publication of *Dabru Emet* in 2000, a document that explored the place of Christianity in Jewish terms. It represents the views of a significant proportion of Jews in English-speaking countries, although there are also many for whom Christianity is unimportant in their Jewish identity or who are critical of the document (particularly some Orthodox Jews).

THE MODERN STUDY OF JEWISH–CHRISTIAN RELATIONS

Several major themes in the last fifty years have emerged from writings that have explored Jewish–Christian relations. Beginning with biblical studies, modern scholarly works demonstrate a willingness to take the Hebrew Bible seriously on its own terms, rejecting the traditional approach of the *Adversus Iudaeos* literature, which had rendered it virtually impossible for Christians to know how to write an Old Testament theology. It is increasingly accepted that Christian biblical theology can only be developed in dialogue with Judaism.

Associated with biblical theology are studies of the New Testament. Profoundly influenced by the writings of the scholars Geza Vermes (b. 1924) and E. P. Sanders (b. 1937), modern scholarship since the 1970s has emphasised that the ministry of Jesus can only be understood in the historical context of first-century Palestinian Judaism, since Jesus was a Jew who taught his fellow Jews, some of whom followed his teaching while others did not. Scholars point out that Jesus' Jewish followers argued amongst themselves about the conditions under which Gentiles might be admitted to this new Jewish movement and with other Jews over issues such as Torah observance and claims about Jesus. The New Testament bears witness to the disputes, which were vigorous and often bitter, but until recently New Testament scholars had almost completely neglected the fact that these arguments were between Jews, about a Jew or about Jewish issues. Traditionally, polemical passages were read as if they were 'Christian' arguments against 'Jews'. Modern scholarship has shown that to read them this way is to misread them and that this misreading contributed significantly to the Christian 'teaching of contempt'.

Rosemary Radford Ruether (b. 1936) argued that Christology in particular was the root cause of the *Adversus Iudaeos* tradition and that antisemitism lay deep within Christian tradition. As she put it, 'Anti-Judaism developed theologically in Christianity as the left-hand of Christology. That is to say, anti-Judaism was the negative side of the Christian claim that Jesus was the Christ.' Ruether suggested that, when Jews refused to accept the Christian teachings regarding Christ, Christians felt obliged to undermine their opponents' views. This was achieved by anti-Jewish Christian teaching and supersessionist polemic.

One of the most influential post-war New Testament scholars is Ed Parish Sanders, whose work is informed by a study of early Judaism in its own right, not just as 'background' to the story of Christian origins. He placed the Christian–Jewish debate at the heart of academic biblical study. Another important biblical scholar is Krister Stendahl, Bishop of Stockholm (1921–2008). In his studies of Paul, Stendahl maintains that the apostle's chief concern was not introspective and individualistic but historical and communal, that is, the question of how, while the Jews remain within the Abrahamic covenant, Gentiles also can be adopted into it; 'justification by faith' means that this can be done without strict Torah observance. Stendahl argues that Paul's experience on the road to Damascus was less a 'conversion' than a 'call'. As a result of these and other New Testament studies, scholarship now tends to describe the relationship between Judaism and Christianity in terms of siblings (the metaphor of elder and younger brothers being the most common) rather than in terms of a father (Judaism)–daughter (Christianity) relationship.

As well as reflection on the New Testament, the study of antisemitism and the Holocaust is also of central concern to Jewish–Christian relations, as illustrated by continuing controversies over the role of Pius XII. Franklin Littell (1917–2009), a Methodist theologian who was in Germany immediately after the Second World War, stresses the failures of the churches, notably Protestant 'peddlers of cheap grace'. He promoted the study of the Holocaust in the development of Christian theology, suggesting that Christian–Jewish conversation would help free it from antisemitism. Karl Barth's writings are also an important topic. Barth's opposition to Nazism and antisemitism was based on the view that the relationship between the Jewish people and the Church was unbreakable because of God's election of the Jew Jesus, which made opposition to antisemitism the duty of every Christian. He compared Jewish–Christian relations to the relationship between the various Christian churches. Barth (1886–1968) has been criticised for using supersessionist language and would not engage in

Jewish–Christian dialogue. In his view, the sole authority of Christ took precedence over any secular political authority and discussions with Jews were subordinate to this principle.

Catholic writers such as Edward Flannery (1912–98) have also examined the history of Christian antisemitism, and Charlotte Klein (1915–85) uncovered surprisingly fixed ideas among some New Testament scholars, even including contemporary writers, who contrasted law and grace in Pauline teaching and continually referred to first-century Judaism as 'late Judaism' (*Spätjudentum*). Among the scholars whose prejudices she revealed are Martin Noth (1902–68), Rudolf Bultmann (1884–1976) and Joachim Jeremias (1900–79). A similar contribution has been made by Katharina von Kellenbach (b. 1960), whose study of certain feminist theologians revealed a prejudicial portrait of Judaism as the antithesis of feminist values, associating it wholly with patriarchy. The writings of Ruether can be cited in this regard, since she maintained a view of the coming of Jesus as heralding the liberation of oppressed women from a patriarchal, oppressive Jewish culture.

As far as the Holocaust is concerned, a number of Jewish thinkers have been particularly influential, especially Richard Rubenstein (b. 1924), Emil Fackenheim (1916–2003), and Irving Greenberg (b. 1933). Rubenstein sets the mechanical non-humanity of the perpetrators of the Shoah in a vast historical context, on the one hand of slavery (essentially making humans into consumables) and on the other the rise of the inhuman city, where functionaries survey the lives of the city-dwellers from behind closed doors. Rubenstein rejects any notion of God acting in history, for after Auschwitz only human beings can create value and meaning, and Judaism has a particular role in this renewal and reintegration.

Rubenstein's argument that belief in a redeeming God – one who is active in history – is no longer credible deeply influenced Christian theologians, among them three Protestant thinkers who have been described as the 'death of God' theologians, T. Altizer (b. 1927), W. Hamilton (b. 1924) and P. van Buren (1924–98).

Fackenheim, himself a survivor, seeks to interpret the significance of the Shoah, where evil went beyond all explanation. God and Israel are still in relationship, and the Jewish people are precluded from despair or abdication of responsibility. Fackenheim's thesis of a 614th commandment for Jews to remain Jewish and thus not to grant Hitler a posthumous victory gained wide recognition among Jews and Christians, and he called on Christians to support Israel as a guarantor for the future survival of the Jewish people and for Jews and Christians to work together for *tikkun olam* (mending of the world). An example of Fackenheim's influence can be seen in the writings of Roy Eckardt (1918–98) who, following Fackenheim, called for a Christian return into the ongoing history of Israel.

Irving Greenberg developed an interest in Jewish–Christian relations, seeing the Holocaust as an event that needs to lead to the re-evaluation of Christian identity and relations with Jews. His concept of 'voluntary covenant', according to which Jews after the Holocaust are no longer commanded but choose to take on the continuity of Judaism, has been discussed and incorporated into some aspects of Christian Holocaust theology.

Roy and Alice Eckardt were profoundly shocked that the Christian churches had for twenty years remained silent about the Holocaust and continued to remain silent about contemporary Jewish existence (Roy called it 'the new Christian silence'). Only, he suggests, by becoming the younger brother once again in the house of God the Father of Israel will the Church be able to live authentically. With his wife Alice (b. 1923), he pleaded for a 180-degree reversal of inherited Christian theology, indeed a 'starting all over again' to eliminate all vestiges of supersessionism. Both saw historic Christian anti-Judaism as directly connected to modern antisemitism and as providing the soil in which the seeds of Nazism could flourish.

The Eckardts also devoted themselves to interpreting the significance of the state of Israel and vigorously defending it against its critics. As a source of Jewish–Christian controversy, Israel has been the subject of much discussion. The most critical scholars include the Christian liberation theologian Naim Ateek (b. 1937) and the radical Jewish theologian Marc Ellis (b. 1952), who take issue with other theologians by suggesting that Holocaust theology has failed by neglecting to analyse the contemporary use of power, which has now passed into Jewish hands in Israel. Ellis sees solidarity with the Palestinian people as Jewish theology's decisive test and suggests that Jews have to learn from the mistakes of Christians.

A number of Christian theologians have attempted to develop a systematic revision of Christian theology, the most detailed study being by Paul van Buren. In his trilogy *A Theology of the Jewish–Christian Reality* (1980–7) he considers the implications that emerge within Christianity when the continuing validity of the covenant between God and the Jewish people is acknowledged. Van Buren argued that the foundational document of the Church is the Hebrew Bible; as a record of God's conversations with Jews, these Scriptures belong to Israel, and Christians are committed overhearers. Because the covenant between God and Israel continues, churches must reformulate all christological statements that denigrate Judaism. He viewed Judaism and the Jewish people as partners with Christians on the same 'Way' to the kingdom of God. Towards the end of his life van Buren somewhat revised his thinking and was concerned about the dangers of relativisation and the undermining of Christian faith. However, his earlier work has been continued by the Catholic scholar John Pawlikowski (b. 1940), who has reflected on issues associated with covenant, mission and especially Christology in light of Jewish–Christian dialogue.

Other recent studies have also considered developments in educational and liturgical materials, particularly in the United States. Philip Cunningham (b. 1953) has studied textbooks used in Catholic schools and religious education programmes and has also written concise introductions to the Sunday readings (following the Roman Catholic lectionary). Mary Boys (b. 1947) has tackled specific implications of Jewish–Christian dialogue (traditionally dominated by male voices) for Christian education and biblical studies. Her most important work, *Has God Only One Blessing?* (2000), addresses Christian supersessionism and suggests new ways for the Christian message to be proclaimed without anti-Judaism.

For their part, a small but growing number of Jewish scholars have considered the theological implications of Jewish–Christian relations for Judaism. The Jewish community does not subject itself to the discipline of public statements like the numerous Christian statements of the Catholic and Protestant churches. In part, this is because of the asymmetrical nature of the relationship, the history of the *Adversus Iudaeos* tradition and the associated teaching of contempt, and in part because of the distinctive nature of Jewish religious polity, which militates against multi-denominational agreed statements. However, the publication of *Dabru Emet* in 2000 and of the book which followed in the same year, *Christianity in Jewish Terms*, symbolises a growing awareness among Jewish theologians of the theological implications of Jewish–Christian relations. An important Jewish study has been penned by David Novak entitled *The Image of the Non-Jew in Judaism* (1983), which analyses the Noachide laws and the significance of Martin Buber and Franz Rosenzweig. His work marks the beginning of a process that will lead to more reflection on a Jewish theology of Jewish–Christian dialogue.

A notable feature of modern scholarly writings is the increasing number of studies either co-edited by Jewish and Christian scholars or consisting of conversations between Jews and Christians. Among the more significant publications are the dialogue between Karl Rahner (1904–84) and Pinchas Lapide (1922–97), *Encountering Jesus – Encountering Judaism: A Dialogue* (1987), and the study guide of the New Testament and rabbinic texts by

Michael Hilton (b. 1951) and Gordian Marshall (1938–2007) entitled *The Gospels and Rabbinic Judaism* (1988).

Educational centres for the study and teaching of Jewish–Christian relations began appearing in the aftermath of the Shoah, but in the last quarter of the twentieth century their number increased rapidly, especially in academic settings. John M. Oesterreicher (1904–93) founded the first such centre in 1953 at Seton Hall University in New Jersey. His Institute of Judaeo–Christian Studies published an influential series of yearbooks entitled *The Bridge* which explored theological concepts that would inform Vatican II's 1965 declaration *Nostra Aetate*.

Starting in 1973, Christian and Jewish leaders in the United States jointly sponsored periodic National Workshops in Jewish–Christian Relations. To date, sixteen have been held in various cities. Local leaders who had collaborated in preparing for the workshop held in Baltimore in 1986 decided that their combined efforts should continue. This led to the establishment of the Institute of Christian & Jewish Studies, one of the larger such centres in the United States. Among the notable achievements of the ICJS was the sponsorship of the group of Jewish scholars who published *Dabru Emet*.

Since the 1980s more and more university-based research institutes have appeared, such as the Centre for the Study of Jewish–Christian Relations (1998) at Cambridge in the United Kingdom. In 2002, the Council of Centers of Jewish–Christian Relations, representing twenty-five academic institutes in North America, was established 'for the exchange of information, cooperation, and mutual enrichment among centers and institutes for Christian–Jewish studies and relations'. The increasing number of such academic centres suggests that contemporary encounters between Christians and Jews have begun to consider questions that require the scholarly resources of universities; this represents an unprecedented development in the long shared history of Christianity and Judaism.

THE APPROACH TAKEN – SOME EXAMPLES

The thread running through this book is the encounter between Jews and Christians, and it is to be hoped that the reader will be surprised to discover the extent of the impact that Jewish–Christian relations have made on shaping intellectual and religious life during the last 2,000 years.

Needless to say, serious attention has been directed to the relationship during the last two millennia, but the tone and character of that attention has changed significantly since the middle of the twentieth century. In the past it has typically been apologetic or polemical, or else has simply consisted of an examination of, for example, the place of Christianity in Jewish thought, and vice versa. The weakness of such an approach is that, while it may enhance the understanding of one religion *or* the other, it fails to do justice to both. Jewish–Christian relations cannot be categorised under Jewish Studies or viewed simply as an aspect of Christian theology. Although closely related to these disciplines (not to mention history, sociology, literature, etc.), the encounter between Judaism and Christianity must be examined in its own right; nor, while it necessarily deals with the subject, is its principal focus the dialogue between the two religions.

This book begins with an examination of the foundational texts in the formative period of both Judaism and Christianity, devoting the first three chapters to the New Testament, the writings of the church fathers and the rabbis. We then consider some of the unexpected encounters that took place during the first six centuries; unexpected because whilst writings about the 'Other' were generally negative there is evidence to suggest that relations 'on the ground' were far healthier than a review of the religious writings might lead us to believe.

The next chapter examines the medieval relationship when lines of demarcation grew sharper and more clear-cut, especially from the twelfth century onwards. During this period although there were outbreaks of tolerance, attitudes were generally negative and there were numerous acts of Christian violence against Jews. The Enlightenment and Jewish emancipation marked a new stage in the history of Jewish–Christian relations and the chapter ends with a consideration of the impact of the pre-modern period, focusing on Christian Hebraism as well as Voltaire (1694–1778) and the French Revolution.

The final section of the book deals with the modern period – the growth of antisemitism and the calamity of the Holocaust, the rise of Zionism and the creation of the state of Israel. Both developments remain central to the contemporary encounter between Jews and Christians. The last chapter considers the significance of the Jewish–Christian encounter for the wider interfaith encounter, beginning with relations with Islam, the third Abrahamic faith, and also considering the encounter with Eastern religions.

The study of Jewish–Christian relations has significance for the study of interfaith relations in general. One of the greatest challenges of the twenty-first century is to generate an effective dialogue between many faiths. The challenge takes place daily, not only in the seminary or the place of worship but also in the classrooms of the primary, secondary and tertiary sectors as well as in popular culture and in the workings of intercommunal and international relations. A better understanding of Jewish–Christian relations may lead to the realisation that, while Judaism and Christianity are separate, they are also profoundly connected. If this can happen between Judaism and Christianity perhaps it can take place in the encounter with other religions as well.

To give the reader an idea of the approach taken in this book we will briefly examine three distinct topics: liturgy, art and Jewish–Christian relations in the United Kingdom.

LITURGY

Liturgy sheds light on different periods of Jewish–Christian relations, notably the formative era, when Christian worship was rooted in Jewish liturgy since Jesus prayed as a Jew. Even after the Christ event, Jesus' disciples continued their Jewish way of worship in a manner that did not distinguish them from other Jews (Acts 2:42–46).

The Lord's Prayer (Matt. 6:9–13; Luke 11:1–4) is one example of Christianity's origins within Judaism. Even today, it provides a fertile area for Jews and Christians to explore; it has become a common subject of discussion in Jewish–Christian dialogue groups because there is nothing in it that is unfamiliar to Jewish ears. Most scholars believe that the prayer's original form was Aramaic and that it has antecedents both in the Hebrew Scriptures and in the liturgy of the early synagogue. This is demonstrated, for example, by Ben Sira 28:2–4 which states, 'forgive your neighbour the wrong he has done and then your sins will be pardoned when you pray'. David de Sola Pool (1885–1970) wrote that it has an 'exact equivalent in the Kaddish [prayer of mourning], except for differences in person'. The prayer begins with the main concerns of the Kaddish and then follows the outline of the *Amidah* (Eighteen Benedictions): praise, petition and thanksgiving. The hallowing of God's name is an essential part of both the Lord's Prayer and the Kaddish, as is reference to the coming of God's kingdom. The *Didache*, a manual of church discipline from the late first century CE, included the instruction that the Paternoster be recited three times each day (8:2), like the Eighteen Benedictions.

The Eucharist itself combines elements of the traditional synagogue service with Passover and *birkat hamazon* (grace after meals); baptism owes its origin to the purifying ritual of the *mikveh* (ritual bath); the Jewish tradition of carrying the scrolls around the synagogue is mirrored in certain Christian liturgies by processing the Gospels around the church; and, in

Eastern rites, the blessed bread (*antidorian*) is sometimes distributed at the end of the liturgy, quite distinct from the bread of the Eucharist, similar to the Kiddush ceremony at the end of a Saturday morning Shabbat service. It should therefore be of no surprise that the term for 'church', *ecclesia*, like the Greek word *synagoga*, is an equivalent of the Hebrew *kahal*, 'assembly'.

It is also possible to discern the Jewish background of the Christian liturgical cycle, as John Paul II's 1998 Apostolic Letter, *Dies Domini*, acknowledged. The observance of the Sabbath did not disappear from Christian practice and in the early centuries Christians observed both Saturday and Sunday, as witnessed in the second and third centuries by Irenaeus (c. 130–c. 200) and Origen (185–254) respectively. Easter and Pentecost are adaptations, with dates modified according to the solar calendar, of Passover and *Shavuot*. Both the festivals of Epiphany and Sukkot include celebrations of water and light, features that are better preserved in Eastern Christianity than in the West, as is true also of elements shared by Jewish and Eastern Christian wedding ceremonies.

In terms of Jewish–Christian mutual interaction it seems that Jewish liturgy and its Christian equivalent were not, respectively, progenitor and offspring but exercised two-way influences. For example, in the Middle Ages aspects of Purim celebrations were clearly influenced by the Carnival and Twelfth Night. When Jewish communities adopted for their rabbinic texts the codex, they were copying what had long been known in the Christian world.

Mutual influence on liturgies continued in modern times. Nineteenth-century Jewish reformers adopted forms of Protestant worship, including the introduction of a sermon, the use of the vernacular for the service, shortening its length, and the use of choirs. One motivation of the first reformers was to prevent Jews joining the Church, and a style of prayer closer to that of the Church was thought to be more appealing. The new rite of confirmation, of which the name, idea and many specific features were borrowed from the Church, was an early and popular innovation. Permitting men and women to sit together in synagogue was an innovation of Isaac Mayer Wise (1819–1900) in New York in 1851, following the practice of most American churches. The Association for Reform in Judaism conducted its weekly service exclusively on Sunday. During the second half of the twentieth century Progressive Jewish and Protestant groups appointed women rabbis and clergy and used inclusive language for prayers.

After the Holocaust, some Christian rites and texts were revised. Texts that might be perceived as antisemitic, most notably the Roman Good

Friday liturgy, were either removed or replaced by alternatives. In 1959 Pope John XXIII changed the disparaging Good Friday prayer for the Jews (*pro perfidiis Iudaeis* or 'for the perfidious Jews'), ending in Paul VI's corrections to the Roman Missal of 1970 (for 'the Jews, first to hear the word of God'). Thus the prayer, which before Vatican II was a prayer for their conversion, became a prayer that Jews will be deepened in the faith given to them by God. It is perhaps unsurprising that the revision of the Tridentine Rite in 2008 caused such consternation in Jewish–Catholic circles because it appeared to be a step back to pre-Vatican II days.

Finally, although problematic for some practising Jews and Christians, interfaith worship has become more familiar. This is often centred on Holocaust commemoration, although it is also increasingly common practice for Christians and Jews to gather for prayer on special occasions throughout the year.

ART

It might seem surprising that art should even be considered in the study of Jewish–Christian relations. In the past, scholars turned to the following biblical verses:

> You shall not make for yourself a graven image, or any likeness of anything that is in the heaven above, or that is in the earth beneath, or that is in the water under the earth; you shall not bow down to them or serve them; for I the Lord your God am a jealous God. (Exod. 20:4–5.)

This command has been interpreted to mean that Jews and Christians would automatically have opposed every form of figurative visual representation. However, the rabbinic writings make reference to the widespread existence of Jewish figurative art, even though opposing views existed. The Targum mentions that figurative art in synagogues was approved as long as it was used not for idolatrous purposes but only for decoration:

> You shall not set up a figured stone in your land, to bow down to it, but a mosaic pavement of designs and forms you may set in the floor of your places of worship, so long as you do not do obeisance to it. (Targum Pseudo-Jonathan to Lev. 26:11)

Figurative art was also a significant part of everyday life in the early Church. Like the rabbis, the church fathers were concerned about the idolatrous nature of art in places of worship. For example, the Council of Elvira (306 CE) stated that there should be no pictures in a church in case the object of worship was depicted on the walls, but Tertullian (2nd century

CE) states that figurative representation was not forbidden because it was not idolatrous.

Both Jewish and Christian leaders worried about the temptations of religious art. Even though they acknowledged the pious purpose of visual art, religious leaders remained concerned that such art, misunderstood or misused, could become a source of sin rather than edification for those same unsophisticated viewers it was meant to aid. Pope Gregory the Great insisted on the value of paintings on the walls of churches to instruct those who could not read the lessons in the books, but showed his concern about the dangers of these images by insisting that his clergy take care to prohibit anyone from mistakenly worshipping the pictures themselves. Similarly, Rabbi Meir ben Barukh (d. 1293) in thirteenth-century Rothenburg warned against Jewish prayerbooks that contained images of animals, since Jews might turn aside to contemplate the pictures rather than inclining their hearts to God. Yet mutual interaction continued. As a result of their equivalents in the Church, Jewish prayerbooks grew in size, elegance, content and authority and even included prayers for non-Jewish rulers.

A general influence of Christian art upon Jewish is especially noticeable in the Middle Ages when illuminated Hebrew manuscripts were influenced by the Gothic style of Western Christian works and Christian workshops may even have produced Bibles and Passover *haggadot* for Jewish clients. Because of their common Scriptures, Christians and Jews often chose to illustrate the same story, such as the Sacrifice of Isaac (Genesis 22), as we shall discuss later in this book, demonstrating that they shared a set of core stories.

At the same time, it was increasingly common for Christians to portray Jews with negative stereotyping and often with outright derision. Even biblical patriarchs such as Abraham and Moses were given negative attributes. For example, Christian artists endowed Moses with horns protruding from his forehead, which, although originally meant to suggest his honour and power (as a result of the Vulgate translation of Exod. 34:35 that describes Moses' face as 'horned', a mistaken interpretation of Hebrew *qaran*, 'shone brilliantly', as *qeren*, 'horn'), soon came to signify ignominy and even disrepute. The horns on the famous monumental sculpture of Moses by Michelangelo (1475–1564) in Rome's San Pietro in Vincoli may not have been originally intended as derisive, but came to be seen by later viewers as a negative attribute, specifically pointing to his Jewishness.

The visual allegory of Ecclesia and Synagoga, female figures fashioned by Christian artists to proclaim Christian replacement of Jews, and Jews as responsible for the death of Christ, became common in Western Christian art. Later on, the illustrations of popular literature, including the famous Jewish characters of Shakespeare (1564–1616) and Dickens (1812–70), Shylock and Fagin, were arguably more antisemitic than the texts themselves.

By contrast to these defamatory images of Jews made by Christians, the Protestant artist Rembrandt van Rijn (1606–69) was known for his unusually sensitive portrayal of Jews, both in portraits and in representations of biblical scenes, based upon Jewish acquaintances he made in his native Amsterdam. Perhaps the most famous of these is his late painting titled *The Jewish Bride*, which represents the bridal couple with both dignity and tenderness.

In the twentieth century, some Jewish artists took up Christian themes, including the Russian artist Marc Chagall (1887–1985), who included images of Jesus' crucifixion (often showing Jesus wearing a Jewish prayer shawl in place of a loincloth) in some of his paintings reflecting on his childhood in a Russian Jewish village, and the sculptor Jacob Epstein (1880–1959), who adapted the image of the *pietà* (Mary holding her dead son) and of the risen Christ as war memorials.

THE UNITED KINGDOM

Christianity has been the dominant religion in the United Kingdom from the sixth century CE and, although Jews may have arrived in Roman times, the first organised Jewish community only started after the Norman Conquest in 1066 when Jews accompanied William the Conqueror from Rouen. Jewish communities were then established in London – on a site still known as Old Jewry – and in Lincoln, Oxford and some other towns.

As elsewhere in Europe, in the twelfth century Christian attitudes towards Jews grew steadily worse as royal power became weaker and less able to protect Jews. The barons, to whom Jews lent money, encouraged anti-Jewish violence and Christian clergy became more hostile. Popular prejudice was reinforced by accusations of 'blood libel' (the accusation that Jews kill a young Christian boy and use his blood in the ritual preparation of unleavened bread or *matzah* for Passover), which originated in England with the case of William of Norwich in 1144. In 1190 massacres of Jews occurred in several cities, most notably in York at Clifford's Tower, and in 1290 Edward I expelled all Jews from the realm. Despite the expulsion, some Marranos came to Britain and Shakespeare's Shylock was perhaps modelled on one of them. *The Merchant of Venice* depicts Shylock as both villain and victim – an avaricious moneylender and Christian-hater but a man who suffers greatly and is forced to convert.

In the seventeenth century the Puritans showed renewed interest in Judaism, perhaps because of the importance they gave to the Old Testament. Oliver Cromwell (1599–1658), himself a Puritan, was aware of the economic benefits of Jewish tradesmen and allowed Jews to return in 1656. Bevis Marks, the oldest synagogue in Britain, was opened in 1701, and in 1760 the Board of Deputies of British Jews, based on a parliamentary model, was founded. During the tenure of Nathan Adler (1845–91) the Office of the Chief Rabbi, based on the Office of the Archbishop of Canterbury, was established.

In the nineteenth century Jews (alongside Roman Catholics and Nonconformists) gained political emancipation, although the Church of England retained certain privileges. Although delayed by the opposition of bishops, in 1858 Lionel de Rothschild was the first practising Jew to be formally admitted as a Member of Parliament. The same century also saw increasing divisions in the Jewish community, notably among Liberal and Orthodox Jews, mirroring Christian divisions such as those between Methodists and the Church of England.

In the latter part of the century, Jewish refugees fleeing Russian persecution came to the UK and between 1881 and 1914 the Jewish population rose from about 25,000 to nearly 300,000. Nazi persecution led to another influx of refugees in the 1930s and some Christians joined protest meetings against persecution, while Christian missionary centres in East London and other cities provided practical help. (The number of Jews in the UK today is about 250,000, although this does not include those of Jewish birth who have no affiliation with a synagogue.) For example, an Anglican vicar, James Parkes (1896–1981), helped mobilise British opinion on behalf of Jewish victims, playing a leading role in helping refugees escape the Nazis. He was devoted to fighting antisemitism and seeking out its origins, which he found in the writings of the early Church, including the New Testament (see, for example, his *The Conflict of the Church and Synagogue: A Study in the Origins of Anti-Semitism* (1934)). Archbishop William Temple (1881–1944) was central in the formation of the UK Council of Christians and Jews in 1942, and all subsequent Archbishops of Canterbury have been CCJ Presidents and have taken an active interest in relations with Anglo-Jewry and in working in partnership with the Office of the Chief Rabbi.

Mission has often been a controversial topic in Jewish–Christian relations, illustrated in famous and popular works of English literature such as the conversion of Shylock's daughter Jessica in *The Merchant of Venice*. Conversionist narratives were especially common in the late eighteenth and nineteenth centuries, highlighting the supersessionist tendencies of Christian society, and are satirised in George Eliot's *Daniel Deronda* (1874–7).

The Church's Mission to the Jews (CMJ) was originally active in the East End of London, working with Jewish immigrants. After the Second World War, CMJ moved to north-west London, where many Jews lived, and the headquarters are now in St Albans. Today it seeks to combat antisemitism and to make Gentile Christians more aware of their faith's Jewish roots, as well as seeking Jewish evangelism. George Carey (b. 1935), when he became Archbishop of Canterbury in 1991, unlike his predecessors declined to be a Patron of CMJ as, he said, this was incompatible with his position as President of the Council of Christians and Jews.

Christian Zionism in the UK influenced the publication of the Balfour Declaration (1917), which declared the support of the British government for the Jewish claim to Palestine. Arthur James Balfour (1848–1930), the Foreign Secretary, and David Lloyd George (1863–1945), the Prime Minister, saw their support of Zionism as the fulfilment of a historical mission. Lloyd George, for example, was influenced by his Welsh Baptist background, with its deeply rooted, literalist biblical interpretation and interest in messianic expectation. He wrote, 'I was taught far more about the history of the Jews than about the history of my own people,' and a romantic interest in the survival of the Jewish people reinforced his political determination that Protestant Britain should control the Holy Places. David Street, in the heart of the Old City of Jerusalem, is one of a number of streets in Israel named after the former Prime Minister.

Today, attitudes towards Israel are the most common cause of division between Jews and Christians, and, although most churches have made significant efforts to eliminate anti-Jewish teaching and are committed to maintaining good relations with the Jewish community, there is a danger that the conflict in the Middle East may spill over into the UK, although bodies such as the Council of Christians and Jews and the Three Faiths Forum try to ensure good communal relations. In 2006, the Archbishop of Canterbury, Rowan Williams (b. 1950), initiated a dialogue with the Chief Rabbis of Israel and set out a framework for regular meetings in Jerusalem and Lambeth.

Yet, despite tensions, Jewish–Christian relations are primarily friendly, epitomised by joint visits between local churches and synagogues. In 1988, the Lambeth Conference issued a detailed statement, entitled *Jews,*

Christians and Muslims: The Way of Dialogue, in which the Church of England repudiated antisemitism and renewed the wish to purge the Church's teaching of all anti-Jewish elements. The document called for a common mission between Jews, Christians and Muslims.

Recent Archbishops of Canterbury and Chief Rabbis have been proactively committed to deepening relations. For example, in 2005 a Lambeth–Jewish dialogue group was established as a joint initiative of the Archbishop of Canterbury and the present author. Since then, it has been co-chaired by the Interfaith Office at Lambeth Palace and the Centre for the Study of Jewish–Christian Relations in Cambridge. The group meets quarterly and its goal, on the one hand, is to predict and pre-empt future tensions and misunderstandings in Jewish–Christian relations in the UK and on the other, to foster greater appreciation of and sensitivity to the needs of one another.

CHAPTER 2

The New Testament

For Christians, the Bible consists of two quite separate but interlocking Testaments, the Old and the New. The New Testament, the second part of the Christian Church's canon, marks the beginning of the separation of Christianity and Judaism.

Written primarily in *Koine* Greek (with occasional Latin and Aramaic expressions) and dating from the mid-first to the early second century CE, the New Testament addresses both Jews and Gentiles. The designation 'New Testament' can also be translated 'new covenant', which derives in part from Jeremiah 31:31–34. Jeremiah anticipated a 'new covenant', distinct from the covenant at Sinai that the Children of Israel often failed to follow. In the Old Testament the term 'covenant' (*berit*) is usually understood as a sacred agreement and expresses the sovereign power of God, who promises in a solemn oath to fulfil his word to his people Israel, who have only to be faithful and obey. In the New Testament the concept is reinterpreted through the experiences of the early Christian community and represents a new phase in the covenant-story of Israel.

The translation from Hebrew into Greek provided a major challenge for the first Christians and had an impact on Christian interpretation of and in the New Testament. See, for example, the cry of dereliction that the Gospels record that Jesus recited in Aramaic on the cross, 'My God, my God, why have you abandoned me?' (Mark 15:34; Ps. 22:1). The Hebrew text of a later verse from the same psalm (22:16/17) as transmitted by the Masoretes reads, 'like lions [they maul] my hands and feet', but the Septuagint (LXX) has, 'they have pierced my hands and feet'. The difference is caused by the smallest letter of the Hebrew alphabet, the *yod*, which if elongated by a tiny amount becomes a *vav*. In arguments between Jews and Christians, the elongation of this one letter has amounted to much more than a technicality, with the phrase being understood to represent either the despair of the Psalmist or the redemptive voice of Christ.

When the LXX became part of the Christian Bible, its standing in the Jewish community, even in Alexandria where it originated and exemplified the creative engagement between Jewish and Greek culture, began to diminish. Conversely, it acquired a special, even inspired, status in Christianity, and the first generations of Jesus followers read the LXX as reflecting the words of God more precisely than the Hebrew.

THE OLD TESTAMENT IN THE NEW TESTAMENT

According to 2 Timothy 3:16, 'all Scripture is inspired by God and profitable for teaching'. Inevitably the Old Testament, to which Jesus and his earliest followers appealed as a divine sanction for their message, was viewed not only as divinely inspired but as the continuing normative authority for the faith and life of the people of God – a view consistent with the contemporary Jewish environment. The New Testament's use of the Old Testament and the claims made about Jesus demonstrate a deep reluctance to posit any breach between Christianity and Israel. This is exemplified by the Gospel of Matthew, which uses explicit fulfilment citations throughout the birth narrative (with variations on the formula, 'this took place in order to fulfil what had been spoken through the prophet') and gives a prominent place to Old Testament quotations, notably from the Pentateuch, Isaiah and the Psalms.

Although the Church decided that the Old Testament and New Testament formed its canon and insisted on the continuity between the Testaments, the connection between the two was a matter of debate. The heretic Marcion (*c.* 90–155 CE), for example, sought to excise any taint of what he labelled 'Judaism' from Christianity and rejected the Old Testament, appealing only to Paul's letters and to an edited version of the Gospel of Luke. Marcion's teaching became regarded as heresy but residual Marcionism survived in a selective, comparative reading of Scripture, a tendency still in existence today in some Christian writings which depict the Old Testament as presenting a wrathful God of law in contradistinction to the New Testament portrait of a loving God of grace.

The overcoming of Marcion may have contributed to the retention of the Old Testament, which remained for the most part in accord with the Hebrew Bible (Tanakh); the differences were relatively minor and concerned, for example, the order of the books and the inclusion of the Apocrypha. Indeed, when the Church was unsure about her scriptural books it often sought answers from Jews.

Since the first Christians were rooted in early Judaism, it is to be expected that the New Testament exhibits many aspects of traditional Jewish interpretation. Both as an authority for the New Testament authors and as a hermeneutical key for New Testament readers, the Old Testament is indispensable for understanding the earliest claims about Jesus. However, unlike classical rabbinic interpretation, which seeks to discover some 'hidden' element in the biblical text itself, the New Testament, with its eschatological orientation, generally applies the biblical text to some aspect of Jesus' life. This is because for the rabbis the biblical text is primary; for New Testament writers, however, Jesus is primary, and it is he whom the Old Testament serves to illuminate. In particular, the New Testament tends to relegate the Pentateuch to a secondary role, whereas it is paramount for the rabbis. The importance of the Prophets is emphasised in the New Testament, notably attesting to the role of Jesus and the Church, whereas the rabbinic tradition sees the Prophets as speaking to the situation of the Exile and redemption.

Christian reliance on the Old Testament spawned contradictory dynamics after the fall of the Temple in 70 CE, which marked a stage on the way to the eventual separation of Judaism and Christianity. Left to ask where God would be found if there were no Temple, Jews were divided; some found the answer in the Torah as taught by rabbis who emphasised study of the Torah and its application in *halakhah* (Jewish law). They developed an Oral Torah, consisting of comments and explanations on and alongside the Written Torah, the Pentateuch. Others found it in Jesus as fulfilment of the Torah, and others found it in the Scriptures alone, whether the Pentateuch/Written Torah (Samaritans) or the whole Bible (Karaites). As Christianity grew increasingly Gentile demographically, some (like Marcion) with tendencies toward Gnosticism questioned the value of the Old Testament. Others saw it as vital testimony to the truth of Christian faith as God's fulfilment of the promises to biblical Israel. In the *Adversus Iudaeos* ('against the Jews') writings of early church theologians, as we shall see later, the distinction between Christian and Jewish understandings of key biblical texts becomes a defining characteristic of Christian self-understanding.

The early Church distinguished between those elements of the Old Testament that continued to carry force after the coming of Christ and those that were no more than a shadow. An example of this process can be seen in the two main strands of New Testament thought about the messianic understanding of Jesus. One strand emphasises a break with Scripture involving a new covenant with God (Luke 22:20; Heb. 8:8–13). This approach depicts Judaism as an old and superseded covenant. A second strand describes Jesus as a fulfilment of what was prophesied in the Bible, which remains in a typological relationship to it (1 Cor. 10:1–11; Matt. 5:17). What was seen as having foreshadowed Jesus Christ in the Old Testament had become overshadowed in him. Thus, the New Testament reinterprets the Old Testament in terms of the person, ministry, death and resurrection of Jesus. It is both the fulfilment of the Old (e.g., Jesus is a new Adam (Rom. 5:12–21)) *and* the template through which the Old was to be interpreted.

JESUS THE JEW

Biblical scholars have spent an impressive amount of energy on the study of the historical Jesus and much of it in the last couple of decades has revolved around the Jewishness of Jesus. The identity of Jesus needs to be dealt with in the study of Jewish–Christian relations because by definition Christians must take a different position than do Jews. The cleavage between Jews and Christians is determined by the fact that Christians accept Jesus as God's Messiah while Jews do not. Yet in the early centuries the picture is far more complex, for most Christians of Jewish origin remained within the very wide Jewish tent, and the dispute that gradually caused the separation over the centuries was not merely about messianic claims but also (perhaps more) about ritual observance for new members of the Jesus followers.

'Whom do men say that I am?' Jesus once asked his disciples (Matt. 16:13). The answers varied, which reveals how even then there was little consensus over his identity. A brief glance towards recent scholarship indicates that scholars are still on this elusive trail and are as far away from consensus as were the disciples. Yet it can be agreed that Jesus was born a Jew, raised a Jew, taught as a Jew and died a Jew. He was indicted by the Roman procurator Pontius Pilate (governed 26–36 CE) as 'king of the Jews' and condemned to death as such.

There is limited but relevant evidence outside the New Testament. For example, a brief reference in the *Annals* by Tacitus (*c.* 55–after 117 CE) mentions his title, *Christus*, and his execution in Judea by order of Pilate. Suetonius (*c.* 70–140 CE) and Pliny the Younger (62–*c.* 115 CE), for their part, testify to the significant presence of Christians in Rome and other parts of the Roman Empire from the mid-sixties onwards, but add nothing to our knowledge of Jesus.

The only clear non-Christian Jewish reference in the first century is from Flavius Josephus (37/8– *c.* 100) in a famous passage from *Jewish Antiquities*, called the *Testimonium Flavianum*. The *Antiquities* provide rare testimony outside the New Testament to central figures in Christian history: John the Baptist (though Josephus does not connect him with Jesus); James the brother of Jesus; and Jesus himself. In a separate passage (*Antiquities* 20.9.1) Josephus mentions 'James, the brother of Jesus (who is called "Messiah")'. Doubts about the authenticity of the *Testimonium Flavianum* go back to the sixteenth century and virtually all scholars are agreed that the received text is a Christian rewriting. Most, however, are prepared to accept that in the original text Josephus did offer a brief account of Jesus, although a reconstruction of what he wrote is necessarily speculative. The full extant text from *Testimonium Flavianum* reads:

About this time there lived Jesus, a wise man if indeed one ought to call him a man. For he was one who wrought surprising feats and was a teacher of such people as accept the truth gladly. He won over many Jews and many of the Greeks. He was the Messiah. When Pilate, upon hearing him accused by men of the highest standing among us, had condemned him to be crucified, those who had in the first place come to love him did not cease. On the third day he appeared to them restored to life. For the prophets of God had prophesied these and myriads of other marvellous things about him. And the tribe of the Christians, so called after him, has still up to now, not disappeared. (18:63)

There were many ways to be Jewish in the first century. Josephus mentions four groups: Pharisees; Sadducees; Essenes; and Zealots. With which of the groups did Jesus have dealings? The Gospels never mention the Essenes, although the Dead Sea Scrolls (which originate from the Essene community) parallel some of the teachings of John the Baptist, who was executed by Herod's son Antipas (*c.* 13 BCE–*c.* 45 CE), the Tetrarch of Galilee, either because John condemned his incestuous marriage (so the Gospels) or as a preemptive strike against John's popularity (so Josephus). Parallel teachings include the proximity of the Final Judgement and the symbolic use of ablutions to depict (re)turning from sin. Like the Essenes, John was also an ascetic.

Jews referred to as Zealots were active from the time of the Maccabees until the last Jewish revolt against Rome in 135 CE. Josephus accuses them of destroying the Temple in the war against Rome, kidnapping Jews as hostages and killing their own people whom they regarded as traitors. The Zealots are hardly mentioned in the New Testament although Luke includes Simon the Zealot among the twelve disciples (but most scholars are sceptical about whether Simon was actually a member of the Zealot political movement).

The Gospels make clear that Jesus' major dealings were with Pharisees and Sadducees. Both groups were in existence by the second century BCE.

Josephus lists the Sadducees as one of the 'three philosophies' (alongside Pharisees and Essenes). They are mentioned in the New Testament in polemics with Jesus (e.g., Mark 12:18–27 and parallels), and as members of the Sanhedrin that tried Paul (Acts 23:7–8). They became a powerful faction in Judean politics, but seem not to have survived the destruction of the Temple in 70 CE. Sadducees were mainly wealthy aristocrats, but the assumption that they were all priests or that all priests were Sadducees (a traditional extrapolation from Acts 5:17) has now been largely discarded. For example, Josephus, a priest, was a Pharisee. The Sadducees were associated with worship at the Temple in Jerusalem and collaborated with Greek and then Roman rule.

The Pharisees were the only Jewish group – other than the Jewish followers of Jesus – to survive the effects of the disastrous Jewish rebellion against Rome. After the Temple was destroyed, they began to reconstruct Jewish faith and so became known as the fathers of Rabbinic Judaism. Their origin is obscure but they seem to have placed a heavy emphasis on the Oral Torah, as well as the Written Torah, and developed interpretations that ordinary people could observe in whatever context they lived. The Pharisees considered themselves the authentic followers of Moses and Ezra, adapting old codes for new conditions.

In the New Testament, the Pharisees are prominent as the main rivals of Jesus in the Gospel accounts of his ministry, yet they actually had more in common with Jesus than other contemporary Jewish groups. They shared many beliefs, such as belief in the coming of the Messiah (see further below), the existence of angels, life after death and the resurrection of the dead, immortality and a Day of Judgement. There were several schools of thought among the Pharisees (e.g., House of Hillel, House of Shammai), and scholars, especially with regard to the polemical interests of the New Testament, now readily acknowledge the importance of a careful reading of the source material pertaining to the Pharisees. The harsh criticism of the Pharisees in the Gospels is recognised as having as much to do with the closeness and rivalry between the communities in which the texts were written (especially the Matthean community) as with anything that happened during the lifetime of Jesus. To consider that Jesus dismissed the whole of Pharisaic Judaism is to attribute to him an impossibly superficial approach. Indeed, the level of overlap and coherence between the teachings of Jesus and those of the Pharisees probably outweighs the areas of difference of opinion.

The conflicts generally centre on interpretation of the Torah, such as Sabbath observance and issues of purity. Interestingly, however, the

Pharisees are notable by their absence from the Passion narratives. Although Paul of Tarsus describes himself as a Pharisee, it is difficult to establish which of his writings reflect specific Pharisaic teachings.

During the Second Temple period, there were many internal arguments about what it meant to be Jewish. Did religious law permit one to acquiesce in the Roman occupation, or to fight it? How did the law reconcile justice and mercy? These must have been common debates, which one can see mirrored in the Gospels' accounts of Jesus' disputes with contemporary religious leaders. We cannot be certain of Jesus' views, for the Gospels are a highly interpretative genre of literature, coloured by their contributors' and editors' reflections on events that had happened forty and more years previously, in the light of the momentous events that had occurred in the intervening years. Even so, Jesus' attitude towards dietary laws as recorded in Mark's Gospel shows little interest in the minutiae of what they require that Jews eat and drink. This unusual interpretation eventually became common for Christians: certainly the food laws gradually became a thing of the past, as accounts in Acts and the Pauline letters illustrate. Moreover, although Jesus' message of the kingdom of God being at hand was clearly within mainstream Jewish tradition, the christological references about him and his meaning are less so. In addition, he spoke with enormous personal authority, performing exorcisms and forgiving sins.

Yet it is important to know that, for all the differences within the divergent interpretations of Judaism at that time, there was also much in common. Two convictions especially bound Jews together. The first was a belief in the one and only God, who accepted no rivals. God made behavioural demands of his people, so Judaism could be described as ethical monotheism. The second was that God had entered into a special covenantal relationship. In the call of Abraham, the Exodus from Egypt and the giving of the Torah on Sinai, God had elected and chosen his own people.

THE MESSIAH

Naturally, the question as to why Jews rejected Jesus as the Messiah became a fundamental preoccupation of the New Testament writers who insisted, one way or another, on continuity between the Church and Israel. In time, the interpretation of Old Testament texts became the subject of debate because, whilst Jews and Christians accepted that some passages referred to the coming of the Messiah, the latter believed them to be fulfilled by Jesus and the former did not. In addition, Christians referred to other texts, which had not previously been viewed as messianic, to explain why the Messiah, who had been expected to bring a Jewish triumph over Rome, suffered and was crucified. An example of this can be seen in the messianic interpretation of Psalm 118:22–3, found in Acts 4:11 ('He is "the stone you builders rejected, which has become the cornerstone"').

As we have seen above, Jesus shared many of the central convictions of the Pharisees, but the beliefs of his early followers that he was Messiah and Son of God led to a parting of the ways with them, as well as with other Jewish groups, which helps explain why the pages of the Gospels are charged with hostility towards the Pharisees.

There is much debate about whether a Messiah was expected in the first century, and, if so, what sort of a Messiah. It has often been argued, for example by Jacob Neusner (b. 1932), that the concept of the Messiah was not a well-known one in the Jewish world at the time of Jesus. Yet messianic movements are mentioned by Judas the Galilean (6 CE) and Theudas (46–8 CE); in Acts 5:36–37 Gamaliel (the grandson of Hillel, end of first century BCE and beginning of first century CE) compares them with the activity of Jesus. The Dead Sea Scrolls seem to have envisaged two Messiahs (King and Priest), including the Davidic Messiah who would fulfil the prophecy of the Lion of Judah (Gen. 49:10). The LXX understands Balaam's oracles (Num. 24:17) in terms of a coming Jewish conqueror ('there shall come a Star out of Jacob, and a Sceptre shall rise out of Israel, and shall smite the corners of Moab, and destroy all the children of Seth'). These hopes may have been the basis for Shimon Bar Kokhba (d. 135), who led a disastrous rebellion against the Romans from 132 to 135 CE. According to the Jerusalem Talmud (Ta'anit iv8, 68d), the most famous rabbi of his generation, Rabbi Akiva (*c.* 40–*c.* 135) believed him to be the Messiah and linked him to the messianic Star, also prophesied in Numbers 24:17. This background provides the context to the New Testament description of Jesus as Messiah.

The Gospel of Mark begins with the declaration of faith: 'The beginning of the good news about Jesus, the Messiah, the Son of God.' Paul, in his earliest writing, 1 Thessalonians, which dates from about 50 CE, calls Jesus the Messiah in his opening greeting (1:1). Yet only once, in the Fourth Gospel, does Jesus claim in so many words to be the Messiah, privately to a Samaritan woman (4:25f.). On two other occasions he accepts the designation, but on neither does he do so forthrightly.

The first occasion is recorded by the Synoptic Gospels (Mark 8:27–31; Matt. 16:13–21; Luke 9:18–22). Jesus asked his disciples what people were saying about him. He then asked what they thought. Peter replied, 'You are the Messiah.' After this, Matthew differs from Mark and Luke. The latter record that Jesus gave them strict orders not to tell anyone; however, Matthew maintains that Jesus welcomed Peter's statement but then went on (as in the two other accounts) to warn them against broadcasting this view. It is followed, in Mark and Matthew but not in Luke, by Jesus rebuking Peter as 'Satan' for not believing that the Messiah must suffer many things and be put to death. This is a mysterious scene. Did Jesus actually accept the title or not? Yes, though with reservations, if we follow Matthew; in the other accounts, the most we can say is that he did not straightforwardly refuse it.

The second occasion takes place after Jesus is arrested and brought before the High Priest, who asks him, 'Are you the Messiah?' Mark records that Jesus said 'I am' (14:61f.) whereas according to Matthew he replied, ambiguously, 'You have said so' (26:63f.). In Luke's account, the whole assembly asks Jesus the question, which he refuses to answer at all, saying, enigmatically, 'If I tell you, you will not believe' (Luke 22:67f.). Here again, ambiguity and enigma prevail.

Both these stories have been modified by the evangelists. For example, Mark's account of Jesus' frank reply to the High Priest leads the interrogator to tear his clothes (14:63). This is picked up by Mark when, as Jesus dies, the veil of the Temple, separating the Holy of Holies from the Holy Place, is torn in two from top to bottom (15:38). This passage should be viewed as a theological reflection rather than historical record, for it is part of Mark's theme of judgement on Jewish religious leaders for failing to recognise God's presence in Jesus. They, and the kind of Temple religion they represent, are doomed in Mark's opinion (he was probably writing around the time the Roman army destroyed the Temple in 70 CE).

The puzzling fact that Jesus was early on called Messiah, yet seems to have used the term of himself only cautiously and rarely, if at all, is compounded when we look at the world of Judaism in his day. Popular imagination holds that many people believed in a coming Messiah, but the evidence suggests that some did whereas others did not. Some scholars believe that the titles 'Son of Man' and 'Son of God' shed light on Jesus' messiahship. 'Son of man' has its origin in a christological explanation of Daniel 7:13 where it refers to a vision of a figure 'like a son of man' coming with the clouds to the Ancient of Days (God). Here the term should be understood as apocalyptic, rather than messianic.

However, 'Son of God' is likely to have been a messianic title (on the basis of 2 Sam. 7:14 and Ps. 2:7 and their interpretation in Qumran). In Jewish tradition, 'son of God' was used to refer to the people of Israel and was associated with election and obedience. In Christianity, 'Son of God' as a title for Jesus has been used to express Jesus' divinity and his special relationship with God. Interestingly, Rabbinic Judaism seems to have deliberately avoided the term 'son of God', perhaps because Christians made extensive use of this concept in their christological reflection.

One important story indicates that Jesus did believe he was the Messiah: his entry into Jerusalem at the beginning of the last week of his life (Mark 11:1–10; Matt. 21:1–11; Luke 19:28–38). Scholars accept the historicity of this account because it is similarly recorded by all the Gospels, although Bultmann warns about its 'fairy tale motif'. The description of the entry is both messianic and kingly. For example, the journey from the Mount of Olives is reminiscent of the expected Last Days (Zech. 14:1–4). Matthew certainly understands Jesus' entry in this way, as his quotation of Zechariah 9:9 makes clear ('Say to the Daughter of Zion, "See, your king comes to you, gentle and riding on a donkey, on a colt, the foal of a donkey"'), but all the Gospels identify Jesus as king whose actions legitimate his claim to authority. The cries of 'hosanna ['help' or 'save now'] to the son of David' also indicate that Jesus' entry was viewed by the crowds as the entry of a king and Messiah, who was expected to redeem his people.

POLEMIC

The problem of polemic provides one of the major challenges in the study of Jewish–Christian relations. The traditional Christian teaching of contempt ('enseignement du mépris', a term coined by Jules Isaac, a French historian who explored the Christian roots of antisemitism) of Jews and Judaism fostered an abuse of the Scriptures, both Old and New, and has been used to justify antisemitism. It is undeniable that some Christian biblical interpretation has promoted hatred, discrimination and superiority. However, is antisemitism to be found in the pages of the New Testament?

This question is complicated by the fact that Jesus was a Jew who taught his fellow Jews, some of whom followed his teaching while others did not. Most of his contemporaries, of course, had never heard of him. After his death, his Jewish followers, encouraged by their experience of the resurrection, argued for the validity of his teaching and their own, against their fellow Jews who had not been persuaded. To complicate the position even further, Jesus' Jewish followers argued amongst themselves about the conditions under which Gentiles might be admitted to this new Jewish movement. In addition, some of the Jewish communities within the Jesus movement – with or without Gentile members – found themselves further at odds with other Jews over issues such as Torah observance and claims about Jesus.

The New Testament bears witness to the debates and arguments that were taking place. These disputes were serious, vigorous and often bitter. Nevertheless, what has often been forgotten or neglected is the fact that the arguments were primarily between Jews, about a Jew or about Jewish issues (even when they concerned Gentile converts). The problem of polemic is magnified when New Testament passages are read as if they were 'Christian' arguments against Jews. To read them this way is to misread them and to ignore the context of the ministry of the earthly Jesus: first-century Palestinian Judaism.

This misreading contributed to the development of the 'teaching of contempt', which will be explored in more detail in the next chapter, on the writings of the church fathers. Yet the Christian Bible shares an intrinsic problem that is common to the Jewish Tanakh (and the Qur'an), namely that polemic, against a named other, once enshrined in documents venerated as Scripture, carries a weight and authority throughout history. Moreover, they are constantly available for use or abuse, to justify the most appalling actions in the name of God. Their very existence is and remains the problem for they cannot simply be expurgated or interpreted out of existence.

However, the polemic can be addressed and the dangers reduced. For example, it can be useful to juxtapose texts from the same Scripture that offer a contrasting approach. When dealing with New Testament accounts of abrasive arguments between Jesus and the Pharisees one might turn to passages that demonstrate their close relationship, such as Luke 13:1. One might compare verses such as 'No-one comes to the Father except through Me' (John 14:6) or 'nor is there salvation in any other, for there is no other name under heaven given among men by which we must be saved' (Acts 4:12) with passages such as 'Other sheep I have which are not of this fold' (John 10:16).

Nevertheless, this approach removes neither the existence of problematic texts, nor their availability. They can always return to haunt the inheritors of such revelations and provide potential new victims, despite the worthiest of efforts. In other words, whilst contextualisation is essential in understanding and re-interpreting a text, it will not erase the polemic.

Thus, although reading difficult texts within their proper historical context will help to avoid 'false' readings – for it *does* make a difference if the reader understands something of the background and develops a keener awareness of the context from which these texts came – this cannot always render a text innocent. The text's original context is not the only necessary source of its meaning or effect. To 'solve' the problem at a historical level does not change the history of a text's effect and interpretation. One of the achievements of the study of Jewish–Christian relations has been the realisation that texts have a history; and a compromised history at that. It is impossible to read the Passion narratives of the Gospels without recognising the antisemitic uses to which past readings of them have been put. When Matthew wrote: 'And all the people answered, "His blood be on us and on our children!" ' (27:25), Jews and Christians struggle to read them from their perspective, not his. Sometimes, then, they have dealt with (meaning, in practice: rejected) long-held readings that have been death-dealing, not life-giving.

The 'history of effects' of texts represents a shift away from the traditional historical critical quest for the original meaning of an original text, towards its reception history (*Wirkungsgeschichte*), that is to say, the history of its impact on Jewish–Christian relations. It is one of the striking features of powerful texts, that they can be read anew in new contexts – for good of course, but also for ill. Even if texts can be found to be part of an intra-Jewish debate *then*, this is not how they have always been read since and not how, in some places, they are still read now.

THE TRIAL NARRATIVES

One particular collection of problematic texts in the New Testament is the portrayal of the events that led to Jesus' death, interpretations of which have fuelled generations of Christian hostility against Jews and the charge of 'Christ-killers'. In general, the Gospels tend to exaggerate the responsibility of the Jewish leaders in Jesus' death and to exculpate Pilate and the Romans in their record of the trial narratives.

Jesus is charged with one offence (a threat to destroy the Temple) of which he is acquitted, but his answers lead to another charge being laid against him – that of blasphemy – of which he is convicted. This, anyway, is how the four evangelists tell it. They clearly do not have access to an accurate record of the proceedings and, in their attempt to provide a comprehensive defence of the accused in the minds of their readers, they are apt to take on other roles in the drama, including those of the prosecution and even that of framing the charge.

There are many strange aspects to this account. Firstly, in a Jewish context the claim to be 'Son of the Blessed' (i.e., God) or to be the Messiah is not blasphemous. Jesus' claim to be the latter is, as we have seen, ambiguous: and historically we know that there were Jews who did make this claim both before and after Jesus, but no record that contemporary Jews considered this blasphemous. More to the point was whether the Romans would consider his claims and actions to be a political threat.

Secondly, the circumstances of the trial appear to be troublesome to the narrators, who present the Roman authority, Pilate, as being very uneasy about condemning Jesus to death and finding it hard to believe that he is guilty of the crime of subversion, or that he constitutes any threat to the Roman administration. This is a strange feature of the presentation because, according to Philo of Alexandria (*c.* 25 BCE–*c.* 50 CE) and Josephus, Pilate was a despotic and ruthless dictator, who was forced to resign from office. Luke similarly mentions 'the Galileans, whose blood Pilate mingled with their sacrifice' (Luke 13:1–4), but most Christian sources seek to absolve him from blame for the death of Jesus. This tendency can certainly be detected in the Gospels but, to a much larger extent, in later writings such as the Gospel of Peter, where 'the Jews' not only wish to see Jesus dead but are also responsible for the actual execution. Most scholars understand this as an attempt to present the Christian message as in no way threatening to the Roman authorities.

According to the Gospel of John, Jesus' trial consisted of a single appearance before two chief priests, whereas the Synoptic version has two trials: a religious trial before the chief priests and the whole Council and a political trial before the Roman Governor. The charge brought against Jesus in the Roman trial is that he claimed to be 'King of the Jews', a title that may suggest his perceived role as leader of the resistance. It was, therefore, a political charge of sedition against Rome.

According to Mark's Gospel, Jesus is brought before a court consisting of the High Priest with all the chief priests and the elders and scribes. Witnesses are brought who say they heard Jesus declare, 'I will destroy this Temple that is made with hands and in three days I will build another not made with hands.' However, the witnesses are 'false', according to Mark, and their testimony does not agree, so the charge fails. Jesus is then questioned by the High Priest who asks him, 'Are you the Christ, the Son of the Blessed?' Jesus replies that he is, and that 'you will see the Son of Man seated at the right hand of Power, and coming with the clouds of heaven' (Matt. 14:62). To this the High Priest responds by tearing his garments and declaring that a blasphemy has been committed and no more witnesses are needed; the whole court then declares the prisoner to be deserving of death.

Matthew's account of this stage of the trial is fairly similar to Mark's. Luke on the other hand makes no mention of the charge about destroying the Temple. This omission may reflect his concern that Christians should not be associated in the minds of Gentile authorities with any kind of political insurrection. Also, Luke's Jesus is unwilling to state that he is the Messiah, saying, 'If I tell you, you will not believe' (Luke 22:67).

At the time the Synoptic Gospels were being written, the Temple had just been (or in the case of Mark was just about to be) destroyed by the Romans, a highly significant issue for the Gospel writers. In the trial narratives, witnesses claim that Jesus threatened to destroy the Temple, but the evangelists claim that he only predicted that the Temple would be destroyed (e.g., Matt. 24:1–2). They want to stress that Jesus predicted this momentous event, but at the same time shield him from the accusation that he was personally involved in a threat of its destruction in order to disassociate him in the minds of the authorities from any kind of insurrection.

But according to E. P. Sanders the question of the charge of destroying the Temple should not be so easily set aside. Both Matthew and Mark record that passers-by at his crucifixion jeer at Jesus for his claim to destroy the Temple. All four Gospels record that Jesus caused tumult in the Temple, making accusations and overturning the tables of the money-changers (a scene described as the 'cleansing' of the Temple). Sanders and J. D. G. Dunn (b. 1939) are among commentators who suggest this is the central issue for the chief priests as the guardians of an economy built around the Temple. According to Sanders, Jesus may have been staging a symbolic destruction because he believed (as did the Essenes and the Zealots) that destruction was to take place after which the Temple would be radically transformed.

It is significant that the Pharisees are entirely absent from this story, and furthermore it is likely that the chief priests, who would have been Sadducees, would have been most disturbed by Jesus' action in the Temple. Although he was not the only charismatic Jewish preacher to be executed during Rome's occupation of Palestine, the Roman and Jewish establishment feared Jesus: he represented a disruption of public order and threatened subsequent Roman reprisals. And he associated freely with the outcasts of society – lepers, prostitutes, the poor and collaborators with the Roman regime (e.g., tax collectors). These would not have been well received by the religious authorities.

But what actually happened was different and the evangelists' concern, writing nearly half a century later, was that Jesus in their story should testify to his status as it was now being perceived in the Christology of the developing Christian community – a community in fierce competition with the Jewish community that survived the destruction of 70 CE. This must have presented quite a difficult literary and theological problem. For the Romans, one might say it was all a much simpler matter: had there been an offence against public order that was sufficiently serious to warrant taking punitive action? Was there any kind of threat to their political authority?

This attempt to underscore Jewish responsibility for the death of Jesus is evident in all four Gospels. Matthew has Pilate convinced of Jesus' innocence and, in a detail that is unique to Matthew, he receives a message from his wife who on the basis of a dream warns him to have nothing to do with the charge against Jesus. Pilate, however, realises he faces a riot and gives in to pressure from Jews to have Jesus crucified, while publicly washing his hands of the whole affair. But at this point we have Matthew attribute to the people as a whole (albeit persuaded by the priests) the notorious statement, 'His blood be on us and on our children' (27:25), which has played such a fateful role in the history of Jewish–Christian relations.

In Luke there is no record of any charges connected with the Temple, but the charge has been filled out in other respects. The authorities report to Pilate that Jesus has been 'perverting our nation, forbidding us to give tribute to Caesar and saying that he himself is a king'. Luke implicates 'the people' more deeply than his fellow evangelists.

In John's Gospel, the focus of his attention is intensely christological and this colours his account of the trial. Pilate questions Jesus, stating that it is the Jewish authorities who are pressing for action, and, in response to the 'King of the Jews' claim, Jesus stresses to Pilate that his kingdom is 'not of this world' which is why he has no forces to command. But he strongly affirms that he is indeed a king (in contrast to his answers in the Synoptic Gospels) and makes the extraordinary statement (John 19:11) that Pilate has 'no power' except what is given him from above. Pilate appears impatient with this talk and says that, as far as he can see, Jesus is innocent. As in the Synoptics he offers a choice of Jesus or Barabbas according to the custom whereby one prisoner can be freed at Passover. But the crowd opts for Barabbas. We have no extra-biblical corroborating evidence for this custom, although we cannot rule out the possibility of an occasional incidence of amnesty granted. The intended irony indicated by the confusion of names, 'Jesus Barabbas or Jesus who is called Messiah' (Matt. 27:17), suggests redactional intent. Finally, on the sixth hour of the Day of Preparation (John's time scheme also differs from the Synoptics'),

Pilate passes sentence on Jesus and then, so we are told, hands him over to the chief priests for crucifixion. (John 19:16). John leaves us in no doubt about who it is he thinks bears responsibility for the death of Jesus.

In sum, the trial of Jesus as recounted in the four Gospels is a very strange affair. It involves a conviction of Jesus for blasphemy by Jews who could hardly have construed his claims as blasphemy at the time, and his sentencing to death by Romans who, according to the evangelists, did not find him guilty of any crime against the state. Yet no other account of a trial has had such a far-reaching and fateful effect on history as this one. The trial is not just a defence of Jesus' innocence but also a prosecution of Jews, the contemporary rivals of the evangelists' communities (especially that of Matthew). The writing of the Gospels represents a time of great bitterness in relations between the nascent Christian community and the rest of the Jewish community who were engaged in redefining and consolidating Judaism in the wake of the war against Rome.

PAUL

As the first Christian missionary to the Gentile world, Paul has played a unique role in Jewish–Christian relations. Convinced that God had called Gentiles to be members of his people, Paul insisted that what had happened through the death and resurrection of Christ was the fulfilment of God's promises to Israel. The passionate zeal and intellectual strength of Saul of Tarsus helped Christianity flourish but, tragically, later generations read his letters out of context, and so lost sight of his emphasis on continuity, instead interpreting his words as an attack on Judaism.

Paul's identity was that of a Jew who, through a variety of circumstances, came to the conviction that Jesus was the Messiah. According to Luke, he was present at the stoning of Stephen, and he himself testifies that, in his religious zeal, he did not hesitate to persecute Christians (Gal. 1:13). While on his way to Damascus, Paul had a transforming experience when he had a vision of Jesus and converted to become a follower.

Some scholars have tried to understand Paul on the basis of Stoic and Cynic trends, rather than from the perspective of Judaism. However, Paul writes as a concerned Jew, such as when he describes the conditions of his people by saying that 'a hardening in part' has come upon Israel (Rom. 11:25), and laments that many Jews have rejected the Messiah. Nevertheless, he is convinced that 'all of Israel will be saved' (v. 26).

Paul's reflection on whether the Jewish people remains divinely chosen, even though most Jews rejected Jesus, has been hugely influential on recent

Christian thought (notably since Vatican II (1962–5)), inspired to a certain extent by the writings of Krister Stendahl about relations with Jews and Judaism. Scholarly views on Paul vary considerably, partly because of the lack of his extant writings – of the thirteen letters attributed to him, we may only be confident that he wrote seven (Romans, 1–2 Corinthians, Galatians, Philippians, 1 Thessalonians and Philemon). All his letters are 'pastoral' – written to deal with issues that were causing concern, either to the churches or to Paul himself. Paul was a practical and pastoral theologian, not a theoretical, and certainly not a systematic, one.

For example, Paul insists, alluding to Isaiah's doctrine of the remnant, that a holy remnant remains even though a large number have failed (Rom. 11:5). Here the remnant he envisages must be the Christians. But later in the same chapter he invokes the image of the olive tree. The old branches have been cut off to make way for the grafting in of new branches from a wild olive. Paul is quite clear that the choice of Israel by God can never be revoked (11:28–29): 'If you cut from what was by nature a wild olive, can be grafted unnaturally onto a cultivated olive, how much more will the branches which naturally belong there be grafted onto the olive tree which is their own?' All right for the end-time. Israel remains the chosen people, and will be grafted back. But what, in Christian eyes, is the status of Judaism at the moment? The trouble is that this horticultural image does not work. Once branches are cut off they are dead and cannot be grafted back after an interval – unless of course they develop a life of their own. It is perhaps for this reason that Paul (like some of his readers) ends by throwing up his hands in despair and proclaiming, 'How rich and deep are the wisdom and knowledge of God, how incomprehensible his decisions and how untraceable his ways!' (11:33).

There is room here for further research and reflection, raising one particularly important question in contemporary Jewish–Christian relations, which we will discuss in a later chapter: what of the ongoing validity of God's covenant with the Jewish people? A growing number of Christians reject the simple and straightforward notion of the Church as the New Israel, replacing the Old as inheritors of God's promises.

In the view of Paul, God seems to have had a remarkable ability to keep faith with both Christians and Jews when they have not kept faith with him, a point of which he is profoundly aware in Romans 9–11. There, he admits that God has temporarily suspended Israel's privileges as his chosen people, for a number of reasons, not least because 'a hardening has come upon a part of Israel' (11:25). Yet he goes out of his way to deny claims that God has rejected people whom he foreknew (11:2), and asserts that their stumbling does not lead to their fall (11:11). And in 11:28, he proclaims that 'the gift and the call of God are irrevocable'.

Related to this conviction is Paul's treatment of the 'Law' (single quotation marks are used as the English translation 'Law' reflects more the Greek (*nomos*) and especially the Latin (*lex*) translations, rather than the original Hebrew term, *Torah*, which means 'instruction'). On the view that the messianic age has come and that Christ is the end of the 'Law' (i.e., that he has fulfilled it), logic demands it should cease to have any effect. The 'Law', in Paul's view, sometimes seems to be a sadistic taskmaster, prescribing for what it cannot cure. Or else it is a tutor to human consciences and actions, unnecessary and, indeed, invalid after the Messiah comes, or even an instrument of condemnation so that the real way of salvation can be expounded. This arises from Paul's conviction that all humanity is to be saved by faith in Christ. Yet Paul had doubtless grown up believing the 'Law' to be God's good gift to Israel, and so a positive note about it is sometimes struck, along with the recognition that it had not foundered. Paul was, however, very clear that it was not binding on Gentiles, though some might keep aspects of it, so as not to give offence or cause other weaker ones to stumble.

An example of the complexity (inconsistency?) of Paul's interpretations can be seen in his reflections on Abraham, in which he uses themes from the Old Testament to argue that Abraham is the model of believers and the father of those adopted into God's family.

In the letter to the Galatians, Paul faces a situation in which emissaries have arrived at the church founded by Paul and successfully persuaded the Galatians to adopt circumcision to confirm their new status as 'children of Abraham'. The Galatians, they argued, would become true inheritors of Abraham's blessing in Genesis by fulfilling the commandment of circumcision, the sign of God's covenant with Abraham.

For Paul, however, Gentile believers in Jesus should not fulfil the commandment of circumcision, an argument based on Genesis 15:6 where Abraham believed God's promise of descendants 'and it was reckoned to him as righteousness'. Rather, through Abraham's faith and his seed (which in Gal. 3:16 Paul explicitly identifies as Christ), Gentiles will receive the promised blessing. In other words, it was through God's promise to Abraham made in response to his faith, not his circumcision, that the Gentiles were to be grafted into Israel and become inheritors of this promise through their own faith in Christ.

In his letter to the Romans, the situation is different. The problem that he wrestles with here is the fact that Israel is rejecting Christ – a situation which is for Paul both the reality and at the same time ultimately unthinkable. This letter presents Paul's mature thought on a number of issues pertinent to Christian–Jewish relations and is one that has made and continues to make a tremendous impact on Christian understanding of Jews and Judaism.

Paul realises the need to counter some of the dangerous implications of his previous logic: 'Do we then overthrow the "Law" by this faith? By no means! On the contrary, we uphold the "Law"' (Rom. 3:31). Here, Paul interprets Abraham as the father not only of the circumcised but also of the uncircumcised who have faith, which was 'reckoned to Abraham as righteousness' before and not after he was circumcised. Ultimately, it is faith not circumcision that is crucial.

The focus now falls on the nature of faith, which is not a form of work for which one receives what is due, but a matter of trusting God, despite one's own evident sinfulness. Here Paul uses the rabbinic hermeneutic principle *gezerah shawah* (literally, 'similar laws', i.e., interpretations based on analogies), linking the word 'reckon' with Psalm 32, where David pronounces blessing on those whose sins are forgiven. Later, he shows Abraham as having faith in God's promise to make him the father of many nations despite the lack of a legitimate heir, the fact that his body was 'as good as dead' and that Sarah was barren. And, likewise, Paul demonstrates his own faith that, despite the evidence, 'all Israel will be saved', affirming that 'God has not rejected his people' (11:12), because 'the gifts and the calling of God are irrevocable' (11:29).

In Romans 9–11, Paul identifies seven enduring characteristics of the Jewish people (9:4–5; absence of a verb implies present tense):

1. It is a mystery that election favours the unlikely younger sons (Isaac and Jacob) in relation to divine mercy (9:6–29) and righteousness grounded on faith (9:30–33).
2. Christ is the *telos* (end, goal) of the 'Law' (10:4) in relation to Moses and Jonah (10:6–8).
3. Isaiah 65:1–2 is interpreted as contrasting the favourable lot of Gentile Christians with 'a disobedient and contentious people' (LXX) in Romans 10:19–21.
4. God has not rejected his people (11:1) but a remnant has always remained faithful (10:2–10).
5. The positive response of Gentiles to the Gospel should make Jews jealous (11:11, 14), for all are sanctified by the first fruits and the root of the cultivated olive tree to which Gentiles are grafted (11:16–24).

6. When 'the full number of the Gentiles comes in all Israel will be saved'; they are beloved because of the patriarchs, 'for the gifts and the calling of God are irrevocable' (11:25–29).

7. Ultimately, this is a mystery whose solution is reserved to God (11:33–36). Paul's thesis is that both Jews and Gentiles sin and fail to achieve the purpose of human existence, and are under divine judgement. But the descent of God's wrath in judgement is offset by the work of Jesus Christ. Through his self-giving in obedient love, Jesus merits divine blessings for all humanity. God's love (*agape*) is revealed through the presence of the Holy Spirit, enabling Christians to attain the destiny of sharing in the risen life of Jesus, yet this new gift does not contradict God's promises to the Jewish people.

Indeed, so strongly does Paul make this point that he offers a severe warning that Gentile Christians should not be haughty or boastful toward unbelieving Jews, much less cultivate evil intent and engage in persecution against them. This remained a critical warning almost totally forgotten by Christians in history. As we shall see in the next chapter, shortly after the New Testament canon was closed Christian writers remembered Jews as 'enemies' but not as 'beloved' of God (Rom. 11:28), and have taken to heart Paul's criticisms, using them against Jews, while forgetting Paul's love for the Jewish people and their traditions.

CHAPTER 3

The writings of the church fathers

The church fathers are the early Christian teachers who gave their name to the patristic age of church history, which lasted from the end of the first century to the early Middle Ages, and to the patristic literature, the main body of Christian texts from these years.

Their writings on Jews and Judaism illustrate a tension that continues to underlie Jewish–Christian relations today. On the one hand, there was acceptance that Jesus was born, lived and died a Jew; on the other, they wrestled with the problem that Jews did not recognise Jesus as the Messiah. The Jewish rejection was extremely embarrassing for the early Church and raised a number of challenges, notably in the formation of Christian identity and in Christianity's relationship not only with Judaism but also with the ancient traditions commonly called paganism. Pagans were generally sympathetic to older religions and held a revulsion for all things new, for antiquity was equivalent to respectability. Even though Judaism was criticised by ancient writers for many reasons, such as its alleged separateness and unfriendliness, it was admired on the grounds of its history. For example, Numenius of Apamea, who lived in the second century BCE, described Plato as an 'Atticising Moses'.

The arrival of Christianity led to some harsh accusations, especially as the Romans considered new cults as suspicious and dangerous. Pagan critics, such as Celsus (*c.* 180 CE), were quick to exploit the Jewish rejection of Christianity: as far as Jews were concerned, the Messiah had not appeared. A philosopher and anti-Christian polemicist, Celsus accused Christians of deserting Jewish tradition even though they claimed to be faithful to its Jewish heritage. He placed the following criticism into the mouth of a Jew, 'Why do you Christians take your origin from our religion and then, as if you are progressing in knowledge, despise these things, although you cannot name any other origin for your doctrine than our law?' (*Contra Celsum* 2:4) The Emperor Julian (r. 361–3) took this argument further and accused Christianity of being an apostasy from Judaism (and he was later known as 'Julian the Apostate').

In response to pagan, as well as Jewish, criticism, the writings of the church fathers demonstrate a hardening of attitudes towards Jews and Judaism. Indeed, as we shall see, the Jew, as encountered in the pages of many of the church fathers, is not really a human being at all; rather, he is, at best, an opponent and at worst, a monster. As a result, it is often difficult to judge whether the anti-Jewish polemical writings of the Church, known as the *Adversus Iudaeos* literature, illustrate a real encounter with Jews and Judaism or whether they should be understood as a literary genre, simply a creation of the Christian imagination, which was used for the primary purpose of attacking the views of pagans or Christian heretics.

The German Protestant scholar Adolph von Harnack (1851–1930) argued that the *Adversus Iudaeos* writings were the result of either internal needs and, therefore, directed at other Christians, or of external needs and directed at pagans. He maintained that the literature was entirely artificial and shed no light on the subject of Jewish–Christian relations. This view has been supported more recently by a number of Jewish scholars such as Jacob Neusner and David Rokeah (b. 1930), who suggest that, from the middle of the second century CE, Christian attention turned to pagans and that the Jews were merely in the middle of a polemic between pagans and Christians.

However, whilst it is likely that the *Adversus Iudaeos* writings were concerned more with strengthening Christian self-identity than with debating with real Jews, they do also shed light on the attitudes of the church fathers towards Judaism. Descriptions of close associations between Christians and Jews are found scattered throughout the patristic literature and indicate face-to-face discussions. William Horbury (b. 1942) has demonstrated in his research that, whilst von Harnack was right in recognising the importance of *Adversus Iudaeos* for formation of Christian identity, he was wrong in supposing that significant contact between Jews and Christians ceased.

THE CHRISTIANISATION OF ROME

During the patristic period, the Roman Empire became Christian, beginning with the conversion of the Emperor Constantine on the eve of the Battle of Milvian Bridge (312) in which he assumed undisputed control of the Western Empire. This was a long and complex process, not to be reduced to the religious policy of a single emperor: but the fact that the emperor was a Christian, and favoured the Church, was important, especially when in 324 Constantine assumed control of the Eastern Empire as well. In the first three centuries the Church occasionally came under political pressure, since the rapid spread of Christianity threatened the traditional pagan cults, sometimes causing social unrest; but the last great persecution by the Roman authorities (303–11) ended with the rule of Constantine and by 380 CE Christianity was the state religion of the Roman Empire.

Before Constantine, Jews were recognised by Rome not so much as members of a national community, but as members of legal *collegia* or associations, which in many cases took the form of synagogues, indicated for example by Tertullian of Carthage's description of Judaism as a *religio licita*, or legal religion. Christians, on the other hand, as they came to be distinguished from Jews by the Roman authorities, did not enjoy a similar legal status. Indeed, they were often persecuted. The difference in legal status of the two communities was based on the Roman cultural principle of *presbyteron kreitton* or 'older is better'; the formal recognition of Judaism was connected with its antiquity, whereas Christianity was 'novel', seemingly without an ancestral foundation. This is one reason why the church fathers were so concerned to maintain a claim on Jewish tradition, and acknowledge their historical links to it.

Under Constantine, the Edict of Milan (313) granted 'both to Christians and to all others full authority to follow whatever worship each desired', but this general extension of a toleration that was already customarily extended to Jews was principally intended in order to restore the position of the Christian Church after persecution. The corresponding edict of toleration for the Eastern Empire is expressed in narrower terms: freedom of worship is extended to those 'who still persist in error', that is, are not Christian.

In the following centuries the setting in which Jews and Christians had dealings with one another changed profoundly and the *Adversus Iudaeos* writings contributed to consequent Christian emperors enacting restrictive measures and movements against Jews. The Theodosian Code (438) began a long process of legal proscriptions which enacted such rulings as forbidding Jews to hold public office. Judaism, however, remained a *religio licita*: freedom of worship was upheld, as were Jews' fiscal privileges. The stance is one of reluctant toleration, in marked contrast to the Code's decidedly harsh treatment of Christian heretics. Officially persecution of Judaism was forbidden but this status was ambivalent: it was intended to preserve (until the second coming of Christ) Jews as witnesses to the truth of the gospel they had rejected; to this end they were to continue in a diminished state, forbidden to have Christian slaves, to proselytise, work for the government, teach in public institutions, or serve in the army; nor were they allowed to build new synagogues, or even (in practice) to make major repairs to existing ones. Under Justinian I (483–565) the Code was consolidated and strengthened with new imperial ordinances (*Novellae*) that introduced anti-Jewish rulings resulting in Jews being listed alongside heretics; they were forbidden to worship, and their buildings were taken over by the Church. Indeed, the late Roman laws sanction the verity of Christian orthodoxy, as opposed to the 'error' of Judaism, heralding later medieval conceptions. Nevertheless, the exercise of the Jewish religion, in contrast to that of pagan cults, was not banned.

Gregory I, known as Gregory 'the Great' (r. 590–604), gave public support to the legal protection of Jews. Although his writings contain many features of the *Adversus Iudaeos* tradition, he intervened on several occasions to prevent violence against Jews, their synagogues and their cemeteries. For Gregory, the context was one of local Roman policy towards Jews but, as the power of the popes grew, local Roman policy began to have more universal influence, demonstrated by his letter to the Bishop of Palermo (598) that began with the words *Sicut Iudaeis*. These opening words provided the formula for all subsequent letters and bulls of papal protection of Jewish rights in Christian Europe during the Middle Ages. Papal statements, however, failed to prevent outbreaks of violence against Jews, though letters and bulls were regularly published. Their frequent reissue by a succession of popes testifies to their limited success in controlling such violence.

CHRISTIAN EXEGESIS

Early Christian writings are traditionally divided into Western and Eastern traditions, a geographical as well as a linguistic division. The Western fathers wrote in Latin, while the Eastern fathers used (primarily) Greek and Syriac (a dialect of Aramaic). In the later patristic age the languages of the Eastern church also included Armenian, Coptic and Ethiopic. The forms of literature used would have been familiar to contemporary Jews, for the books follow literary models attested in earlier Jewish writing, including biblical commentary, homily, church orders (comparable with the Qumran literature), hymns and prayers. Apologetic, doctrinal and historical treatises develop Greek models previously used by Philo and Josephus.

One of the central questions the early Church attempted to answer concerned the identity of Christ. At one level, the answer involved doctrine such as the dogma of the Trinity and of Christ's person. On another, it required an examination of the life of Christ, which transformed the Old Testament into a witness to Christ. Consequently, the relationship between the Old and New Testaments was a subject of much discussion. The church fathers insisted simultaneously on the continuity and the discontinuity of the Old and the New. Continuity centred upon the claim that the God of the Old Testament was the same as the God of Christ, and discontinuity proceeded from the belief that the Old Testament pointed to a future event – to Christ.

In the last chapter we mentioned that in the second century CE Marcion argued (unsuccessfully) that Christianity should reject the Old Testament (as well as much of the New). In response, Irenaeus, one of the most important early theologians, claimed a unity of the Testaments, interpreting passages in terms of types and allegories. Typology established a correspondence between biblical persons and events, taking seriously the historical setting. Allegory is a figurative reading that sees the literal text as standing for something else. For example, typologically, the Exodus anticipated liberation from sin and death in baptism; allegorically, the Song of Songs depicted the soul's relationship to Christ (while for Jews it described God's relationship with Israel).

Christian allegorical interpretation was based on Jewish allegory, notably that of Philo of Alexandria. For Philo, allegory alone led to true knowledge of the eternal God. Christian theologians looked to Philo as a model which they used in developing Christian doctrine. The first systematic school of Christian exegesis appeared in Alexandria in the second century and theologians such as Clement (*c.* 150–*c.* 215) and Origen incorporated Philo's allegorical approach in their writings so that he became well known in the Latin patristic tradition. Perhaps it was for this reason that he was neglected in Jewish circles until the sixteenth century when the Italian Jewish scholar Azariah de' Rossi (*c.* 1511–*c.* 1578) revived interest in Philo.

From the fourth century, a more literal and historical approach was developed by the Antiochean School of exegesis (which also has a number of parallels with traditional Jewish exegesis), epitomised by the Syrian church father, Ephrem the Syrian (*c.* 306–73). From the fifth century, the church fathers start using and copying older exegetical commentaries and patristic exegesis becomes progressively less original. Procopius of Gaza (465–530) collated a biblical commentary of already existing exegesis and introduced the compilations of commentaries on each verse of the Bible known as the *catenae* (Latin for 'chains'). Similar in structure to some of the rabbinic commentaries such as Midrash Rabbah, the *catenae* list quotations or paraphrases, on a verse-by-verse basis.

THE CHURCH FATHERS ON JEWS AND JUDAISM

The writer of 1 Peter commended Christians to be 'ready always to offer an explanation and defence' (3:15), and it is not coincidental that during the same period Jews were similarly counselled to 'be alert to study the law, and know how to make answer to an unbeliever' (M. Avot 2:14).

Faced by pagans, the church fathers sought to vindicate the legitimacy of the Old Testament. They laid claim to the Jewish Scriptures in the face of the seemingly prior claims of Jews, emphasising the accuracy of biblical prophecy, which was adapted to show that the prophets foretold the rejection of Jews and the revelation of Christ to the Gentiles. They also emphasised the antiquity of Scripture and its superiority over pagan literature. In his refutation of Celsus, for example, Origen develops the theme of Jewish stubbornness to explain their rejection of Jesus. He adopts Jewish apologetic, probably taken directly from Philo, that Abraham and Moses were older than Plato and the origins of Greek wisdom.

Some church fathers complained that Christians were far too influenced by Jewish readings of Scripture. For example, Cyril of Jerusalem (*c.* 375/80–444), Patriarch of Alexandria from 412 CE until his death, criticised both Jews and pagans:

> The Greeks plunder you with their smooth tongues . . . while those of the circumcision lead you astray by means of the Holy Scriptures, which they pervert *if you go to them* [my emphasis]. They study Scripture from childhood to old age, only to end their days in gross ignorance. (*Catechetical Lectures* 4.2)

It is interesting that Cyril describes how some Christians visited Jews, presumably to discuss Scripture. Such visits indicate a close relationship between Jewish and Christian congregants, even as late as the fifth century, witnessing that Judaism continued to influence the Christian interpretation of Scripture. Perhaps not coincidentally, according to the church historian Socrates (*c.* 380–450) Cyril was personally responsible for the expulsion of Jews from the city of Alexandria following a riot that occurred there in 415.

Cyril's comment suggests that the description of Jews by Augustine of Hippo (354–430) simply as 'our satchel bearers [. . .] who carry the books for us who study them' (*Commentary* on Ps. 40:14) was as inaccurate as it is derogatory. In *Contra Faustum Manichaeum*, a polemic against the Manichean leader Faustus (*c*. 340–before 400), Augustine depicts Jews as children of Cain whose dispersion and woes were God's punishment. Just as the blood of Abel called out to God from the earth, so did the blood of Christ; just as Cain was cursed but lived under divine protection, so did Jews – they served as witnesses to their own evil and to Christian truth. Even so, they were not to be harmed but preached to with love. Their blindness to the acceptance of Christ marked them as no longer the elect of God. Instead, the Church was the New Israel by adoption through Christ, while Jews served as 'witnesses' to the victory of the Church as the True Israel. God preserved them in their adversity to demonstrate the truth of the Old Testament as foretelling the coming of Christ. This theology continued until the sixteenth century.

We now consider the writings of a number of the key church fathers in a little more detail.

Justin Martyr (c. 100–65)

Justin is an important source for the study of Jewish–Christian relations in the early patristic period primarily because of his work, *Dialogue with Trypho*, which recounts a debate between Justin and a Jew. Scholars disagree as to whether there actually existed a Jew called Trypho but, at the very least, Justin records contemporary debates with Jews through the mouth of Trypho. Of course, to some extent, the arguments placed into the mouth of Trypho are superficial – Trypho asks a question in order for Justin to answer. However, the view of most scholars is that the *Dialogue with Trypho* represents a real encounter and reflects the Church's debate with Jews and Judaism.

In the dialogue Justin demonstrates a good knowledge of Judaism in response to Trypho's questions about Christianity. Justin is aptly described as an apologist and he sought to defend Christianity using philosophical terminology. Given that the criterion of truth was antiquity, Justin, like earlier Jewish apologists, insisted that the Greek philosophers had drawn upon the Hebrew Scriptures. The following passage illustrates the sorts of issues with which Justin was dealing. Trypho begins by asking the position of those Christians who believe in Christ but who continue to follow traditional Jewish observance. Although the passage condemns Jewish practice, it also provides evidence that some Christians continued to follow Jewish observance, a fact that not only contradicts Justin's argument that Judaism was worthless but indicates a closer relationship between Jews and Christians than Justin admits:

But if some, even now, wish to live in the observance of the institutions given by Moses, and yet believe in this Jesus who was crucified, recognising Him to be the Christ of God, and that it is given to Him to be absolute Judge of all, and that His is the everlasting kingdom, can they also be saved, he [Trypho] inquired of me.

And I [Justin] replied, 'Let us consider that also together, whether one may now observe all the Mosaic institutions.'

And he answered, 'No. For we know that, as you said, it is not possible either anywhere to sacrifice the lamb of the Passover, or to offer the goats ordered for the fast; or, in short, to present all the other offerings.'

And I said, 'Tell me then yourself, I pray, some things which can be observed; for you will be persuaded that, though a man does not keep or has not performed the eternal decrees, he may assuredly be saved.'

Then he replied, 'To keep the Sabbath, to be circumcised, to observe months, and to be washed if you touch anything prohibited by Moses, or after sexual intercourse.'

And I said, 'Do you think that Abraham, Isaac, Jacob, Noah, and Job, and all the rest before or after them equally righteous, also Sarah the wife of Abraham, Rebecca the wife of Isaac, Rachel the wife of Jacob, and Leah, and all the rest of them, until the mother of Moses the faithful servant, who observed none of these [statutes], will be saved?'

And Trypho answered, 'Were not Abraham and his descendants circumcised?' . . .

Then I returned answer, 'You perceive that God by Moses laid all such ordinances upon you on account of the hardness of your people's hearts, in order that, by the large number of them, you might keep God continually, and in every action, before your eyes, and never begin to act unjustly or impiously . . . Yet not even so were you dissuaded from idolatry: for in the times of Elijah, when God recounted the number of those who had not bowed the knee to Baal, He said the number was seven thousand; and in Isaiah He rebukes you for having sacrificed your children to idols. But we, because we refuse to sacrifice to those to whom we were of old accustomed to sacrifice, undergo extreme penalties, and rejoice in death – believing that God will raise us up by His Christ, and will make us incorruptible, and undisturbed, and immortal; and we know that the ordinances imposed by reason of the hardness of your people's hearts, contribute nothing to the performance of righteousness and of piety. (chapter 46)

Justin argues that it is impossible to keep all the commandments and that, even if they are narrowed down to the four listed by Trypho, neither the patriarchs nor the matriarchs observed them. In fact, according to Justin, circumcision, as well as the other precepts, was only given to Moses as a means of preventing sin, but even these were not sufficient to prevent injustice. He concludes that the biblical ordinances add nothing to the practice of righteousness but were given 'on account of the hardness of the heart of your people'.

For Justin, the divine rebuke should be applied to contemporary Jews, not just biblical Israel; likewise, he applies the divine blessings to Christians only. As with many church fathers, anti-Judaism was an integral part of his writings, for 'Jews no longer understand the Scriptures' (*Dia.* 9:1). Christianity has replaced Judaism. Indeed, Justin is the earliest exponent of the teaching that the Church appropriated the Old Testament. Only Christians could offer true interpretations for they are the heirs to all God's promises and are the True Israel (*verus Israel*). For instance, Justin Martyr wrote:

Let all of us Gentiles come together and glorify God, because He has looked down upon us; let us glorify Him by the King of glory, by the Lord of hosts. For He hath taken pleasure even in the nations, and He receives the sacrifices more gladly from us than from you. What account should I, to whom God has borne testimony, then take of circumcision? What need of that other baptism to one, who has been baptized by the Holy Spirit? I think that by these arguments I shall be able to persuade even those who are of slight intelligence. For the words have not been fitted together by me, nor adorned by human art, but they were sung by David, proclaimed as good news by Isaiah, preached by Zechariah, written down by Moses. You recognize them, Trypho? They are laid up in your scriptures, or rather, *not in yours but in ours* [emphasis added], for we obey them, but you, when you read, do not understand their sense. (*Dia.* 29)

This passage illustrates four key features of early Christian exegesis. Firstly, Gentiles have been brought into Israel; secondly, circumcision (which represents Jewish practice in general) is no longer required; thirdly, Scripture not only provides proof-texts supporting the Christian message but no longer belongs to Jews – Jewish interpretation is demonstrably false and only Christians offer correct interpretations; fourthly, the biblical commandments were given because of Israel's hardness of heart and have been replaced by faith in Jesus as the only means of salvation.

Arguments found in the *Dialogue* continued to be used in later *Adversus Iudaeos* literature, which makes it probably the most important and comprehensive anti-Jewish document in the patristic writings, sowing the seeds for anti-Jewish attitudes that came to dominate the thinking of the churches from the fourth to the twentieth century. Justin also describes Jewish hostility against and cursing of Christians, which we will explore in the next chapter.

Justin's *Dialogue* also provides the first real expression of the idea that Jewish social misfortunes (such as the consequences of the failed Bar Kokhba revolt in 132–5 CE) are the consequences of divine punishment for the death of Jesus; as a result, Jews will never be able to escape suffering in human society, remaining confined to a marginal and miserable existence. This theology became the source for the 'wandering Jew' imagery prevalent in later Christian popular thinking, folklore and art.

Melito of Sardis (c. 140–85)

Melito was Bishop of Sardis, a city that was also home to one of the oldest and possibly largest Jewish communities of Asia Minor. His major work is a liturgical homily on the Passion, *Peri Pascha*, which compares the celebration of Passover with that of Easter and shows signs of direct debt to the Passover liturgy and the *Haggadah* (from the Hebrew for 'to tell, relate'), a term that refers to the retelling of the story of the Exodus from Egypt. Melito's interpretation of Jewish symbols such as the *afikomen* (a piece of *matzah* which is used during the *seder* meal) and his exposition of unleavened bread and bitter herbs illustrate personal knowledge of contemporary Jewish Passover celebrations. The homily is seen by many scholars as a response to the activity of the Jewish community and its influence on the local Christians who celebrated Easter on 14th Nissan – the same day as the Jewish Passover.

For Melito, the events of Jewish history merely served as prototypical models for the great event of Easter; having fulfilled this role with the coming of Christ they serve no useful spiritual purpose. This is the beginning of the Christian theology of supersessionism that regarded Judaism as a religious wasteland.

Melito is notorious for his charge of deicide – killing God – which became a recurring theme in the history of Christian anti-Judaism. He argued that not only had Jews rejected Christ, they killed him. Whilst his emphasis on Jewish culpability is not unusual among early Christian writers one is struck by his sharp language and preoccupation with Israel's 'crime', as the following passage demonstrates:

> He [Christ] is the Pascha of our salvation.
>   It is he who in many endured many things:
>   It is he that was in Abel murdered
>   and in Isaac bound
>   and in Jacob exiled
>   and in Joseph sold
>   and in Moses exposed

and in the lamb slain
and in David persecuted
and in the prophets dishonoured.
It is he that was enfleshed in a virgin,
    that was hanged on a tree,
    that was raised from the dead,
    that was taken up to the heights of the heavens.
He is the lamb being slain:
    he is the lamb that is speechless;
    he is the one born from Mary the lovely ewe-lamb:
    he is the one taken from the flock,
    and dragged to slaughter,
    and sacrificed at evening,
    and buried at night;
    who on the tree was not broken,
    in the earth was not dissolved,
    arose from the dead,
    and raised up man from the grave below.
It is he that has been murdered.
    And where has he been murdered? In the middle of Jerusalem.
    By whom? By Israel.
    Why? Because he healed their lame
    and cleansed their lepers
    and brought light to their blind
    and raised their dead.
    That is why he died.
    Where is it written in law and prophets,
    'They repaid me bad things for good
    and childlessness for my soul,
    when they devised evil things against me and said,
    "Let us bind the just one,
    because he is a nuisance to us"' (Isa. 3:10)?
What strange crime, Israel, have you committed?
    You dishonoured him that honoured you:
    you disgraced him that glorified you:
    you denied him that acknowledged you:
    you disclaimed him that proclaimed you:
    you killed him that made you live.
What have you done, Israel? Or is it not written for you.
    'You shall not shed innocent blood' (Jer. 7:6, 22:3)
    so that you may not die an evil death?
    'I did', says Israel, 'kill the Lord.
    Why? Because he had to die.'
    You are mistaken, Israel, to use such subtle evasions
    about the slaying of the Lord.

> He had to suffer, but not by you:
> he had to be dishonoured, but not by you:
> he had to be judged, but not by you;
> he had to be hung up, but not by you
> and your right hand.   *(Peri Pascha, 69–75)*

Melito's poem – he has been called the first poet of deicide – marks a significant shift from earlier years when it was the attitude towards the 'Law' that epitomised the gulf between Jew and Christian, not the accusation that the responsibility for the death of Jesus lay with Jews. In the New Testament, the impression persists that the crucifixion was part of the pre-ordained purpose of God (e.g., Luke 24:7, 46; Matt. 26:53ff.; John 12:23) despite the Jewish acceptance of responsibility according to Matthew 27:25 or a sinister Jewish presence in the background of the fourth Gospel. However, for Melito the focus has shifted to the fulfilment of prophecy in the person of Jesus and to Jews as the killers of Christ.

Origen (185–254)

Origen is one of the most well known of the early church fathers although he is not, in a strict sense, a church father because he was denounced as a heretic at the Fifth Ecumenical Council of Constantinople (553 CE). Origen helped organise and systematise Christian biblical interpretation and produced the Hexapla, which consists of a harmony of the Hebrew text and the Greek translations of the Scriptures. He was the first church father to devote himself fully to the study of the Bible, and this led him to meet Jews and engage with Jewish interpretation of Scripture.

Despite hostility, Christians still looked to Jews for help in translating and interpreting Scripture. Origen was unusual because, although he rejected Judaism, attacking for example the observance by Christians of Jewish festivals, he also recognised the importance of the Jewish tradition for Christian scholarship. Nevertheless, in his view Jews refused to believe in Jesus as the Saviour because they lacked a spiritual sense of the Scriptures which would allow them to go beyond the literal meaning.

For Origen, Jews and Gentiles reversed roles. The historical Israelites ceased to be Israelites while the believers from the Gentiles became the New Israel. Jews were the chosen people but 'through their fall salvation is come to the gentiles'. Jacob now represents the Church and Esau the Jew. The difference between Judaism and Christianity, according to Origen, is that Christians perceive the mysteries, which are hinted only at in the Bible, whereas Jews are capable only of a literal reading of the text. Jews 'make impious and ignorant assertions about God' because they do not understand Scripture in its spiritual sense but interpret it according to the 'bare letter' (*Principles* 4.2.1; *Romans* 8.7). In an age where Christian life was still socially blended in close proximity to Jewish practice and belief, Origen represents a major step towards the establishment of a separate Christian identity.

Origen's writings make clear that messianic prophecy was one of the principal battlegrounds between Christians and Jews; he refers to discussions over:

- the virgin birth (Isa. 7:10–14 – *Against Celsus* 1:34)
- the birthplace of the Messiah (Mic. 6:1 – *Against Celsus* 1:51)
- the Messiah riding on an ass (Zech. 9:9 – *Against Celsus* 1:46)
- the suffering servant (Isa. 53 – *Against Celsus* 1:54)

Origen recommends Christians to study Scripture as an aid in responding to Jews:

And I try not to be ignorant of their various readings, lest in my controversies with the Jews, I should quote to them what is not found in their copies, and that I may make some use of what is found there, even though it should not be in our scriptures. For if we are so prepared for them in our discussion, they will not, as is their manner, scornfully laugh at gentile believers for their ignorance of the true readings as they have them. (*Epistle to Africanus* 5)

Origen was presented with a dilemma: on the one hand, Jewish knowledge of the Scriptures and of rabbinic exegesis was greatly desirable; on the other hand, Jews were 'Christ-killers', blinded by literalistic interpretations of biblical texts. Origen defended Jews against pagan attacks and occasionally referred to Jews and Christians together as 'all of Israel' (*Against Celsus* 6:80), awaiting the salvation of God. Origen's theology of Judaism is therefore complex and inconsistent. On the one hand, his derogatory rhetoric and supersessionist remarks place him among the emerging *Adversus Iudaeos* thinkers of the early Church. On the other, Origen's appreciation for Jewish insight and thought is immense.

Antioch and John Chrysostom (c. 350–407)

The Jewish community of Antioch was founded in the middle of the second century BCE, and, as in other cities in the Eastern Empire, Jews held an important place in the city's life. Antioch was also the birthplace of Gentile Christianity and represents a bridge between Judaism, Jewish Christianity and Gentile Christianity. It is mentioned in Acts as the scene of the first mission to the Gentiles: according to Luke (11:26), 'in Antioch they first called the disciples "Christians"'. In the fourth century CE, Antioch was relatively pluralistic with Jews, Christians and pagans living within its confines and many of the main buildings were Hellenistic shrines.

John Chrysostom, 'the golden tongue', was born into a wealthy and powerful family. He studied under the well-known rhetor Libanius, and was baptised in 368. Chrysostom retreated to the desert to study with monks, was ordained in 382 and in 398 summoned to Constantinople to become patriarch, but in 403 was deposed and exiled.

Chrysostom delivered eight angry sermons entitled *Adversus Iudaeos*, in 386/7 at an early stage of his career. They were bitter and polemical but also demonstrate a close relationship between his Christian congregants and the local Jewish community which Chrysostom feared would threaten his authority. Although the target of Chrysostom's attacks is the Christian 'Judaiser,' the Jew is the victim. His homilies show that many Christians in Antioch participated in Jewish festivals and fasts, believed that synagogues were endowed with numinous aura and viewed Jews as a continuation of the biblical Israel.

Chrysostom's main concern was that many Christians wanted to follow aspects of Jewish practice, were tolerant to those Christians who did so and failed to see a significant difference between Judaism and Christianity. He expressed frustration that Jews did not return the favour and keep Christian rites. Chrysostom also protested that Christians attended the synagogues during the festivals, stayed away from the church and celebrated Easter with their Jewish neighbours. He complained that Christians regarded the synagogue as a place to take an oath even though it was the home of idolatry and the devil and the idea of going to synagogue was itself blasphemous. He wanted to refute the charge that only Jews knew the Hebrew Scriptures and that Christians possessed only a copy, while Jews had the original.

His sermons denigrated Jews and Judaism, but when we read them more than 1,600 years later we need to remember their context. Firstly we should bear in mind that the purpose of Chrysostom's rhetorical training and his use of invective was not to argue logically or truthfully but to vilify. Invective was not taken literally by the listeners, who would have regarded it as a form of entertainment. He was a skilled preacher who was aware that a congregation tended 'to listen to a preacher for pleasure, not for profit, like critics at a play or concert'. It needs little knowledge of history to establish that controversy in today's world of political correctness and external good manners is conducted beneath a veneer of civility that was completely lacking in the ancient world. Examples are given of ferociously aggressive contemporary insults and intolerably abusive language.

Yet there were no angry crowds storming the synagogue as a result of Chrysostom's sermons; he simply aimed to win back Christians who had deserted the churches. His attacks should also be seen in the context of his attacks against other groups. For example, his description of Judaism as a disease was used several days earlier with reference to the Arians; his description of Jewish fasting as a form of drunkenness was elsewhere applied to the moral laxity of Christians; his description of the synagogue as a gathering place for 'whores, thieves and the crowd of dancers' was also used in an attack against Julian the Apostate.

One further point needs to be made. Neither Chrysostom, nor his contemporaries, were aware that they lived at the beginning of a period of Christian domination. The Emperor Julian had only been killed twenty years earlier and the persecutors of the Church were flourishing shortly before. There was fear of another Julian, another Valens, even another Diocletian. Ambrose (339–97), a contemporary of Chrysostom, knew some magistrates who could boast of having spared Christians.

However, the impact of Chrysostom's *Adversus Iudaeos* sermons can be seen in later generations who enjoyed Chrysostom's rhetoric but either did not recognise, or ignored, the oratorical conventions. Sections of the homilies were excerpted into the Byzantine liturgy for Holy Week and later writers drew freely from the homilies. They were translated into Russian in the eleventh century (at the time of the first pogrom in Russian history under Prince Vladimir (956–1015)), and were read in medieval Europe, in Byzantium, and especially in Russia where Jews were subject to repressive laws. Jews were now viewed as semi-satanic figures, cursed by God and specially set apart by the civil government.

Chrysostom begins his homilies with an admission. He had originally intended to speak against the Arians, but a more urgent 'disease was upon us'. He clarifies the cause of his concern: 'the festivals of the pitiful and miserable Jews are soon to march upon us, one after the other and in quick succession: the feast of trumpets, the feast of Tabernacles, the fasts [. . .]'. He continues:

Let me also say this to those who are our own – if I must call our own those who side with the Jews. Go to the synagogues and see if the Jews have changed their fast: see if they kept the pre-Paschal fast with us: see if they have taken food on that day. But theirs is not a fast: it is a transgression of the law, it is a sin, it is trespassing. Yet they did not change. But you did change your glory and from it you will derive no profit; you did go over to their rites. Did the Jews ever observe our pre-Paschal fast? Did they ever join us in keeping the feast of the martyrs? Did they ever share with us the day of the Epiphanies? They do not run to the truth, but you rush to transgression. I call it a transgression because their observances do not occur at the proper time. Once there was a proper time when they had to follow those observances, but now there is not. That is why what was once according to the Law is now opposed to it . . . (*Adversus Iudaeos* 4.3)

Chrysostom then states that the destruction of Jerusalem by the Romans was part of God's punishment for the Jewish rejection of Christ. For Chrysostom, like many church fathers, the destruction of the Temple in 70 CE and the failure of Bar Kokhba's revolt in 132–5 were signs of the divine rejection of the Jewish people. The Romans renamed Jerusalem *Aelia Capitolina*, building a temple dedicated to Jupiter on the site of the Jewish Temple and forbidding Jews from entering the city. This partly explains the great anxiety felt by Christians when the Emperor Julian decided to rebuild the Temple in 363. He was, however, killed in battle the same year and the work was apparently stopped by the outbreak of fire. Even though Julian's reign lasted only two years, his writings and actions had a great impact upon the church fathers who feared that a new Julian could arise at any time, even after 380 CE when the Empire was officially proclaimed Christian:

Even if a man be completely lacking in understanding, should it not be clear and obvious to him why Jerusalem was destroyed. Suppose a builder lays the foundation for a house, then raises up the walls, arches over the roof, and binds together the vault of the roof with a single keystone to support it. If the builder removes the keystone, he destroys the bond, which holds the entire structure together. This is what God did. He made Jerusalem what we might call the keystone which held together the structure of worship. When he overthrew the city, he destroyed the rest of the entire structure of that way of life. But the Jew totally rejects this testimony. He refuses to admit what Christ said. What does the Jew say? 'The man who said this is my foe. I crucified him, so how am I to accept his testimony?' But this is the marvel of it. You Jews did crucify him. But after he died on the cross, he then destroyed your city: it was then that he dispersed your people: it was then that he scattered your nation over the face of the earth. In doing this, he teaches us that he is risen, alive, and in heaven . . .

I did enough to complete my task when I proved from all the prophets that any such observance of ritual outside Jerusalem is transgression of the Law and a sacrilege. But they never stop whispering in everybody's ear and bragging that they will get their city back again. Even if this were true, they could not escape the charge of transgressing the Law. But I gave you abundant evidence to prove that the city will not be restored nor will they get back their old commonwealth and way of life. (*Adversus Iudaeos* 4.6)

John Chrysostom's writings have perhaps been the most damaging and influential in the popular imagination and his denunciations of Judaism gave the Church for centuries a pseudo-religious basis for persecuting Jews. Indeed, some Christians considered themselves chosen to assist God in fulfilling the curse upon Jews, feeling free to engage in attacking Jews with a divine seal of approval.

Jerome (c. 342–420)

Alongside Origen, the most famous church father who knew Hebrew and was familiar with Judaism was Jerome, author of the Vulgate translation. Jerome devoted himself to biblical study and the preparation of a new Latin version of the Bible. He settled in Bethlehem and worked on his translation of the Old Testament taken directly from the Hebrew which, he became convinced, represented the authentic voice of Scripture, *Hebraica veritas*. This resulted in the accusation that he followed Jews and earned him disapproval from, among others, Augustine.

Jerome immersed himself in Hebrew studies, meeting Jewish teachers, acquiring Jewish texts, and learning all that he could about the Hebrew language and Jewish exegesis of Scripture. This involved close contact with Jews; indeed, he had written to Pope Damasus (r. 366–84) describing a visit from a Jew bearing scrolls from the local synagogue to help him in his researches. Scholarly converse with Jews continued in Bethlehem. That in itself was extraordinary given the climate of the times; even more remarkable was his composition of *Hebrew Questions on Genesis* which, according to Robert Hayward (b. 1943), represents the most ordered and sustained attempt by any Christian writer, up to Jerome's time, to transmit Jewish scholarship to the Church. There is not one instance where Jerome prefers the LXX reading over the Hebrew text. His purpose seems nothing less than an attempt to justify his dealings with Jews and Judaism, when the ecclesiastical and civil authorities were marginalising them. As if this were not enough, *Hebrew Questions* aims to show his detractors that Jewish understanding of the Scriptures is often correct. The originality of his thesis demanded that Jerome defend, from first principles, his dealings with Jews and their teachings, and his acceptance of the latter.

From his Jewish teachers, Jerome acquired knowledge of exegetical traditions, which he incorporated into his writings and his many letters; most of these can be traced in extant Jewish sources, while others may represent otherwise lost Jewish interpretations of Scripture. While judging some Jewish traditions as true, others he calls fables; he attacks Jewish rituals, sneers at Jewish prayer, is downright hostile to 'Judaising' Christians, and repeats stock Christian objections to Judaism. Respect for individual Jewish scholars he could offer; positive regard for Judaism and its practices seems to have been beyond him.

The Syriac fathers

Since the writings of Jerome and other church fathers developed at the same time as the Hebrew and Aramaic literature of the Talmud and midrash, some patristic awareness of rabbinic tradition is perhaps to be expected. Particularly striking, however, is the general overlap between patristic and rabbinic exegetical tradition in the Syriac writings, such as the poetry of Ephrem the Syrian which has much in common with midrash and Targum.

Syriac is a form of Aramaic and linguistic similarities contributed to close relations between Jews and Syriac Christians, which displayed both shared traditions and also sharp antagonisms. This is illustrated by the fifth-century *Doctrine of Addai*, which on the one hand accuses Jews of killing Christ but on the other indicates that Christians had friendly relations with Jews and may have attended synagogue. Because Syriac Christianity retained its original Semitic expression, it was less affected than Christianity in the rest of the Roman Empire by the need to negotiate the thought-world of Hellenism, and it also remained open to Jewish traditions.

The principal Syriac version of the Scriptures (and still the authorised version of the Syriac-speaking churches) is called the *Peshitta*, the Old Testament of which was probably made from a Hebrew original in the early part of the second century for the Jewish community in Edessa; it betrays the influence of Targumic interpretations. Recent research suggests that some books in this version (such as Chronicles) may have been translated into Syriac by Jews and that translations of the Pentateuch and Prophets show affinity with post-biblical Jewish exegetical tradition. Interestingly, this seems to have been a two-way process for, in the case of Proverbs, the Targum depends upon the *Peshitta*.

Some Syriac writers such as Aphrahat (mid-fourth century CE) and especially Ephrem betray extensive knowledge of Jewish exegetical traditions in their writings. The poet Ephrem employed literary techniques similar to those of contemporary Jewish poetry (such as regular syllable stresses and acrostics interwoven into a biblical text). His hymn cycles (*madrashe*) display many affinities with rabbinic exegesis, such as his treatment of the 'robe of glory' lost by Adam and Eve but regained through baptism, and his identification of Melchizedek with Shem, son of Noah. Familiarity with and dependence upon Jewish exegetical tradition did not prevent scathing attacks on Jews. Ephrem, who also attacked Marcion and the Gnostics, engaged in fierce polemic with Jews – with whom, especially in Nisibis, he was in close proximity. Like all Christian writers of his time, Ephrem is unambiguous about the redundancy of Judaism. He is, however, unusually bitter in lambasting Jews for their collusion both in the crucifixion and in more recent persecutions.

Even so, influence of this contact between Jews and Syriac Christians may be perceived in other less polemical Christian writers, notably Eusebius of Emesa (d. *c.* 359), whose quotations of 'the Syrian' and 'the Hebrew' in his commentaries often demonstrate information derived from a Jewish source. *Piyyutim* – Jewish hymns that embellish statutory prayers – also provide examples of positive Christian interaction with Jewish writings, notably in Byzantine poetry. The *kontakion* hymns composed by the sixth-century poet Romanos Melodos (d. 555?), perhaps Byzantium's greatest liturgical poet and born quite possibly to Jewish parents, are similar in form to the Hebrew *qerovah* adopted by his Jewish contemporary Yannai. The *kontakia* deal mainly with biblical events and consist of a short prelude followed by a number of longer strophes in identical metre, separated by a repeated refrain, and united by an acrostic.

For all his zeal against Christian heretics, Romanos displays a remarkably temperate attitude to Jews at a time when official toleration was diminishing. He has no doubt that Jews are in error, but accepts that at the Last Day they will be judged. They will certainly bewail their error in not recognising the Christ and confessing the Trinity, but they will not be punished for it. Equally, in his treatment of the Passion of Christ he singularly fails to lambast 'the Jews', preferring the less inflammatory 'the lawless'. In advocating a position that upholds the integrity of the Christian revelation without denying the ongoing special dispensation accorded to Jews, Romanos represents a significant and constructive voice of continuing relevance.

As well as poetry, Jewish and Christian religious buildings shared many of the same characteristics, both with each other and with the architecture of other religions. The synagogue may have developed as a place for communal Jewish worship during the Babylonian exile (586–538 BCE), but the earliest synagogue thus far excavated (Delos, Greece), dates from the first century BCE. The earliest excavated example of a church dates from the third century CE, in Dura-Europos (on the border of present-day Iraq and Jordan). In one street, archaeologists uncovered three separate houses, accommodating a Mithran sanctuary, a synagogue (from 245 CE) and a church (*c.* 230 CE).

In ancient Eastern churches in particular, there are inherited similarities with the design of a synagogue, which can still be seen today, for example in the Coptic church in Giza, on the outskirts of Cairo. In the middle of the church building one finds a large, U-shaped, walled-in platform. This is distinct from similar features in Western churches because of its location and the fact that, unlike them, it does not possess a throne for a bishop and seats for the clergy. Contemporary literary sources, such as Ephrem, describe this feature as a 'bema', which was where the Bible was read and the sermon delivered. It is generally agreed that the church 'bema' is a copy of the synagogue 'bima' which was a similarly designed platform in the middle of the synagogue, from which the Torah and Prophets would be read.

Another example is the synagogue at Sardis (3rd–4th centuries CE), which is basilican in form with a colonnaded forecourt leading to the Jerusalem-facing entry wall. The arrangement parallels Old St Peter's in Rome (*c.* 320–30). The spatial resemblance between these two houses of worship is remarkable, indicating that the architectural precedent of the Roman basilica was more influential than theological differences between the two religions in the patristic era.

CHAPTER 4

The writings of the rabbis

Scholars disagree about when the 'rabbinic period' in Jewish history really began. Perhaps it started as early as the fifth century BCE, with the return to Jerusalem of Nehemiah and Ezra, or as late as the second century during the reign of the Hasmonean dynasty. What is certain is that the rabbinic way of life was a new stage in the development of Judaism. In contrast to the Hasmoneans who concentrated on national issues such as the removal of foreigners (be they Romans or Greeks) from Jewish soil, and the Sadducees who were Temple centred, the rabbis emphasised Torah and *halakhah* (Jewish law).

The progenitors of the rabbis were the Pharisees, and the success of the Pharisees, and later the rabbis, enabled Judaism to survive without a homeland and without a Temple. Indeed, unlike other Jewish groups it was the rabbis' ability to respond to the catastrophe in 70 CE that enabled them, eventually, to dominate Jewish life. The rabbis replaced sacrifice and pilgrimage to the Temple with study of the Scripture, faith, prayer and deeds, eliminating the need for a sanctuary in Jerusalem and making Judaism a religion capable of fulfilment anywhere. All succeeding Judaism is ultimately derived from the rabbinic movement of the first centuries.

One result of their endeavours is the title given by Muslims to Jews (and Christians), 'the people of the Book' (*Ahl al-Kitab*), although Jews are more likely to describe themselves as 'people of the books', for there are many sacred books. The Jewish books begin with the Torah, continue through the biblical, legal and homiletical literature and extend to medieval codes, philosophical works and the literature of the mystics. In addition, every area of this vast literary corpus is complemented by detailed commentaries and annotations. Thus, rabbinic emphasis on study resulted in a huge number of works, so that if today you read the Bible or the Talmud you read it alongside the interpretations of generations of rabbis.

The foundation of all Jewish writings is the Torah, which in its narrowest sense refers solely to the Pentateuch – the Written Torah (*Torah she-bikhtav*) consisting of Genesis, Exodus, Leviticus, Numbers and Deuteronomy. Equally important, however, is the Oral Torah (*Torah she-be²al peh*), a body of teaching also deriving, according to tradition, from Moses on Sinai, which gives the true interpretation of the Written Torah and which is now found in written form in the Mishnah and Talmud.

> Moses received the Torah from Sinai, and he delivered it to Joshua, and Joshua to the elders, and the elders to the prophets, and the prophets delivered it to the men of the Great Synagogue. They said three things: Be deliberate in judgment; and raise up many disciples; and make a fence to the Torah. (M. Avot 1:1)

The Torah as recorded in the Mishnah and the other rabbinic sources is, according to the opening of the tractate Avot, transmitted directly from Moses, who received it from God on Sinai, and passed it on to the early rabbis (men of the Great Synagogue). This concept of transmission justified the notion of the Oral Torah, that is, all the tradition orally transmitted from the time of Moses and eventually recorded in the body of rabbinic literature.

For the rabbis, the Torah was the object of continual study and interpretation, 'Turn the Torah over and over again, for everything is in it. Contemplate it and grow old and grey over it' (M. Avot 5:25). They felt it was their duty to explore and expound the divine truth and in so doing lead their lives in accordance with the divine will.

Rabbinic literature consists of a diverse body of texts, with different aims, style and content, written, edited and collated from the destruction of the Temple in 70 CE until the medieval period (the next chapter will discuss the writings of the medieval Jewish scholars, such as Rashi (1040–1105) and Maimonides (1135–1204)). The classical period is generally considered to be the first six centuries CE and the texts were written in different places; the two main centres of Rabbinic Judaism were Palestine and Babylonia.

Rabbinic Judaism gradually gained strength and by the third century CE it was probably the dominant force in Palestinian Judaism. Rabbinic Judaism was carried to Babylonia in the third century CE by Palestinian scholars who soon eclipsed in prestige their counterparts in the Babylonian academies of Sura and Pumbeditha. The rabbis also largely succeeded in bringing the Jews of the Western Greek-speaking Diaspora under their aegis. The process by which they achieved this remains obscure, but it must have involved, at least during the first few centuries of the common era, interaction and competition with the expanding Christian mission.

Marcel Simon (1907–86) argues strongly that competition for converts between Christianity and Judaism continued until the conversion of

Constantine in 312 CE. However, other scholars have disagreed, suggesting that the universal mission of the early Church was unparalleled in the history of the ancient world. Martin Goodman (b. 1953), for example, finds no evidence for a universal mission in first-century Judaism, although he accepts that in a later period proselytism did occur (but claims that this was a reaction to Christian mission). The lack of agreed scholarly opinion on the extent of Jewish missionary activity mirrors the different views about seeking converts expressed by two of Rabbinic Judaism's most famous rabbis, Hillel and Shammai, around the beginning of the Common Era. Shammai was concerned that if Jews had too much contact with the Romans, Judaism would be weakened, and this attitude was reflected in his strict interpretation of conversion and Jewish law in general. Hillel did not share Shammai's fear and therefore was more liberal in his views. Hillel favoured the admission of proselytes into Judaism even when they made unreasonable demands, as one proselyte did by demanding that the whole Torah be taught to him quickly 'while standing on one foot'. Hillel accepted this person as eligible for conversion, whereas Shammai dismissed him as not serious about Judaism (BT. *Shabbat* 31a).

As a result of the fundamental rabbinic principle that 'the law of the land is the law' (*dina d'malkuta dina*), a characteristic feature of Rabbinic Judaism is its ability to digest the mores and customs of the surrounding culture, as many scholars, notably the British theologian Louis Jacobs (1920–2006), have shown. As we shall see in the next chapter, this facilitated some surprisingly constructive encounters between Jews and Christians.

Both Rabbinic Judaism and Christianity have their roots in the religious diversity of late Second Temple Judaism, a process which Daniel Boyarin (b. 1946) has called 'co-emergence', and their relationship is complicated and uncertain. In the opening centuries the rabbis largely succeeded in neutralising the Christian mission to Israel, perhaps partly by applying the category of 'heretics' (*minim* – see below) to Christians so that they could be excluded from the synagogue and Jewish social life. Jewish Christians represented one Jewish sect who rivalled the rabbis. As we saw, the Christians, when they found themselves in a position of political power from the time of Constantine onwards, persecuted Jews in various ways, closing their schools, dispersing their leaders, censoring or even, in the Middle Ages, destroying the Talmud (only one complete manuscript of the whole text (Munich 95) is now extant) and other rabbinic texts, and forcibly converting their followers.

The date of the split between Judaism and Christianity has been the subject of much debate: some scholars see it beginning as early as Paul of

Tarsus, others as late as Constantine, or even later. J. D. G. Dunn (*b.* 1939) has suggested that the separation between Judaism and Christianity should be described as 'the partings of the ways'. We saw in the last chapter that in the late fourth century CE Chrysostom bitterly attacked his Christian community for supporting, socialising with and even participating in local Jewish religious activities. It should be noted that not only were Christians in late fourth-century Antioch able to participate in synagogue life but that contemporary Antiochene Jews also allowed them to participate. The full involvement of Christians in Jewish life should be taken into consideration when discussing the timing of the separation of Christianity from Judaism.

The term 'the rabbis' does not describe a definitive group of people. They were generally teachers in the synagogue or study houses, but belonged to different communities from different time periods. Palestinian rabbis are often titled 'Rabbi' and were led by a patriarch, whereas Babylonian rabbis are often titled 'Rav' and were led by an exilarch. However, there was movement between the two centres and a number of Babylonian rabbis lived or worked in Palestine. The different generations of rabbis are indicated by certain names. The first generation were called *tannaim* – 'teachers'. They belonged to the 'tannaitic era', which is traditionally dated up to 200 CE and associated with the writing of the Mishnah, a comprehensive compendium of (primarily) rabbinic law from the early third century CE. The Mishnah formed the base-text of the Talmud (literally 'Teaching'), which consists primarily of debates and discussions of God's laws. The Mishnah makes no clear reference to Christians or Christianity, which may be a reflection of general early rabbinic indifference towards non-Jewish or non-rabbinic religions. The eschatological prediction that 'the Kingdom will convert to heresy (*minut*)' (M. *Sotah* 9:15), presumably referring to Constantine's conversion to Christianity, is a later interpolation which may be dated to the fourth century.

The second generation of rabbis were known as the *amoraim* – 'commentators', and they are associated with the Talmud and midrashic writings. As a major source-text of Judaism, the Talmud has long been at the centre of Jewish–Christian controversies. However, references to Jesus and Christianity, which we will discuss shortly, are sparse in the Talmud and related literature. This may reflect self-censorship by the redactors who lived (until the seventh century and the rise of Islam) under increasingly oppressive Christian rule.

In fact, pagan and non-Jewish cults as a whole are rarely mentioned in the Talmud, but simply bundled into the catch-all category of *avodah zarah* ('foreign worship'), a halakhic (legal) designation of all polytheistic and idolatrous cults. One passage (BT. *Avodah Zarah* 6a and 7b) suggests that Christianity belongs to the category of *avodah zarah*, although it is not explained in what respect it should be regarded as idolatrous, polytheistic or 'pagan'. The assimilation of Christianity with other religions into the single category of *avodah zarah* may explain its apparent rarity in the Talmud. A few halakhists argued that Christians are not *avodah zarah* worshippers, but this view is rare (although it is found in some medieval writings, e.g., Menachem Ha-Me'iri and increasingly among post-Emancipation authorities). (By contrast with Christianity, Islam is generally not categorised as *avodah zarah*, and is hence a legitimate non-Jewish religion.)

Another approach was to use the term *shittuf*, which means 'partnership' or 'association' of an additional power with God, to describe Christianity (and Islam). It was applied to religions that are not considered idolatrous but are viewed as combining elements of Judaism and paganism, resulting in a contamination of the absolute monotheism revealed at Sinai. However, because a *shittuf* religion has not degenerated into polytheism and idolatry, it was not condemned, and contacts with its representatives were deemed acceptable. A pragmatic position eventually emerged in the medieval period that, while *shittuf* compromised monotheism and was thus prohibited to Jews, it was not incompatible with the Noachide laws and thus Christians were not actual idolaters (Tos. *Sanhedrin* 63b and BT. *Bechorot* 2b).

The category most frequently associated with Christians is *min* (pl. *minim*), literally 'type(s)', a term generally applied to (Jewish) heretics, most likely including Jewish Christians, and by extension applicable (in some cases) to non-Jewish Christians, although the extent to which the term *min* in the Talmud should be identified as 'Christian' has been grossly overestimated. One *min*, Jacob of Sikhnin, is said to have healed 'in the name of Jesus' and conveyed an exegetical teaching of Jesus to Rabbi Eliezer (early second century). The former subsequently regretted his action (BT. *Avodah Zarah* 16b–17a, 27b); he is certainly to be identified as Christian.

The final genre of literature we should define is midrash, a Hebrew term for asking, searching, inquiring and interpreting. It has been argued by some Christian scholars, such as Raymond Brown (1928–88), that there also exists a specifically Christian form of midrash, notably in the New Testament. In Rabbinic Judaism, midrash consists of an anthology and compilation of homilies, including *aggada* (Jewish lore) and *halakhah* (Jewish law). Consequently, midrash is considered a religious activity as well as a commentary on a particular book of the Bible – it is the rabbis' attempt to fill in the gaps of meaning and to elucidate Scripture where its meaning seems to be ambiguous. The purpose of their interpretations is to uncover what has always been there, but had previously been unseen or undiscovered. An example of Christian midrash can be found in the differing birth stories in Matthew and Luke. The two stories may be described as Christian midrash because they look at the historical facts – the birth of Jesus – and add related stories which interpret and amplify the original historical event. Brown argues that Christian midrash builds a bridge between the stories of the Old Testament and the life of Jesus.

There are, in midrash, no wrong interpretations. This is reminiscent of the story told of the leader writer for *The Times* who settled down to his task with a long blank sheet of paper on which he had written in the middle the single word 'however'. Yet, on some questions, it is possible to detect a general thrust sufficient for certain conclusions to be drawn as broad principles, always provided that confident assertion is tempered with a healthy degree of scepticism.

Midrash sometimes sheds light on the Jewish–Christian encounter, demonstrating rabbinic awareness of Christianity. For example, a midrash on the phrase 'let us make man' (Gen. 1:27) may represent an early Jewish response to Christian teaching about the relationship between the Father and the Son. In *Dialogue with Trypho*, Justin claims Jews misrepresent Scripture and complains to Trypho that

> you [i.e., Jewish interpreters] may not, by changing the words already quoted, say what your teachers say, either that God said to Himself, 'Let us make . . .' as we also, when we are about to make anything, often say, 'Let us make' to ourselves; or that God said, 'Let us make . . .' to the elements, namely the earth and such like, out of which we understood that man has come into being. (*Dia.* 62)

Justin's rejection of a Jewish interpretation of Genesis 1:27 is likely to refer to the following midrash:

> 'And God said, let us make man . . .'. With whom did He take counsel? Rabbi Joshua ben Levi said, 'He took counsel with the works of heaven and earth, like a king who had two advisors without whose knowledge he did nothing whatsoever . . . Rabbi Ammi said, 'He took counsel with His own heart.' It may be compared to a king who had a palace built by an architect . . . (Genesis Rabbah 8:3)

The American Jewish scholar Burton Visotzky (b. 1951) claims that there even exist New Testament quotations in the rabbinic writings, and suggests that the following rabbinic passage paraphrases 1 Corinthians 1:11, 'in the Lord, woman is not independent of man nor man of woman' and represents a response to Paul. The rabbinic commentary reads:

The heretics asked R. Simlai, How many gods created the world? He answered them, Me you are asking? Let us ask Adam, as it is said, *for ask now of the days that are past, which were before you, since the day that God created Adam . . .* (Deut. 4:32). It is not written, since gods created [pl.] Adam but *since the day that God created* [sing.] *Adam.* They said to him, But it is written, *In the beginning God* [*elohim* is a plural construct] *created* (Gen. 1:1). He answered them, Is *created* written [as a plural]? What is written here is *created* [sing.]. R. Simlai stated, Every place that the heretics rend [a verse from context to make their point] has the appropriate [textual] response right next to it. They returned to ask him, What of this verse, *Let us make man in our image, after our likeness* (Gen. 1:26) [in which the subject, verb and objects appear in the plural]. He answered them, It is not written, So God created [pl.] man in his image [pl.] but *God created* [sing.] *man in his own image* (Gen. 1:27). His disciples said to him, Those you pushed off with but a straw, but what shall you answer us? He told them, In the past Adam was created from dust, while Eve was created from Adam. From Adam onward, *in our image, after our likeness* (Gen. 1:26); it is impossible for there to be a man independent of woman, nor is it possible for there to be woman independent of man, neither is it possible for both of them to be independent of the Shekhina. (JT. *Berakhot* 12d–13a)

HISTORICAL CONTEXT

In Palestine after 135 CE, Galilee became the chief locale of rabbinic activity, centred on a strong Jewish leadership which lasted until the fourth century. After two unsuccessful revolts against Rome (66–70 CE and 132–5 CE), Jewish attitudes were on the one hand respectful of such a powerful empire as Rome, especially given experience of the dangers of opposition, and on the other wishing to be free from such dominion. Nevertheless, the lack of any significant Jewish revolts for the next few centuries suggests a certain degree of both caution and security. Contact with Christians in this region would have occurred and we find a scattering of references to Christians.

In Palestine, Jewish Christians were a weak minority, and Eusebius reports that when the Romans laid siege to Jerusalem in 66 CE Jewish Christians fled to Pella, in Jordan. Although this flight has been questioned by scholars (and Jewish Christians were certainly living in Jerusalem after the war), Eusebius' report does indicate a step away from Judaism, and gradually Jewish Christians began to lose their influence in the evolving Church.

Later, during the Bar Kochba revolt, the Jewish Christians opposed Bar Kochba because he claimed to be the Messiah. To the Christians the appearance and claims of Bar Kochba appeared as another Jewish rejection of Christ. For Jews, the failure of the Jewish Christians to offer support to the revolts, combined with their questioning and eventual rejection of circumcision, *kashrut* and other aspects of Jewish life, resulted in their increasing distance from Judaism. Although some groups of Jewish Christians continued to exist, over the next couple of centuries their numbers and influence continued to decline.

By the time of Justin Martyr around the middle of the second century, the presence in the Christian movement of Jews who continued to observe Jewish practices had become a hotly disputed point within the Church; and by the end of the second century they were viewed as heretical by the majority church and given the name Ebionite or Nazarene.

Jewish reaction to Jewish Christians is not easy to determine but negative attitudes became increasingly common, particularly as relations between Jews and Christians hardened. Yet, just as we cannot speak of a uniform Christianity at this stage in history, so we cannot speak of a uniform Judaism, and we must, therefore, entertain the possibility that attitudes to Jewish Christians varied between different Jewish communities. Moreover, it seems clear that the Nazarenes saw themselves as operating from within the Jewish community, as their commentary on Isaiah, quoted by Jerome, appears to imply. Some rabbinic references may also support such an internal Jewish profile. Jerome appeared to give voice to this quest for a dual identity when he stated polemically that the 'Nazarenes' sought to be both Jews and Christians but were in fact neither.

Jews probably remained in the majority in Palestine until some time after the conversion of Constantine in the fourth century. In the following centuries boundaries between Judaism and Christianity became clearer and it is in this context that the Palestinian Talmud was compiled.

In Babylonia there had been for many centuries a Jewish community, which would have been further strengthened by those fleeing the aftermath of the Roman revolts. Contact with Christians in this region would have been slight, and in the early third century, when Babylonia came under the rule of Sassanid Persians, Zoroastrianism was imposed as the state religion. This was short-lived and Jews regained some autonomy, but in the fifth century experienced persecution, as did Christians.

It is in this 'dual' climate that much of the rabbinic literature was compiled, continuing up to the Arab conquest in the seventh century when both Jewish centres came under a single leadership.

As we saw in the previous chapter, once Christianity was established as the religion of the Roman Empire in the fourth century, the situation for Jews became more difficult, though this was a gradual process because the energy of Christian Europe was directed towards defeating pagans and

Christian heretics. During this time the Church produced an abundance of anti-Jewish (*Adversus Iudaeos*) writings and Judaism was a frequent subject for discussion in the patristic writings (far more so than Christianity in rabbinic literature). *Adversus Iudaeos* resulted in little violence against Jews, nor did it stir much of a Jewish response, possibly because until then Christianity, whilst seen as a contemporary oppressor of Judaism and ranking as the third or fourth of the four kingdoms predicted by Daniel, was viewed with little theological interest.

Yet there is evidence to suggest that Jewish commentators were aware of Christian exegesis, and they produced some writings that might be termed *Adversus Christianos*, such as the polemical text *Toledot Yeshu*. Thus, although the rabbinic writings are cautious in their comments on Christianity because of Christian censorship and fear of retribution, it is possible to find implicit, and occasionally explicit, repudiation of Christianity. For example, Rabbi Johanan felt it necessary to explain that Jews did not fast on Sunday 'on account of the Christians' (BT. Ta'anit 27b).

RABBINIC WRITINGS ON JESUS

Overall, there is little overt engagement with Christianity or Christians in the rabbinic writings. The nature of the material and the circumstances in which it was compiled and written means that responding to Christianity was not always a primary subject of concern. Where there are possible references they are often uncertain, and such suggestions must be carefully supported. What is significant is that polemic was taken up in later medieval writings, although, given the languages in which this polemic was written, it was primarily for internal educational purposes rather than external attacks on Christians.

It is important to consider the internal features of rabbinic texts when searching for references to Christianity. Most groups outside Judaism are rarely mentioned, and references to external historical events are few so that it is not always certain whether an apparent allusion to Christianity is an illusion. We will first consider one more example, presented in the style of 're-written Bible' (i.e., a retelling of the biblical narrative with expansions), which discusses the hanging of a corpse and demonstrates the difficulty in identifying rabbinic passages as referring to Jesus.

Rabbi Meir used to say: what is the meaning of '*for a curse of God is he that is hung*' (Deut. 21:23)? [It is like the case of] two brothers, twins, who resembled each other. One ruled over the whole world, the other took to robbery. After a time the one who took to robbery was caught, and they crucified him on a cross. And every one who passed to and fro said, 'It seems that the king is crucified'. Therefore it is said, '*a curse of God is he that is hung*'. (Tos. *Sanhedrin* 9:7)

This passage forms part of a longer section on hanging and the proper disposal of a corpse. What might at first seem a striking passage on crucifixion is, in fact, less notable in its wider context. The starting point of the Mishnah is the meaning of the biblical passage from Deuteronomy, and one must understand it in the context of the whole quotation of the verse, which reads: 'his corpse must not remain all night upon the tree; you shall bury him that same day, for anyone hung on a tree is under God's curse. You must not defile the land that the Lord your God is giving you for possession.' Therefore, it is to be found in the context of the proper time for disposal of a body. Rabbi Meir asks what the passage means. Hanging upon a tree was commonly interpreted to denote crucifixion, as indeed the Targumic (Aramaic) translation of this passage interprets it. The existence of twin brothers leads to mistaken identity, and the passage explains that it is a disgrace for a king to be left hanging on the cross. In that sense the passage merely highlights the proper respect due to bodies.

An alternative interpretation may be suggested, that the passage refers to Jesus, and describes the relationship between Jesus and God in terms of two brothers. 'One ruled over the whole world' would be a reference to God, while the one 'who took to robbery' and was 'crucified' would be Jesus. The mention of the cross (*zaluv*) is striking, paralleling the discussion by Paul in Galatians 3:13 ('Christ has redeemed us from the curse of the law, being made a curse for us: for it is written, Cursed is every one that hangs on a tree'). Hanging on a tree may indicate crucifixion but, since this was a common Roman punishment, it is by no means certain on this evidence alone that the passage refers to Jesus. It will in part depend on to what extent we see evidence of any contact between Jews and Christians at this time.

Nevertheless, elsewhere in the rabbinic writings, there are some explicit references both to the figure of Jesus and to Christians, which influenced later rabbinic reflection on and criticism of Christianity. References to 'Jesus the Christian' (*Yeshu ha-notzri*) are generally polemical, and represent later literary creations rather than the legacy of some early historical tradition. They formed the basis of the compilation of the sixth-century *Toledot Yeshu*. Sometimes Jesus is not mentioned by name; instead he is referred to obliquely, or by use of a cipher such as Balaam, the biblical figure who became an object of rabbinic criticism.

For example, in a commentary on Numbers 23:19 ('God is not a man, that he should lie; neither the son of man, that he should repent: hath he said, and shall he not do it? or hath he spoken, and shall he not make it good?'). Rabbi Abahu of the third century CE, known for his opposition to the *minim* (see below), interprets this verse as a rejection of the divinity of Jesus and the claims of his followers.

R. Abahu said: If a man says to you 'I am God,' he is a liar; if he says, 'I am the son of man,' in the end people will laugh at him; if he says 'I will go up to heaven,' he says, but shall not perform it. (BT. Ta'anit 65b)

Although this passage does not expressly mention Jesus it is quite clearly a direct riposte to the Christian claims about:
• Jesus as the 'son of man'
• Jesus going 'up to heaven'
• Jesus as God.
Another example, from a tenth-century midrash called *Aggadat Bereshit*, condemns the *minim* (i.e., 'heretics') who argued that God had a son. Although it does not mention Christianity explicitly it is a clear response to Christian teaching:

How foolish is the heart of the *minim*, who say that the Holy One, Blessed be He, has a son. If, in the case of Abraham's son, when He saw that he was ready to slay him, He could not bear to look on in anguish, but on the contrary at once commanded, 'do not lay your hand on the lad'; had He had a son, would He have abandoned him? Would He not have turned the world upside down and reduced it to *tohu v-vohu* ['void and unformed'; Gen. 1:2]? (chapter 31)

These examples might have been intended as a guide to Jews when debating with Christians and responding to Christian claims.

In other texts, Jesus is depicted as a pupil of Rabbi Joshua ben Perahia, expelled by his master because of his lewdness, and subsequently apostasising to idolatry (BT. *Sotah* 47a, BT. *Sanhedrin* 107a). He was tried, executed and hanged on the eve of Passover by the Jewish high court, for practising magic and luring Jews into idolatry (BT. *Sanhedrin* 43a). It is difficult to relate these stories to anything contained in the Gospels, the detailed contents of which are ostensibly unknown to the Talmudic authors (save for occasional exceptions such as the Sermon on the Mount and a pun on the word *evangelion*, in BT. *Shabbat* 116a–b).

Although, as has already been noted, the references to Jesus in rabbinic writings are few, they may represent a wider tradition of Jewish polemic against Christianity. Although negative assessments of Christianity can be found in ancient authors, the first extant attack on Christianity came from the second-century pagan Celsus, as recorded by Origen. The first Jewish tract that focused on polemic against Christians (as opposed to references such as those already noted) was the (probably) sixth-century work *Toledot Yeshu* ('family history of Jesus'), a parody of the Gospels. A central feature of this and other Jewish anti-Christian texts is to question the divinity of Jesus, and in particular his birth from a virgin.

Three aspects about Jesus are particularly mentioned: his illegitimate birth, his skills as a magician or miracle worker, and his trial and crucifixion. Jesus is commonly alluded to by the names ben Stada or ben Pandira or variants of these names, although the precise meaning is unclear. The explanation is given in BT. *Sanhedrin* 67a (paralleled in BT. *Shabbat* 104b):

Ben Stada is ben Pandira. Rab Hisda said, 'the husband was Stada, the paramour was Pandira'. The husband was Pappos ben Jehudah, the mother was Stada. The mother was Miriam, the dresser of women's hair (*miriam m'gaddela nashaia* [a pun on Mary Magdalene]), as we say in Pumbeditha, 'such a one has been false (*stat du*) to her husband'.

The text explains that the name ben Stada is the same as ben Pandira (which is also found written as Pantera or Pantira). Neither name has a clear origin, and probably the rabbis themselves were unsure, providing here an explanation for Stada, identified with ben Pandira for Stada, the name of the husband of his mother and Pandira the name of her lover (according to Hisda). However, this opinion is questioned because the husband's name is Pappos ben Jehudah and, therefore, Stada must have referred not to the father but to the mother. There are a number of possible explanations for the name Pandira, but none is convincing: e.g., from the Greek *pentheros*, 'mother-in-law', the Greek for 'a panther', or the Greek *parthenos*, 'virgin'. Again, the opinion is questioned because the mother was called Miriam, 'the dresser of women's hair'. The conclusion is that Miriam is her proper name and Stada her nickname because *stat du* means 'she has gone astray' from her husband. The rabbinic description of Miriam (in other words Mary) as a 'dresser of women's hair' appears to be a confused reference to Mary Magdalene as the Aramaic words are *miriam m'gaddela nashaia*, but although there is some awareness of Jesus' connection with Mary Magdalene the details are confused.

In other passages the rabbis state that Jesus knew magical spells and possessed magical powers. This should not be surprising since miraculous stories were also told about the rabbis, but the miracles of Jesus were less important than the substance of his teachings and those of his followers who taught in his name. Josephus' *Testimonium Flavianum* contains reference to Jesus as 'a performer of startling deeds'.

Jesus is described as having learnt his magical craft in Egypt, from where he brought these spells on his flesh, in other words, through tattoos. Egypt was well known in ancient times as a place of magic and it is unlikely that the rabbis were aware of the Matthean tradition, which describes how Jesus, as a baby, was taken from Nazareth to Egypt to avoid being killed by Herod (2:13–14). To describe Jesus as having learnt magic in Egypt is simply to imply that he was a powerful magician. The reference to tattooing parallels second-century pagan and Christian writings, which refer to magicians writing spells on their flesh; perhaps also relevant is Paul's description of himself as bearing the marks of Jesus 'branded on my body' (Gal. 6:17).

The Talmudic passage deals, at the literal level, with remembering magical spells. It begins with the premise that since ben Stada (Jesus) brought magical spells from Egypt in an incision in his flesh the practice might be allowable. However, the response is that since ben Stada is a fool his case proves nothing. The accusation of madness is probably simply a denunciation of Jesus, although the rabbis may be exploiting the reported opinions of Jesus' relatives who 'went out to take charge of him for people were saying that he was out of his mind' (Mark 3:21).

Let us summarise what we are told about Jesus in the rabbinic writings:

- He was known to the rabbis as the one who 'deceived Israel', who was tried and executed for doing so, who had disciples, and in whose name those disciples performed cures and miracles.
- He was born out of wedlock and his mother was called Miriam, a dresser of women's hair. Her husband was Pappos ben Jehudah and her lover Pandira. She was said to have descended from princes and rulers and to have been a prostitute with carpenters.
- Jesus had lived in Egypt, where he learnt magic, and as a magician led Israel astray and caused the multitude to sin.
- He was a revolutionary, was described as near to the kingdom and had five disciples. He mocked the words of the wise and was excommunicated for heresy.
- He called himself God as well as the son of man and claimed that he would go up to heaven.
- He was tried in Lud (near present-day Tel Aviv) before the *beth din* (Jewish court) on the grounds of being a deceiver and teacher of apostasy. Witnesses were concealed so as to hear his statements and a lamp was lit above him so that his face might be seen.

- He was executed in Lud, on the eve of Passover, which was also the eve of the Sabbath. He was stoned, hung or crucified. Beforehand, a herald proclaimed that he was to be stoned and invited evidence in his favour; but none was forthcoming. Under the pseudonym of Balaam he was put to death by Pinhas the robber (Pontius Pilate) and at the time of his death was 33 years old.
- He was punished in Gehinnom (Hell).

It is worth highlighting that the rabbis made no mention of his messiahship. Although hostility was directed towards the figure of Jesus, of the historical person little (if any) trace remains. His entire life was depicted as one of deceit and his death was one fit for a criminal. In the rabbinic mind the person of Jesus and his actions caused the secession from their midst of a new and potentially life-threatening religion. When the rabbis accused Jesus of deceiving Israel they meant it literally, for Christianity not only led some Jews 'astray' but as it became more powerful threatened the very existence of Judaism. Overall, the rabbinic writings have preserved only a very vague and confused recollection of Jesus and, although his name was held in abhorrence as that of a dangerous heretic and deceiver, extremely little was known of him.

BIRKAT HA-MINIM

The *Amidah* prayer is the central component of rabbinic liturgy, recited at every service, and its recitation compensates for the absence of the Temple and its sacrifices. The *Amidah*'s text remained fluid for the first few centuries of the common era and aspects of the Jewish and Christian liturgy, such as the *Kedushah* and the *Sanctus/Trishagion* probably share a common source. Both the Jewish *Kedushah*, derived from the Hebrew for 'to be holy', and the Christian *Sanctus* (also meaning 'holy') adapt the words of the seraphim in Isaiah 6:3. The *Amidah* consists of the Eighteen Benedictions (or the *shmonei-esre*, a term that covers both benedictions and maledictions); the twelfth of these, called the *Birkat Ha-Minim* (the malediction of the sectarians/heretics), became the object of Christian criticism and censorship throughout the ages.

The Talmud (BT. *Berakhot* 28b–29a) records that the *Birkat Ha-Minim* was established under Rabban Gamaliel II's direction in the late first century CE. Its original purpose has been the subject of significant speculation. The suggestion that it was a specific response to Christianity, explaining John's references (9:22, 12:42, 16:2) to the eviction of Christians from the synagogue, is now largely rejected. Justin Martyr (e.g., *Dia.* 16:4 and 96:2),

Epiphanius (*c.* 315–403, *Haereses* 29:9)) and Jerome refer to it unambiguously, and they know that it curses Jewish Christians, calling them *minim* and Nazarenes. Jerome (in his commentary on Isa. 2:18) stated that 'three times each day in all the synagogues [Jews] under the name of Nazarenes curse the name "Christian" '.

Four classes of offenders are mentioned in the rabbinic texts: *minim*, *meshummadim* (apostates) *masoroth* (betrayers) and *epikorosim* (free thinkers, Jewish and non-Jewish). *Minim* seems to have been a very broad term, perhaps referring to different groups at different times. *Min* need not always refer to a Christian, but where the word does occur a polemical discussion is about to begin. The ruling laid down in the Tosefta states:

Slaughtering by a *min* is idolatry; their bread is Samaritan bread, their wine is wine offered to idols, their fruits are not tithes, their books are books of witchcraft and their sons are illegitimate. One does not sell to them or receive from them or take from them or give to them. (M. Hullin 2:20–21)

The precise application of *birkat ha-minim* seems to have depended on the historical context. *Minim* at times seems also to refer not to a specific group but rather to Jewish heretics in general. For Jews living in Christian lands, whose text did not include the more specific *notzerim*, *minim* often did designate Christians. The curse has been described as a test formula for the purpose of detecting those who might secretly be inclined to heresy, since heretics would obviously not want to state publicly a malediction against themselves. It is worth noting that the Mishnah, compiled towards the end of the second century, does not mention the formula.

The following passage describes the application of the *birkat ha-minim*:

Rabbi Ahi and Rabbi Judah ben Pazi were seated together in the synagogue. One of them came and recited the prayers but he altered one of the benedictions. They came and laid the question to Rabbi Simon. Rabbi Simon said to them in the name of Rabbi Joshua ben Levi, 'A congregation may be unconcerned if someone alters two or three benedictions. They do not have him read them over again.' He taught it differently: 'Generally, they do not have him recite it over again, except in the case of one, who does not say, "who makes the dead live", "who humbles the arrogant ones", and "who builds Jerusalem". [In that case] I should say that he is a *min*.' Samuel the Small recited the prayers and altered the end of 'who humbles the arrogant ones'. He remained staring at them. They said to him, 'the sages did not imagine this'. (JT. *Berakhot* 5.4.9c)

The passage shows how the Eighteen Benedictions developed into what might be described as doctrines of faith. Three are given special prominence and it is the refusal of a Jew to pronounce any of these three that is the focus of the discussion. The three examples of deviation represent the three movements that threatened Rabbinic Judaism. Each is regarded as the way of the *minim* and minimal flexibility is allowed towards those who adhere to the deviation.

The first assertion, 'who makes the dead live', refers to one of the divisions between the rabbis and the Sadducees. The latter rejected the belief in physical resurrection.

The third assertion, 'who builds Jerusalem', refers to those Jews who reject Jerusalem as their spiritual homeland, and as the city which they will eventually return to and rebuild.

The second, 'who humbles the arrogant ones', is a malediction that might originally have referred to the Christians. The term 'the arrogant ones' actually refers to the Roman Empire. However, when the malediction is taken as a whole, it might include the cursing of Christians. We can derive this conclusion from the Cairo Genizah version which is probably datable to the ninth century. It reads:

For apostates (*meshummadim*) may there be no hope unless they return to Your Torah; And the kingdom of arrogance may You quickly uproot in our days; And may the Christians (*ha-Notzerim*) and the *minim* perish in an instant. May they be erased from the book of life; And alone with the righteous may they not be written. Blessed art thou, O Lord, who humblest the arrogant ones.

In the Genizah version the word *Notzerim* might refer to a special sect, but seems to be a play on the word 'Nazarene' and is most likely to denote Christians. We have already noted Jerome's comment that the term Nazarenes was applied to Christians but it is not clear that this is earlier than the general sectarian designation. It is possible that, with the rise in Jewish anti-Christian disputation literature, the reference to the Christians was added to the *Birkat Ha-Minim*. It is also possible that *minim* was a title not directed at any specific enemies but a general term for condemnation.

CHAPTER 5

Biblical interpretation: Another side to the story

In the previous two chapters we saw that whilst Jews and Christians shared many of the same Scriptures they read them in dramatically different ways. Christian writers were astonished at what they considered to be Jewish 'blindness': their failure to see and comprehend the truth that was proclaimed in their own sacred texts. Jewish writers were perturbed by Christian interpretations not rooted in the original Hebrew, or removed from their historical and textual context, or that abandoned completely the simple meaning of the words in favour of other significance. Although there existed an abundance of examples of texts, which were primarily polemical and many of which were vituperative, there is also another more positive story to tell. This story demonstrates a more constructive and mutually beneficial encounter between Christians and Jews during these formative centuries. In this chapter we will identify a two-way encounter between Jewish and Christian biblical commentators who were often aware of each other's interpretations, for good, not just for ill.

The Bible and its interpretations are key to understanding the relationship between Judaism and Christianity because Jews and Christians shared (and continue to share) a biblically orientated culture. A number of similarities between Jewish and Christian interpretations can immediately be noted, such as an insistence on the harmony of Scripture and an emphasis on the sanctity of the text. Consequently, both Jewish and Christian interpretations were understandable to many adherents of both religions, as is noticeable in patristic and rabbinic writings and in early Jewish and Christian art.

Another similarity shared by the church fathers and rabbis is that they sometimes asked the same question of the biblical text. This occurred because both the rabbis and the church fathers were very close readers of the biblical texts and interested in the detail of Scripture. This is illustrated by Origen who commended his community to 'observe each detail of Scripture, which has been written. For, if one knows how to dig into the

81

depth, he will find a treasure in the details, and perhaps also the precious jewels of the mystery lie hidden where they are not esteemed'. (*Homilies on Genesis* 8:1). It is not entirely by chance that Origen uses the metaphor of 'digging' beneath the text to make sense of it. The metaphor also aptly describes rabbinic hermeneutics, which seeks to derive meaning from the detail of Scripture. Origen is representative of both the patristic and the rabbinic traditions when he writes that 'the wisdom of God pervades every divinely inspired writing, reaching out to each single letter' (*On Psalms* 1:4). Similarly, Rabbi Ben Bag Bag, who lived in the first century CE, writes for the church fathers as well as the rabbis when he states, 'turn, turn and turn it again, and you will find something new in it' (M. Avot 5:21).

It has been argued, however, by scholars such as Jacob Neusner, that although Judaism and Christianity share some of the same Scriptures these writings form part of a larger canon: the Old Testament and New Testament for Christians; the Written and Oral Torah for Jews. It has also been suggested that significant differences in their approaches arose as a result of the fact that Jews and Christians were interested in different books of the Bible – for instance, Christian interest in the Prophets compared to Jewish interest in the Pentateuch. It is also worth mentioning the contrast between the Christian dependence on the Greek Septuagint and the Jewish dependence on the Hebrew Masoretic text. Thus, it is suggested, Jews and Christians read different texts.

Although there are differences between the Jewish and Christian Scriptures, such arguments can be overstated. It is clear that the rabbis and the church fathers developed their own distinctive literary methods but their approaches did not prevent particular interpretations from being understood in both communities. Simply put, much of the discussion that has taken place between Christians and Jews over nearly two millennia has been centred upon the interpretation of the same biblical story (albeit in different translations). This led to the occurrence of exegetical encounter between Jewish and Christian commentators from the formative period onwards.

There are a number of ways that it is possible to identify an encounter between commentators. Firstly, we should look out for an explicit reference to a source, perhaps an explicit reference to an opposing view. This is often (although not always) found in Christian literature and especially in the *Adversus Iudaeos* writings. However, there is a danger that Christian references to Jews and Judaism were simply part of a literary genre. We therefore need to show caution even in cases where a church father explicitly refers to a Jewish source. Nevertheless, patristic references to Jewish teachers and exegesis or rabbinic references to the *minim* should be taken seriously, particularly if they exist alongside other criteria.

The second indication of an exegetical encounter is when, in the course of their interpretations, Jewish and Christian exegetes refer to the same scriptural quotation. Although it is possible that the exegetes may have chosen the same quotation separately, the choice is unlikely to have been purely coincidental. A third sign is the use of the same words, symbols and images, especially if the interpretations share the same extra-biblical descriptions. Clearly, the literary form can be chosen without recourse to another exegete's interpretations, since it may include telling stories, asking questions, offering instruction, and so on. A fourth indicator is if Jewish and Christian exegetes reach the same or opposite conclusions (when those conclusions are not dependent upon the literal meaning of the text). It can be argued, of course, that exegetes may reach the conclusion by separate means, but this criterion becomes particularly applicable when found alongside other criteria.

Finally, and probably most importantly, is a reference to a well-known subject of controversy between Jews and Christians. If the *Adversus Iudaeos* literature were directed either internally towards Christians or externally towards pagans, one would expect little or no evidence of Jewish interest. If, however, Jewish interpretations indicate an awareness of the Christian polemic one could conclude, first, that Jews were paying attention and, second, it was felt that a Jewish response was required.

CASE STUDY OF AN ENCOUNTER: INTERPRETATIONS OF GENESIS 22

The willingness of someone to give up his own life for a greater cause is well known in religious writings. Both Judaism and Christianity extol self-sacrifice, illustrated by one of the most famous stories in the Bible – the Sacrifice of Isaac. The focus of the story is normally understood as Abraham's relationship with God and how his faith in and commitment to God were demonstrated by his willingness to sacrifice his long-awaited son at God's command.

As a piece of writing, the biblical account has everything. It has tension and drama. Enough action for a five-act play. Yet it is compressed into eighteen verses. It is packed with energy and dynamism. It is a paradigm of Aristotle's catharsis, arousing both terror and pity. It deals with the biggest themes and touches the deepest emotions. And it seems to have a happy ending.

It has every thing except one – an immediately apparent, morally acceptable and topically relevant message. How could Abraham reconcile the bizarre demand by God to sacrifice his son with the divine promise that he would be the ancestor of a people who would spread throughout the world?

As well as being a well-known biblical story, Genesis 22 is treated only once in the Hebrew Bible and there exists no internal biblical exegesis to complicate the examination of post-biblical exegesis. In addition, there are few differences between the various Greek translations and the Hebrew text: Jews and Christians read, almost word for word, the same story whether in Hebrew or Greek. Thus Jewish and Christian exegetes started with a common text, which ensures that interaction cannot be explained by textual transmission.

The Sacrifice of Isaac has been an important story for both Jews and Christians from a very early period. For Jews, from at least as early as the third century CE, the passage has been read on Rosh ha-Shana, the Jewish New Year, and in daily morning prayers (*shacharit*). For Christians, from around the same period, the Sacrifice of Isaac has been mentioned in the Eucharist prayers and the story read in the period leading up to Easter. A wide variety of themes, central to both Judaism and Christianity, emerge from the commentators' interpretations, including the prediction of Christ's coming, fulfilment of Scripture, atonement and forgiveness.

We will now consider some examples.

Verses 1–2: God tests Abraham

And after these things God tested Abraham, and said to him, 'Abraham!' And he said, 'Here am I.' He said, 'Take your son, your only son, whom you love, Isaac, and go to the land of Moriah, and offer him there as a burnt offering upon one of the mountains which I shall tell you.'

The church fathers shared with the rabbis a number of interpretations that explain the reasons for the test, such as a concern to respond to the charge that God desired human sacrifice. Another shared interpretation explains that the test enabled Abraham to be honoured throughout the world. Both the fathers and the rabbis explained that its purpose was to exalt Abraham. For instance, the rabbis stated that the episode educated the world about the excellence of Abraham. One interpretation declares that it took place to 'make known to the nations of the world that it was not without good reason that I [God] chose you [Abraham]' (*Tanhuma Buber Ve-yera* 46; *Tanhuma Yelamdenu Ve-yera* 22).

Both the rabbis and the church fathers were interested in God's choice of words, 'your son, your only son, whom you love, Isaac'. They asked the same question – why did God not simply say 'Isaac'? – and came to the same conclusion, agreeing that the purpose of the drawn-out description of Isaac was to increase Abraham's affection. According to the rabbis, God's words not only indicated the extent of Abraham's love for Isaac but also made the test even more severe. Their purpose was 'to make Isaac more beloved in his eyes' (Genesis Rabbah 55:7). Gregory of Nyssa (330–*c.* 395) offered a similar interpretation, which can also be found in the writings of a number of church fathers:

See the goads of these words, how they prick the innards of the father; how they kindle the flame of nature; how they awaken the love by calling the son 'beloved' and 'the only one'. Through these names the affection towards him [Isaac] is brought to the boil. (*De Deitate*)

Another example of a shared interpretation is the common use by Jewish and Christian exegetes of dialogue as a means of explaining the reason for God's command. The church fathers created an imaginary account of what Abraham might have said to God, but did not. The rabbis, on the other hand, constructed a conversation that Abraham did have with God. Gregory of Nyssa proposed the following imaginary words, spoken by Abraham to God:

'Why do You command these things, O Lord? On account of this You made me a father so that I could become a childkiller? On account of this You made me taste the sweet gift so that I could become a story for the world? With my own hands will I slaughter my child and pour an offering of the blood of my family to You? Do you call for such things and do you delight in such sacrifices? Do I kill my son by whom I expected to be buried? Is this the marriage chamber I prepare for him? Is this the feast of marriage that I prepare for him? Will I not light a marriage torch for him but rather a funeral pyre? Will I crown him in addition to these things? Is this how I will be a "father of the nations" – one who has not produced a child?'
Did Abraham say any such word, or think it? Not at all! (*De Deitate*)

The dialogue enabled Gregory to invite his congregation to consider what their reaction might have been had they received such a command. He suggests that, had Abraham hesitated and challenged God, his reaction would have been representative of that of the fathers in his congregation. However, as befits a theatrical performance, Gregory brings Abraham's imaginary questioning to an end with the closing statement that, unlike everyone else, Abraham said no such thing. He did not complain or think of complaining. The dialogue enabled Gregory to exalt Abraham and promote him as a model to follow. Whilst Gregory's congregants would, he suggested, 'argue with the command', Abraham 'gave himself up wholly to God and was entirely set on [fulfilling] the commandment'.

The rabbis also used dialogue in their interpretation and, like Gregory, developed an element of theatre:

God said to Abraham:	'Please take your son.'
Abraham said:	'I have two sons, which one?'
God:	'Your only son.'
Abraham:	'The one is the only son of his mother and the other is the only son of his mother.'
God:	'Whom you love.'
Abraham:	'I love this one and I love that one.'
God:	'Isaac.' (Genesis Rabbah 39:9 and 55:7)

The purpose of the rabbinic dialogue was quite different from that of Gregory. In addition to arousing the amusement of the audience, the interpretation reveals that Abraham either deliberately misunderstood the command or attempted to delay its implementation. Whilst the rabbis offered a similar literary form, in other words the use of dialogue, its purpose is in marked contrast to the conclusion of the church fathers, who did not once question Abraham's desire to fulfil God's command.

In the next interpretation the subject of priesthood, a well-known source of controversy between Jews and Christians, is discussed in the context of Genesis 22. This disputed subject was central to the interpretations of both the church fathers and the rabbis although, not surprisingly, their conclusions were diametrically opposed. The rabbis discussed Abraham's response to God's command and depicted him as asking God whether he had the authority to sacrifice Isaac.

He [Abraham] said to Him, 'Sovereign of the Universe, can there be a sacrifice without a priest?' 'I have already appointed you a priest' said the Holy One, Blessed be He, 'as it is written "You are a priest for ever." (Ps. 110:4).' (Genesis Rabbah 55:7)

God explains that Abraham had already been appointed a priest and cites Psalm 110:4 in support. The rabbis concluded that Abraham was suitable for priesthood and kingship:

On two occasions Moses compared himself to Abraham and God answered him, 'do not glorify yourself in the presence of the king and do not stand in the place of great men' (Prov. 25:6). Now Abraham said, 'Here I am' – ready for priesthood and ready for kingship and he attained priesthood and kingship. He attained priesthood as it is said, 'The Lord has promised and will not change: you are a priest forever after Melchizedek' (Ps. 110:4); kingship: 'you are a mighty prince among us' (Gen. 23:5). (Genesis Rabbah 55:7)

Once again, Melchizedek is mentioned and the rabbis extol Abraham, making a favourable comparison between him and Moses. The reason why Melchizedek is important to the rabbis is that the priesthood was taken away from him and bestowed upon Abraham (and in another rabbinic passage Melchizedek is said to reappear in the messianic era (BT. *Sukk.* 52b)).

The interpretations of Origen provide an interesting contrast. He begins by describing Isaac not only as the victim but also as the priest, because whoever carried the wood for the burnt offering must also have borne the office of priest. Isaac was like Christ, yet Christ was a priest 'for ever, according to the order of Melchizedek' (Ps. 110:4; *Homilies on Genesis* 8:9). As well as quoting Psalm 110:4, Origen also makes the same comparison as the rabbis between Abraham (and Isaac) and Moses. Abraham, he states, was superior to Moses.

Origen's reference to Psalm 110:4 is significant; it parallels the rabbis' quotation and at the same time mentions Melchizedek, who was also an important figure in the early Church. Melchizedek's significance is illustrated by the fact that he is mentioned nine times in the letter to the Hebrews and highlights the superiority of Christ's priesthood over the Levitical priesthood. Hebrews also quotes Psalm 110:4 to reveal the obsolete character of Jewish worship and ritual that followed the Levitical order. Since Christ was viewed as High Priest 'after the order of Melchizedek' and 'not after the order of Aaron', Christ's priesthood was superior to that of the Levites.

The significance of Melchizedek and of Psalm 110:4 would not have been lost on either Origen or the rabbis. As far as Origen was concerned, the eternal priesthood of Christ was foreshadowed by the priesthood of Abraham and Isaac, while in contrast the rabbis argued that Abraham, rather than Melchizedek, was a priest for ever and that this authority could not be transferred elsewhere. The rabbinic interpretation is a riposte to Christian teaching because it argued that if Moses, the greatest prophet of all, was not worthy to be called king and priest, no one else (i.e., Christ) could be king and priest.

The rabbis used the comparison between Moses and Abraham to show that the latter was suitable not only for priesthood but also for kingship, implying that no other person could be chosen. Abraham, and by extension

Jews, would retain this authority for ever; in other words, it could not be taken away or appropriated by another figure.

Verses 6–8: Abraham and Isaac's journey to Moriah

And Abraham took the wood of the burnt offering, and laid it on Isaac his son; and he took in his hand the fire and the knife. So they went both of them together. And Isaac said to his father Abraham, 'My father!' And he said, 'Here I am, my son.' He said, 'Behold, the fire and the wood; but where is the lamb for a burnt offering?' Abraham said, 'God will provide himself the lamb for a burnt offering, my son.' So they went both of them together.

The figure of Isaac is the key by which to unlock an exegetical encounter between Jewish and Christian commentators in their interpretations of Genesis 22. In the interpretations of the church fathers, Isaac is portrayed as a youth (unlike some early post-biblical writers such as Josephus and Philo who portray him as an adult). Cyril, for example, describes him as 'small and lying in the breast of his own father' (*Glaphyra on Genesis*), and Eusebius comments that Genesis 22:13 'did not say, "a lamb", young like Isaac, but "a ram", full-grown, like the Lord' (*Catena* 1277). Other church fathers, such as Chrysostom, portray Isaac as slightly more mature, but nevertheless retaining his youthfulness: 'Isaac had come of age and was in fact in the very bloom of youth' (*Homilies on Genesis*).

Thus two opinions existed in the writings of the church fathers. The first saw Isaac as a child and the second viewed him as a youth or young man. It is clear that, although there is a discrepancy between the two, the church fathers agreed that whilst Isaac played an important role he remained young and had not yet reached full adulthood.

The rabbinic position was quite different. The rabbis stated that 'Isaac was 37 years of age when he was offered upon the altar' (Genesis Rabbah 55:4). Another interpretation gave his age as 26 years (Genesis Rabbah 56:8) and a third proposed 36 years (Targum Pseudo-Jonathan). It is significant that, whilst the precise age varied, the rabbis were consistent in their portrayal of Isaac as an adult. None of the rabbinic interpretations, in direct contrast to those of the church fathers, hinted that Isaac might have still been a child. He was a fully developed and mature adult.

The church fathers also consider in some detail the significance of Isaac carrying the wood, viewing it as a model of Jesus carrying the cross. Evidence of a typological association between the wood and the cross can already be seen as early as the second century CE in the writings of Melito,

Bishop of Sardis. Melito points to a large number of parallels between Isaac and Jesus:

- Isaac carrying the wood to the place of slaughter was a reference to Christ carrying the cross.
- Isaac, like Jesus, knew what was to befall him.
- By remaining silent both indicated their acceptance of the will of God.
- Isaac 'carried with fortitude the model of the Lord'.
- Both Isaac and Jesus were bound.
- Each was led to the sacrifice by his father, an act that caused great astonishment.
- Neither was sorrowful at his impending sacrifice.

For Melito, Isaac represents Christ and is a model of Christ, who was going to suffer. On the one hand, Isaac paralleled Christ; on the other, he looked forward to Christ. As the *Epistle of Barnabas* stated, Jesus 'fulfilled the type' that was established in Isaac (7:3), pointing forward to the even more amazing deed in the sacrifice of Christ. Melito stated, 'Christ suffered, [but] Isaac did not suffer,' demonstrating, first, that the sacrifice of Isaac was not complete, and, second, that it prefigured the future sacrifice of Christ. What is important is that Isaac was not sacrificed but remained only the model, waiting to be fulfilled by Christ.

Typology, then, was the reason why the church fathers viewed Isaac as a child. He represented an outline, an immature image of what lay ahead. The child (Isaac) was to be fulfilled by the adult (Christ). The rabbis, on the other hand, maintained that Isaac was an adult. His action was not to be interpreted in the light of any later event but had significance in its own right.

Like the church fathers, the rabbis also commented on Isaac carrying the wood; the following appears remarkably similar:

'And Abraham placed the wood of the burnt-offering on Isaac his son.' Like a man who carries his cross on his shoulder. (Genesis Rabbah 56:3)

This interpretation, in Genesis Rabbah, one of the oldest and most well-known midrashim from fifth-century Palestine, betrays an exegetical encounter. The reference to a cross (*zaluv*), the principal Christian symbol, is an explicit reference to Christianity, which the rabbis have appropriated and dressed in a Jewish garb.

The rabbis depict Isaac as a mature adult who was willing to suffer and give up his life at God's command. The emphasis was not on whether Isaac had actually been sacrificed but on his willingness to be sacrificed, not on martyrdom but on self-offering. Isaac was not forced to offer himself as a sacrifice but willingly gave himself to Abraham. For example, in one interpretation the rabbis portray Isaac speaking to God, as follows:

Sovereign of the Universe, when my father said to me, 'God will provide for Himself a lamb for the burnt offering', I raised no objection to the carrying out of Your words and I willingly let myself be bound on top of the altar and stretched out my neck under the knife. (Lamentations Rabbah, Proem)

Isaac's willingness to give up his life represents a rabbinic response to the Christian teaching that Christ was willing to give up his life for Israel, illustrated by Cyril of Alexandria's interpretation:

And the child, Isaac, was loaded with the wood for the sacrifice by the hand of the father until he reached the place of the sacrifice. By carrying his own cross on his shoulders outside the gates (John 19:17–21) Christ suffered, not having been forced by human strength into His suffering, but by His own will, and by the will of God. (*Glaphyra on Genesis*)

For the rabbis, the willingness of Isaac to give up his life is reinforced by the suggestion that he was informed in advance of the sacrifice and continued the journey with Abraham. Unlike the church fathers, who laid stress on the fact that Abraham did not tell his son of the impending sacrifice, the rabbis argued that Isaac's awareness of what was to happen served to emphasise his full participation in the sacrifice. According to the church fathers, however, Abraham gave no indication to Isaac of the impending sacrifice.

The emphasis on Isaac's self-offering led the rabbis to associate Genesis 22 primarily with Isaac rather than with Abraham (who remained the central figure for the church fathers), and the biblical story was called 'The Binding of Isaac' (Akedah). For the rabbis, the self-offering of the adult Isaac was sufficient to provide benefit (*zecut avot*) to Isaac's children (the Jewish People) for future generations. For the church fathers, the story was called the Sacrifice of Isaac, because the child Isaac was an outline of the adult Christ and his self-offering foreshadowed the saving sacrifice of Christ.

The rabbis suggested that because Isaac was a fully grown adult, in contrast to his father who was an old man, he must have metaphorically 'bound himself' for, if he had so desired, he could have prevented his elderly father from binding him. Isaac's request to his father to bind him implied that he was not forced into it.

In their view, so willing was Isaac to give up his life that they described the Akedah in terms such as 'the blood of the binding of Isaac' or 'the ashes of Isaac'. This is startling because the biblical account explicitly states that the angel stopped Abraham from harming his son and commanded him 'not to do anything' to Isaac. An illustration of this interpretation can be found in the *Mekhilta de Rabbi Ishmael*:

'And when I see the blood, I will pass over you' (Exod. 13:12 and 25) – I see the blood of the Binding of Isaac. For it is said, 'And Abraham called the name of that place, "the Lord will see".' Likewise it says in another passage, 'And as He was about to destroy the Lord beheld and repented Him' (1 Chron. 21:15). What did He behold? He beheld the blood of the Binding of Isaac, as it is said, 'God will for Himself see to the lamb.' (Pisha 7 and 11)

This interpretation clearly suggests that Isaac's blood was shed – an opinion repeated in the *Mekhilta de Rabbi Shimon ben Yochai*, which states that Isaac 'gave one fourth of his blood on the altar'. According to the rabbis, blood and ashes were an intrinsic aspect of atoning ritual since biblical times and their adoption in rabbinic interpretations of Genesis 22 consequently links the Akedah to atonement and the Temple. For example, there is a tradition that states that the Temple was rebuilt where Isaac's ashes were found (BT. *Zebulun* 62a).

Remarkably, the rabbis even suggested that Isaac died, according to the eighth-century CE text *Pirkei de Rabbi Eliezer*, which describes the death of Isaac and his resurrection, which took place soon after:

When the sword touched his neck the soul of Isaac took flight and departed but when he heard the voice from between the two cherubim saying, . . . 'do not lay a hand' his soul returned to his body and [Abraham] set him free, and he stood on his feet. And Isaac knew the resurrection of the dead as taught by the Torah, that all the dead in the future would be revived. At that moment he opened [his mouth] and said, 'Blessed are You, O Lord, who revives the dead.' (chapter 31)

These examples show that rabbinic interpretations of the Binding of Isaac cannot be properly understood without reference to the Christian context. In other words, the rabbis were not only aware of, but were influenced by, Christian exegesis. And this was a two-way process, for Christian authors, as we have previously seen, were also influenced by rabbinic interpretations. The large number of shared interpretations, as well as examples of exegetical encounters, indicates the close relationship that existed between Jews and Christians for many hundreds of years. This relationship was based on a shared Scripture.

THE ARTISTIC EXEGETICAL ENCOUNTER

Up to now we have focused on homily, commentary and poetry, but biblical interpreters are not only preachers and teachers but also artists. Biblical interpretation is like an electric cable, made up of several individual wires, which together are capable of conducting spiritual and creative energy of great intensity. When they are brought together a connection is made; when left independent, they remain isolated. Combined, they provide light; left alone, their contribution is limited. Only one wire is normally traced and discussed — the literary interpretation of a biblical text. As a result, artistic interpretations are relegated to the role of poor cousin and, when studied, are viewed with the lens of the writer, not from the perspective of the artist. Yet artistic interpreters offer their own distinctive interpretations, which shed light on Jewish–Christian relations.

Genesis 22 was one of a small number of popular biblical images found in Jewish and Christian art in late antiquity. Gregory of Nyssa, for instance, wrote:

I have seen many times the likeness of this suffering in painting and not without tears have I come upon this sight, when art clearly led the story before the sight. (*On the Son of God and the Holy Spirit*)

Augustine of Hippo also discussed this subject:

The deed is so famous that it recurs to the mind of itself without any study or reflection, and is in fact repeated by so many tongues, and portrayed in so many places, that no-one can pretend to shut his eyes or his ears from it. (*Reply to Faustus the Manichaean* 22.73)

Christian artistic exegesis

The earliest Christian artistic representations of Genesis 22 can be seen in the Roman catacomb frescoes, which illustrate the theme of deliverance. For instance, in the Callixtus catacomb, dated from the first half of the third century CE, Abraham and the child Isaac offer thanks for their deliverance. Another (late) third-century fresco located in the Catacomb of Priscilla illustrates the same theme. It shows the boy Isaac carrying wood and Abraham pointing to a tree. Abraham is looking up to the heavens, perhaps hearing the word of God.

Two other fourth-century frescoes have very similar images. In the late third- or early fourth-century fresco in the Catacomb of Peter and Marcellinus (Fig. 1) Abraham holds a knife in his raised right hand and at his feet is the child Isaac – naked, kneeling and bound for the sacrifice. The ram appears on the far side of the altar, which is alight, and the image is above a scene of the paralytic carrying his bed. Cubiculum C in the Via

1. Catacomb of Peter and Marcellinus (3rd century).

Latina, from the late fourth century, reproduces this image almost exactly. The altar has wood burning upon it; nearby is the ram, which appears to be looking for Abraham who has a sword in his hand. Abraham is looking around (perhaps at an angel?) while Isaac is kneeling with his hands behind his back. Below is a representation of a servant with a donkey, possibly at the foot of the mountain.

In addition to frescoes, we commonly find images of the Sacrifice of Isaac in early Christian sarcophagi. The Mas d'Aire Sarcophagus from the third century is the earliest. It shows the child Isaac, bound and kneeling. Abraham grasps his hair from behind and raises the knife to strike. Abraham's eyes are not on Isaac but on the ram, which is standing at his side, almost nuzzling him and appearing eager to be sacrificed. In a Luc-de-Béarn sixth-century sarcophagus, a man and woman are watching the sacrifice. The woman, who has her hand to her mouth to indicate dismay, may be Sarah. The appearance of Sarah at the sacrifice is mentioned in the poems of Ephrem and other Syriac writings but rarely in the Greek or Latin fathers. She is also portrayed in the chapels of the El Bagawat (Egypt) necropolis, which are dated from the fourth century CE.

In El Bagawat's chapel of Exodus, Isaac stands with his arms crossed while his mother Sarah stands at his side and lifts her arms to the sky in an act of prayer. The ram stands under a tree and the hand of God is seen to the right of the name 'Abraham'. In the Chapel of Peace (Figs. 2 & 3) a hand (of an angel?) is throwing two knives in the air and another is held by Abraham. Isaac, a child, is unbound and his arms are outstretched, perhaps in supplication. Archaeologists have suggested that mother and son are holding incense. Sarah has a halo around her head and Abraham, Isaac and Sarah are all identified. As a result of the inclusion of Sarah, the artists of El Bagawat extend the biblical story to a whole family affair.

Two of the most famous church mosaics in late antiquity in Ravenna – San Vitale and San Apollinare in Classe – associate Genesis 22 with the offerings of Abel and Melchizedek and link the biblical narrative to the liturgy of the Eucharist. In San Vitale we find a mosaic portrayal of Abel and Melchizedek sharing a church altar near which are placed the bread and wine. Nearby appear the three angels announcing the promise of a son while Abraham offers them a calf and Sarah stands in the doorway of a tent. To the right is a representation of the Sacrifice of Isaac. In this, Isaac is kneeling on the altar and Abraham's sword is raised but the hand of God appears to prevent the sacrifice. At Abraham's feet is the ram looking at Abraham, striking a typical christological pose. These mosaics flank the real church altar where the Eucharist was celebrated. The biblical figures are linked by the following prayer:

> Be pleased to look upon these offerings with a gracious and favourable countenance, accept them even as you were pleased to accept the offerings of your just servant Abel, the sacrifice of Abraham, our patriarch and that of Melchizedek, your high priest – a holy sacrifice, a spotless victim.

Jewish artistic exegesis

One of the most famous Jewish representations of the Akedah is found in the third-century CE Dura-Europos synagogue. Externally, this synagogue was modest in the extreme, being located in a private house that could not compare architecturally with the city of Sardis. However, its uniqueness lay in its interior wall decorations. The city itself was founded by Seleucus I in approximately 300 BCE and remained a Seleucid outpost until the mid second century BCE when it was captured by the Parthians. For the

2. El Bagawat Chapel of Peace (5th century).

3. Line drawing of sacrifice of Isaac in El Bagawat Chapel of Peace.

next three centuries it flourished as a centre for east–west trade. In the second century CE it was captured by the Romans but it was destroyed by the Persians in 256 CE and never resettled. Dura-Europos contained sixteen temples catering to the needs of an eclectic pantheon of Roman, Greek and Persian gods. It also contained a modest Christian chapel. In the synagogue there are more than thirty scenes covering the four walls of a 40 ft room. The image of the Akedah (fig. 4) is found over the opening for the ark, the Torah shrine. This was the most prominent feature of the synagogue and was always built on the Jerusalem-orientated wall.

Our eye moves from left to right focusing first on the menorah, the palm branch (*lulav*) and the citron (*etrog*). At the centre we see the Temple and, to the right, the Akedah. The symbols of Sukkot and the Temple suggest a vision of a future feast of Tabernacles to be celebrated in Jerusalem by all nations, as described in Zechariah 14. The Temple could be viewed in terms of the future as much as the past and might represent a new Temple to be built on the site of the destroyed Temple. The synagogue building had been dedicated 170 years after the destruction of the Second Temple and restoration was a realistic dream, as Julian the Apostate would make clear 120 years later.

Examining the characters in more detail we can see that a primitively drawn Abraham, knife in hand, stands resolutely with his back to the onlooker, as does the little bundle of Isaac lying on the altar. This is emphasised by the shock of black hair that we see on both figures rather than facial features. Isaac is clearly a child and appears unbound. In the distance a tiny figure, also with a shock of black hair, stands before a tent, with an opening on the top. This figure has been variously interpreted as Abraham's servant, Ishmael, Abraham himself in his house and Sarah. However, arguments are readily available that render each proposal unlikely. For instance, the figure appears to be wearing a man's clothing and is therefore unlikely to be Sarah; he is not wearing the same clothes as Abraham (and therefore unlikely to be Abraham); the traditions concerning hostility between Isaac and Ishmael were influenced by the rise of Islam (seventh century), which rules out Ishmael. It is possible that the character is another depiction of Isaac, as the tent is touching the altar upon which Isaac lies and the figure is the same size as Isaac and shares his black hair. Remembering that Sarah died straight after the Akedah (Genesis 23) and that the first time Isaac was comforted was when Rebecca was brought to him and taken into his mother's tent (Gen. 24:67), this seems plausible. The open hand of God appears beside the tent; this representation is the earliest surviving image of the hand of God.

4. Dura-Europos Torah shrine (3rd century).

5. Beit Alpha Synagogue (6th century).

There are a number of changes to the biblical story, such as Isaac being unbound, the third character and the presence of the hand of God, but the representation is in part closer to the biblical text than some other artistic representations. In the lower foreground the rather large ram waits patiently, tethered to a tree, its central location emphasising its importance to the artist. Although the rabbis suggested that the ram had been created on the sixth day of creation and had been waiting ever since for its moment of destiny (e.g., *Pirkei Avot* 5:6), they did not give a great deal of attention to it nor did they describe it being tethered to a tree. Indeed, there appears no Jewish literary source for this artistic interpretation. However, the fourth-century Coptic Bible mentions a 'ram tied to a tree', which may indicate that Jewish artistic interpretation retains a tradition no longer found in Jewish literature. This suggestion is supported by artistic evidence elsewhere, both Jewish and Christian, which depicts the ram tied to a tree.

In the mosaic floor of a sixth-century synagogue called Beit Alpha, a sequence of three scenes, bordered like a carpet, leads to the Torah located in a wall orientated towards Jerusalem: the Akedah, the zodiac with Helios and his four horses, and the ark.

Our view of the Akedah (fig. 5) moves from left to right, from the donkey to the ram to Isaac; from the accompanying youths to Abraham. The Hebrew, naturally, moves from right to left identifying Isaac, the ram and the command issuing from the hand of God. Abraham throws Isaac into the fire on the altar while the hand of God, as at Dura-Europos, prevents the sacrifice. A large ram is standing erect, tied to a tree, although following the biblical story it is also caught by one horn.

Perhaps the most remarkable figure is the child Isaac, floating beyond Abraham's fingertips. Does Abraham hold him close, or at arm's length in preparation for the loss? Isaac is suspended and his arms are crossed but not bound, swinging precariously between the flames of the sacrifice and his obedient father. The trial is still Abraham's – but not unequivocally, for we focus on the helpless, dangling figure of the son.

The ambiguity of the mosaic raises the question of Isaac's willingness. As mentioned earlier, the rabbis emphasise Isaac's voluntary obedience by describing his maturity and giving his age as 26, 36 or 37 years. The artistic portrayal of Isaac as a child suggests that he has little active role in the sacrifice. It is even possible to view him as a reluctant participant. Once again, we can see that artistic interpretation possesses its own emphasis, significantly different from the literary interpretation.

Another portrayal of the Akedah is found in an early fifth-century synagogue in Sepphoris, capital of the Galilee. The mosaic floor is the most important part of the synagogue that has survived, covering the building's entire floor and consisting of fourteen panels. The central band depicts the zodiac. Each of the twelve signs, which surround the sun, is identified with the name of the month in Hebrew. Most have images of young men, the majority clothed but some naked; the four seasons are depicted in the corners accompanied by agricultural objects characteristic of each season.

The Akedah is depicted in two panels (fig. 6) and includes a Greek inscription. According to the archaeologists, the image shows the two servants who remain at the bottom of the mountain with the ass. One holds a spear while his other hand is raised slightly in a gesture similar to the depiction of Ezekiel in Dura-Europos. The other servant sits under a tree, holding the ass.

There is no other instance of a servant making the special sign, so perhaps, rather than a servant, the figure may be Abraham instructing the servant to remain behind. In this gesture, the palm is turned outward and the second and third fingers are held extended while the thumb, the fourth and the fifth fingers are doubled back against the palm. The most familiar analogy is the Christian gesture of benediction, found commonly in Byzantine art.

The right-hand panel is badly damaged and depicts the head of an animal tethered to the tree by its left horn; below are two upturned pairs of

6. Sepphoris Synagogue (5th century).

shoes – a small pair for Isaac and a large pair for Abraham. Isaac's small pair of shoes again emphasises that, for the Jewish artistic exegetes, he was a boy. The idea of removing shoes is probably derived from other biblical passages such as Moses at the burning bush (Exod. 3:5). The artist is suggesting that when Abraham and Isaac reached the sacred spot they would have removed their shoes out of respect for the sanctity of the site; the image provides an alternative exegetical tradition.

In sum, the Akedah was part of an extensive tradition of synagogue decoration. It is highly unlikely that its existence in three synagogues was mere chance. Isaac is always portrayed as a child, which reminds us that artistic interpreters do not necessarily follow literary interpretations. In this case, the exegetes emphasise the helplessness of the child and not the voluntary self-offering found in rabbinic literature. They also expand the role of the ram. Whereas in the biblical story the ram appears to have been on Mount Moriah by chance, and it is rarely mentioned in the rabbinic writings, the artistic representation emphasises the significance of the ram through its size and prominent position.

It is clear from this brief study that artists offer their own interpretations of Scripture, as evidenced by portrayals of Genesis 22. An examination of the literary interpretation on its own, although illustrative of the diversity of literary tradition, does not tell the whole story. The diversity of Jewish and Christian representations is striking. The artists who created images based on the biblical story should be viewed as exegetes in their own right, offering their own interpretations, some of which conflict with the better-known interpretations found in the writings of the church fathers or the rabbis.

There are a number of similarities between the representations of Jewish and Christian artists, some of which show variations from the biblical text such as the ram being tied to a tree (rather than caught by its horns in a bush), and Christian artistic interpretations sometimes follow the same pattern as Jewish (or vice versa). They demonstrate a positive Jewish–Christian encounter in late antiquity and provide further evidence of Jews and Christians working together in ancient times.

Some religious leaders have criticised these artistic representations, seeing in their diversity the possibility of danger and error. Luther complained that 'the picture commonly painted about Abraham about to kill his son is incorrect' (*Luther's Works: Lectures on Genesis*, ed. Jaroslav Pelikan, St Louis: Concordia, 1964, p. 110). In fact, the portrayals of Genesis 22 exhibit not errors, but interpretations of the biblical text. Sometimes these interpretations mirror literary developments; on other occasions, they are not found elsewhere. In the words of the church father Gregory of Nyssa, valid for Jewish as well as Christian art, there are occasions when 'art clearly led the story'.

CHAPTER 6

Medieval relations

The medieval period, which for this study is defined as between the tenth and the seventeenth centuries, was a time of violence and prejudice as Christian society became increasingly intolerant, especially from the twelfth century, not just toward Jews but toward everyone deemed deviant.

In the chapter on the church fathers we noted that Jewish rights granted by the Theodosian and Justinian Codes were progressively removed. In the medieval period this process accelerated. Legislation enabled local authorities to outlaw Judaism, close synagogues and enforce baptisms (despite some church council opposition). For example, the Fourth Lateran Council in 1215 addressed a variety of political and doctrinal issues, including the position of Jews in Christendom. Some laws were renewed, such as the law forbidding Jews to appear in public during Easter, especially on Good Friday (a ruling said to prevent mocking of Christians but also perhaps partly for the Jews' own protection). Other laws were new, such as that which compelled Jews (and Muslims living under Christian rule) to wear distinctive dress, in order to avoid 'prohibited intercourse' (especially sexual relations).

The practice of demarcating a religious minority by requiring its members to wear distinctive clothes originated in Islam, which imposed dress restrictions on both Jews and Christians in the time of Omar II (717–20). When discriminatory dress regulations entered Christian canon law in 1215, it testified to a society in which it was assumed that the category to which every individual belonged (nobles, serfs, clergy, etc.) should be identifiable by dress. Restrictions on Jewish dress continued for many hundreds of years and, although they had been removed throughout most of Europe by the eighteenth century, the Nazis restored dress restrictions against Jews during the Holocaust.

The medieval period witnessed significant anti-Jewish violence, and during the First Crusade in 1096, despite some protection offered by local bishops, between 5,000 and 10,000 Jews perished. From the twelfth century, accusations against Jews escalated, including charges of Jewish ritual murder of Christian children, host desecration and causing the Black Death. This was also the time of the Inquisition, the burning of thousands of Talmuds and other Jewish books, the preaching of conversionist sermons at which Jewish attendance was compulsory, and enforced public disputations.

Yet Jewish communities continued to flourish during these centuries, and hostility is only one factor among many that determined medieval Christian–Jewish relations. For all the Christian hostility and violence and the inevitable anti-Christian Jewish response, there were also outbreaks of tolerance and positive interaction between Jews and Christians (and, in the Iberian Peninsula, Muslims). Salo W. Baron (1895–1989) criticised 'the lachrymose conception of Jewish history', a view of Jewish historical experience under Christian rule as a vale of tears, of unrelieved oppression and suffering, a view fostered by the tendency of medieval Jews to write chronicles not during normal times but precisely during times of crisis, in order to memorialise the dead or to encourage the survivors.

POLEMIC: CHRISTIAN

In the medieval Christian mind, the terrifying concept of the antichrist, the satanic princely ruler and arch-enemy of Christ in the end-times, became a recurrent anti-Jewish motif. Rooted in Persian and Babylonian mythology and adapted from Jewish sources, Christian notions of the antichrist were first applied to historical enemies of the Church such as the Emperor Nero (37–68) and the Gnostics. While medieval and Reformation polemicists intermittently identified political opponents such as individual popes and emperors, Jews were constantly linked to the antichrist. Popular imagination envisaged the antichrist as a demonically conceived Jew. Medieval Christian art, drama and sermons followed suit.

The myth of blood libel (the accusation that Jews would kill a young Christian boy and use his blood in the ritual preparation of *matzah* for Passover) stems partly from perceptions of Jews as servants of the antichrist. Its origins appear in antiquity where Josephus relates that Antiochus Epiphanes (r. 175–164 BCE) was told that Jews engage in human sacrifice within the precincts of the Temple; similarly the early Latin apologist Felix Marcus Minucius (early third century CE), testifies to accusations of Christians murdering a child during a ceremony admitting new adherents into the Christian faith.

The earliest historical example of the libel is the case of William of Norwich in 1144. When the twelve-year-old boy's body was found, his uncle blamed the Jews of Norwich, but this accusation did not result in any action. It was only with the arrival in 1150 of the monk Thomas of Monmouth that the local tale became infamous. Thomas wrote an account of the life of William, of his Passion and the miracles that took place around his tomb, and later around the shrine in Norwich cathedral. In the next few centuries, similar accusations arose around the country, such as in Lincoln in 1255 when a boy (known later as Little St Hugh) was supposedly imprisoned, tortured and killed by Lincoln's Jews in mocking re-enactment of the crucifixion. The blood libel led to the execution of nineteen Jews and Geoffrey Chaucer (*c.* 1342–1400) wrote about the Lincoln blood libel charge in *The Prioress's Tale*. After 750 years, in 2005, the cathedral acknowledged Lincoln's role in perpetrating medieval anti-Jewish prejudice by hosting a unique Shabbat service for the local Jewish community when special prayers of penitence were offered.

Despite official secular and ecclesiastical investigations in the thirteenth century by Emperor Frederick II (r. 1215–50) and Pope Innocent IV (*c.* 1200–54) that denied any possibility that Jews used human blood, accusations continued against Jews in Europe into the twentieth century. Indeed, in the 1930s the Nazis revived the charges that Jews killed children and used their blood. Today, similar accusations are occasionally repeated in the Middle East, wrapped in anti-Zionist garb.

In medieval art, anti-Jewish prejudice was pervasive. Jews were depicted as associates of Satan and the antichrist, shown with a sow, either sucking on her teats or performing other obscene acts. They had pointed chins, forked beards, distorted facial features (such as hooked noses) or physical deformities, and wore peculiar or foreign-looking costume such as peaked-shaped hats (*Judenhüte*) or yellow badges of identification. Jews as Christ-murderers and as mockers, torturers or executioners were also frequently shown in representations of the Passion.

As already mentioned, medieval Christian artists fashioned female figures called Ecclesia and Synagoga to represent Christianity's relationship to Judaism. The figures of triumphant 'Ecclesia' and defeated 'Synagoga' symbolised the Christian claim that Judaism was obsolete. Depictions present the proud Ecclesia standing erect in contrast to the bowed, blindfolded figure of the defeated yet dignified Synagoga (e.g., the thirteenth-century stone figures in the cathedrals of Strasbourg and Notre Dame, Paris). Like Leah of the weak eyes (Gen. 29:17), Synagoga was blind, failing to recognise the light of Christ; her crown had fallen and her staff broken, while Ecclesia was the younger and beautiful sister, Rachel. In the Later Middle Ages Synagoga becomes a more contemptible and commonly found figure in anti-Jewish Christian art, sometimes portrayed in the clutch of a devil who rides on her neck and forces her to turn away from Christ.

Another common form of medieval Christian anti-Jewish polemic can be found in the growth and popularity of disputations, a form of discourse where one party refutes the validity of the other in order to invalidate the foundation of the other's faith. Whilst disputational literature can be seen in the earlier writings of the church fathers (e.g., Justin Martyr's *Dialogue with Trypho*) as well as the rabbis (whose writings also witness disputation with pagans and *minim*), the medieval period marked the development of public disputations. Gatherings in Paris (1240), Barcelona (1263) and Tortosa (1413–14), for example, took the form of trials in front of an audience of nobility and clergy. Christian participants were often baptised Jews who argued that passages in the Talmud were blasphemous to Christianity and were stumbling blocks to Jewish conversion. They also attempted to prove the truth of Christianity out of rabbinic writings (especially the Zohar), as Raymond Martini (*c.* 1220–85), for example, does in his *Pugio Fidei*. Jews who participated in these disputations in defence of the Jewish communities included Nahmanides (1194–1270) and Joseph Albo (1380–1430).

Although disputation literature declined towards the end of the medieval period, it continued to be written during the Reformation and Renaissance and through to the eighteenth century. The 1769 exchange between Moses Mendelssohn and Johann Kaspar Lavater (1741–1801), about the extension of civil rights to Jews, is one example.

One consequence of the medieval public disputation was the condemnation of the Talmud. In 1236 Nicholas Donin (first half of thirteenth century) presented to Pope Gregory IX (r. 1227–41) a list of charges against the Talmud, most seriously that it contained blasphemous statements about Jesus and was filled with expressions of hostility against Gentiles. The Pope ordered that copies of the Talmud be seized and examined. King Louis IX of France (r. 1226–70) complied; at Paris in 1240, following a public disputation, twenty-four wagonloads of rabbinic commentaries were burned in Paris. This was not an isolated incident; similar attacks continued for many centuries. The Dominican Johannes Pfefferkorn (1469–1522), also a baptised Jew, led early sixteenth-century attacks, instigating throughout Italy the seizure and burning of all copies of the Talmud in 1559.

The Franciscans and the Dominicans were specially trained for controversy with Jews and Muslims, studying Hebrew, Arabic and rabbinic commentaries. Many delivered conversionist sermons, such as Abner of Burgos (*c.* 1270–1340). Baptised as Alfonso of Valladolid, he called for Jewish conversion, attacked the Talmud, and urged anti-Jewish measures, including conversionist preaching and segregation of Jews from Christians.

Sometimes expulsions followed the disputation. Two major waves of expulsions took place at the end of the thirteenth and the end of the fifteenth centuries. The expulsion of all Jews from England in 1290 was unusual at this point in its completeness. Edward I (1239–1307), King of England (1272–1307), initially used Jews as a source of funds, particularly for his Crusades and to support the *Domus Conversorum* (House of Conversion), a home in London for Jews who converted to Christianity, which had originally been established by Henry III in 1232 and was not abolished until 1891. When Jews did not convert *en masse*, and their financial contribution to the throne became limited through fiscal exploitation, Edward expelled the entire community. Although he cited Jewish usury as a central reason for expelling them, religious motives were also apparent: the expulsion decrees insist on the offence caused to Christians by the presence in their midst of those who denied Christ. Some rulers, such as the French kings in 1306, expelled Jews only to readmit them later. Several other Christian rulers took advantage of expulsions to welcome Jews into their lands, as happened in Italy (Naples and Rome) and in Poland, where Jews suffered fewer restrictions than elsewhere in Europe. Indeed, the period from the fifteenth to the mid-seventeenth century was known as a Golden Age, resulting in flourishing art and culture.

Usury was a major issue in the medieval period. Differentiating themselves from both Jewish and Roman practice, the taking of interest beyond the principal of the loan was prohibited by the church fathers. The Third Lateran Council of 1179 ordered the excommunication of usurers and the annulment of wills that dispensed usurious gains. This position clashed dramatically with the realities of urban growth and commercialisation of the European economy from around 950. It also existed in tension with the interests of secular rulers who licensed interest taking by setting regional rates of interest and licensing specific groups to undertake moneylending and pawnbroking. It is in these late medieval centuries that Jews were simultaneously excluded from many occupations and encouraged to engage in financial services. Although moneylending at interest was a widespread and necessary economic reality, it became a byword for Jewish evil, and for the harm that Jews intended to inflict on Christians.

ANTI-JEWISH VIOLENCE AND THE CRUSADES

Unlike the patristic period which witnessed sporadic incidents of violence between Christians and Jews, the medieval period was marked with lengthy periods of sustained Christian violence against Jews. The Black Death, which ravaged the European population from 1347 to 1351, witnessed the suffering and devastation of Jewish communities at the hands of Christians. The epidemic, which killed at least a third of the European population, hit the densely settled urban communities – where most Jews lived – particularly badly. Rumours began to circulate about a Jewish plot to poison wells and cause the plague. Pope Clement VI (r. 1342–52) attempted to quash these accusations and encouraged urban authorities to protect Jews by issuing a papal bull stating, 'Let no Christian dare to wound or kill these Jews or to seize their property.' Like *sicut iudeis*, this was an official doctrine of toleration, the rules of which were that Jews should be protected whilst living a life of dispersion, subjugation and inferiority that reflected their reprobate status in God's sight. But it was much more lenient and tolerant than the Church's policy toward pagans or their own Christian heretics.

Nevertheless, in hundreds of cities massacres of whole communities resulted, especially in the Rhineland – Frankfurt, Mainz and Cologne – but also further east, notably in Prague.

However, it was the Crusades (eleventh–sixteenth centuries) which became the byword for medieval fanaticism and violence against Jews and Muslims. The first of these holy wars was preached by Pope Urban II (r. 1088–99) in 1095 as an armed pilgrimage to the East to free Jerusalem from the Saracens. The Second and Third Crusades were expeditions aimed to re-establish the successes of the First in the Holy Land. Other Crusades were aimed at conquering pagan lands, as for example from the middle of the twelfth century in the Baltic. Crusader preaching concentrated on whipping up Christian emotions against unbelief or deviant forms of Christian belief.

Urban's call resulted in the gathering of princely armies as well as irregular bands of crusaders, whose departure for the Holy Land in 1096 preceded that of the official crusaders. On their land route through Germany they encountered prosperous Jewish communities in cities like Speyer, Worms, Mainz, Cologne and Trier. In all these cities the bishops concerned tried to prevent anti-Jewish violence. Not only were they anxious to uphold public order in their cities, they were committed to maintaining official church policy which did not permit Jews to be attacked or forcibly converted. In Speyer casualties stayed low, but many Jews died in Worms and Mainz and in the villages outside Cologne to which the archbishop had sent them for safety. Others were forcibly baptised or died by their own hands as martyrs sanctifying God's holy name (*Kiddush ha-Shem*) rather than undergoing baptism. The princely armies did not persecute Jews in Europe.

Contemporary Hebrew accounts chronicled a powerful story of self-immolation, although some scholars question to what extent such acts of martyrdom took place. Nevertheless, martyrdom entered Jewish folklore during this period and David Blumental (b. 1938) has argued that it remains pivotal to Jewish–Christian relations. The Crusades offered examples to follow, which were commemorated in Jewish liturgy; and among Christians they aroused puzzlement and even demonisation of Jews as child-killers. The Hebrew narratives of the 1096 massacres, which were written within about fifty years of the event, graphically depict the ritual slaughter of whole Jewish families. Although there is much scholarly debate about the historical reliability of these sources, corroboration from the Latin sources would suggest that many Jews died in this way. Similarly, there is disagreement about whether, when Jerusalem fell to the crusaders in 1099, numerous Jews were killed alongside Muslims; recent work has suggested that wholesale slaughter of Jews did not occur.

Extensive loss of Jewish life was prevented by individual Christian leaders such as Bernard of Clairvaux (1090–1153) during the Second Crusade in 1146 when he stopped anti-Jewish preaching, demanding that Christians adhere to traditional church policy protecting Jews. Although he argued against inflicting physical harm on Jews, Bernard's sermons and mystical writings reveal standard anti-Jewish motifs that were well established in Christian tradition: he emphasised Jewish carnality, the inability of Jews to exercise proper reason, and their stubborn disbelief.

In the Third Crusade, the Jews of York were massacred in 1190 in Clifford's Tower, while King Richard I (r. 1189–99) was absent from England organising his own departure for the Holy Land. As far as later Crusades are concerned, major violence against Jews was usually stemmed by those in authority.

What explains anti-Jewish violence by crusaders? One scholar of the period, Anna Sapir-Abulafia (b. 1952), suggests that crusading preaching, calling upon Christians to re-take the Holy Land and take vengeance on Muslims, easily spilled over into the desire to avenge the death of Jesus on those who were judged to be guilty of the crucifixion. Crusaders wondered why they should seek out Muslims in the Holy Land when there were Jews at home. In addition, the reality of crusading meant that large armies needed to get hold of provisions along the way. It is likely that crusaders felt it only right that Jews should in this way help finance the Crusades. The idea that Jews should suffer financially on behalf of crusading endeavours intensified partly because, by the end of the twelfth century, Jews had become important players in providing crusading loans. After the massacre of Jews in Clifford's Tower, the evidence held in York Minster of debts to Jews was destroyed.

The Crusades have had a continuing impact on Jewish–Christian relations. Even the word 'crusade' conjures up for Jews (and Muslims) the image of unjust religious persecution. When US President George Bush called for a 'crusade against terrorism' after the 9/11 suicide bombings in 2001, he was taken aback by the controversy that followed on account of his choice of words.

POLEMIC: JEWISH

Because of the one-sided nature of the relationship between Christians and Jews, it is to be expected that Jewish polemic was less common and far more nuanced. As we saw in the last chapter, references to Christianity in the Talmud are few, yet there are passages in classical Jewish texts, including the Talmud, that depict a violent picture: rabbinic descriptions of the messianic age as one of catastrophic blood-letting for the Gentiles or their subjugation to Jewish rule (*Pesikta Rabbati*, Piska 36); a Talmudic dictum that a non-Jew who studies Torah is liable to the death penalty (BT. *Sanhedrin* 59a); Kabbalistic teachings that the Gentile nations of the world are to be identified with the cosmic forces of evil, their souls derived from demonic powers (e.g., Zohar I:121a–b, III:72b–73a).

As for explicit anti-Christian polemic, there certainly existed Jewish tracts against Christians such as *Toledot Yeshu*, a parody of the Gospels attested from the tenth century but probably originating in the sixth century. After the rise of Islam we find examples of anti-Christian texts such as *The Alphabet of Ben Sira* (probably ninth century), which contains the tale of the miraculous birth and prophecy of the ancient writer Ben Sira, intended as a parody of the life of Jesus. The lewdness of some aspects is apparent as is the attempt to discredit the virgin birth. Jewish polemical literature appears to have mostly developed in Islamic lands, and its language was Arabic, reflecting the influence of Arabic polemical literature. Where we have Hebrew texts, such as a Genizah fragment (ENA, n.s. 50, fol. 9), they sometimes reflect an Arabic original. The earliest medieval polemicist was Dāwūd ibn Marwān al-Muqammas (ninth century), a Jew who converted to Christianity and, upon returning to Judaism, wrote two polemical works against Christianity. In his theological study *Ishrūn Maqāla* he included anti-Christian material. In the tenth century, Saʿadia Gaon (882–942) also included anti-Christian arguments in his writings but without composing a separate treatise.

The influence of Islam in writings on Christianity can be found among Jewish philosophers such as Maimonides who lived his entire life in Muslim countries. He insisted that, unlike Islam, Christianity was idolatry; consequently the Talmudic laws severely regulating Jewish interaction with Gentiles applied to contemporary Christians. Later Jewish thinkers tried to modify this view. At the conclusion of his *Code of Jewish Law* (*Mishneh Torah*), discussing Jewish messianic doctrine, Maimonides argues that Jesus only imagined he was the Messiah, but, instead of improving the lot of the Jewish people, made it incomparably worse. On the other hand, Maimonides argued that Christianity, along with Islam, providentially spread knowledge of God and Scripture throughout the world, thereby preparing the way for the true Messiah. Maimonides' statement that 'The pious of the Gentile nations have a share in the world to come' (*Code, Laws of Kings* 8.11) has been frequently cited by modern Jews as evidence of Jewish inclusiveness, sometimes contrasted with the Christian doctrine *non salus extra ecclesiam* (outside the Church there is no salvation), although it is not certain whether Maimonides would have included Christians in his definition of 'the pious of the Gentile nations'. The Yemenite philosopher Netanel ibn Fayyumi (d. *c.* 1164), went further and asserted the authenticity of the prophecy of Muhammad, as revealed in the Qurʾan, and at least the possibility that there are additional authentic revelations: 'He sends a prophet to every people according to their language.'

One subject that led to virulent Jewish criticism was a belief, which had become central to Christian theology by the early Middle Ages, that Christ was born of a virgin, who was intact at the time of his conception and remained so after his birth. Jewish polemical texts suggested that the concept of virginity masked Mary's adulterous pregnancy. *Toledot Yeshu* inverted Christian belief and called Mary impure (*Nidda*). Jewish rejection of virgin birth also formed part of the denial of the incarnation.

One of the most popular polemical works in the medieval period was the *Book of Nestor the Priest*, possibly written by a Christian priest who had converted to Judaism. It rejected the idea that God would have dwelt in a 'womb, in the filth of menstrual blood, in confinement and imprisonment and darkness for nine months'. Conversely, in medieval Christian polemical writings, such as the writings of Odo of Cambrai (*c.* 1100), rejection of the virgin birth was imputed to Jewish interlocutors. The popularity of these texts ensured that Jewish anti-Christian polemic was a tradition that was to have a long history.

We should also consider whether there was Jewish violence against Christians, in response to Christian violence against Jews. For the most part, of course, medieval Jews were simply not in a position to harm their Christian neighbours, and the frequent charges of ritual murder of Christian children remain in the realm of fantasy and projection. Yet there are references to occasional incidents of Jewish-inspired violence: for example, contemporary Christian documents accuse Jews of supporting the Persians against Christian armies in their invasion of Byzantine territory, including Palestine (and Jerusalem) in the seventh century.

According to the Jerusalem monk Antiochus Strategos, once the Persian army had breached Jerusalem's fortifications in 614, Jewish rebels joined the Persians in the sack of Jerusalem and the Persian commander, Shahrbaraz, recognised their assistance by giving them the opportunity to massacre surviving Christians, who were hiding out in cisterns. They offered the Christians an opportunity to save their lives by denying Christ and becoming Jews but they refused, preferring to 'die for Christ's sake rather than to live in godlessness'. According to Antiochus' account, Jews killed the Christians and demolished 'with their own hands [...] such of the holy churches as were left standing'. Is it inconceivable, whether because of temperament or tradition, that Jews could ever have been the killers and Christians the martyrs?

POSITIVE INTERACTION

Not all the interaction between Christians and Jews was confrontational, as demonstrated by numerous Jewish and Christian writings that show signs of interdependence. For example, the Christian teaching that Scripture had four different senses – usually called 'historical' (the actual events), 'tropological' (moral instruction), 'allegorical' (doctrine linked with a non-literal reading), and 'anagogical' (teaching about the mystical spiritual realm) – was well established by the twelfth century. In Jewish thought, an analogous conception of four senses – *peshat* (simple meaning), *remez* (philosophical allegory), *derash* (homiletical application), and *sod* (mystical symbol) – crystallised late in the thirteenth century, undoubtedly influenced by the Christian teaching.

Other examples of Christian influence can be seen in the commentary of the Jewish medieval scholar Nahmanides. Similarly, the Spanish exegete Isaac Abravanel (1437–1508) had a broad knowledge of Christian exegetical literature and was influenced by the commentaries of the Franciscan Alfonso Tostado (*c.* 1400–55). Jewish commentators also copied Christian literary structures, dividing the biblical text into small sections of paragraphs and verses, even though the text was traditionally divided differently.

The Hasidei Ashkenaz, a Jewish pietistic group in twelfth- and thirteenth-century Germany, is another example of the influence of contemporary Christianity on Judaism. The *hasidim* adopted what they considered to be praiseworthy Christian pietistic practices, such as exposure to cold and flagellation as forms of penance/penitence, like their Christian counterparts. Earthly love became for them an allegory for the love of God, with the ideal being a monastic absence of passion.

For their part, some medieval Christian scholars argued that greater attention should be given to the 'historical' meaning of the text and studied Hebrew with Jews (perhaps contributing to the Jewish tendency at this time to distinguish between the homiletical interpretation and the simple meaning of the biblical text). Michael Signer (1946–2009) has identified contact between scholars, notably in the biblical commentaries of the School of St. Victor in the twelfth century, which are filled with references to Jewish interpretations, not for polemical but for purely intellectual purposes. These contacts are derived from both textual interaction and oral conversation.

The Victorine scholars took rabbinic tradition seriously and Hugh of St. Victor (d. 1142), who established the Victorine tradition of literal interpretation and historical study of Scripture, was inspired in part by Rashi. Rashi's commentaries were meant for the ordinary educated Jew, but they soon became known to Christians, such as Hugh, who rather like Rashi set himself the task of rehabilitating the literal sense of Scripture. Hugh knew Hebrew and frequently cited Jewish sources, including the commentary of Rashi's grandson, Rashbam (*c.* 1080/5–1158). Andrew of St. Victor (d. 1175) entered into conversations with Jews and recorded their understanding of biblical words and phrases in his own commentaries, including passages in the Talmud and midrash. Although he rejected Jewish explanations that asserted the eschatological restoration of Jews, he juxtaposed Christian and Jewish interpretation frequently and sympathetically, and his exegesis marks a significant advance in the development of Christian biblical interpretation based on Hebrew and Jewish sources.

Comments about Christian interpretations appear both explicitly and implicitly in the writings of Rashi. The commentary on Psalms has several 'answers to the Christians' (*Teshuvah L'minim*), and in the introduction to the Song of Songs Rashi emphasises that Israel will endure 'exile after exile' and that God still loves them deeply. As well as the Victorines, Nicholas of Lyra (*c.* 1270–1349) quotes the commentaries of Rashi throughout his comprehensive *Postillae perpetuae* on the Hebrew Bible and, through him, Rashi became an important source for Luther's exegesis.

As well as interaction between Jewish and Christian commentators, both Judaism and Christianity faced similar philosophical difficulties. They found anthropomorphism, for example, equally problematic, which led to interesting interaction between scholars such as Maimonides and the Dominican scholastic Thomas Aquinas (*c.* 1225–74). Both argued that biblical images capture the human experience of God, not how God is in Godself. Furthermore, God is timeless (literally, there is no duration in God) and therefore immutable (there is no change in God). Maimonides' *Guide for the Perplexed* was translated into Latin and was familiar to Aquinas, who refers to 'Rabbi Moses the Egyptian' with respect. As well as Maimonides, Aquinas read works by Jewish thinkers such as Avicebron (*c.* 1020–*c.* 1070).

Yet, like other scholastics, Aquinas held ambiguous attitudes towards Jews and Judaism. For example, although he discouraged some anti-Jewish measures and opposed undue fiscal harshness towards Jews (such as the removal of children from parents as contrary to Natural Law), in *Summa contra Gentiles* he created an encyclopedic manual for missionaries against Muslims and Jews. He also supported imposing the Jewish badge, upheld coerced conversions, and proposed substituting manual labour for moneylending.

This ambiguity is also found in the writings of the French philosopher Peter Abelard (1079–1142), who regarded Judaism as philosophically and spiritually inferior to Christianity, yet expressed compassion for Jewish suffering. Abelard had personal contact with Jews, knew some Hebrew and argued that nuns should learn Hebrew. In his work *Dialogus inter philosophum, Judaeum et Christianum*, his ficticious Jew empathised with Jewish oppression and envisaged a biblically promised blissful future, but Abelard also believed that the minutiae of Jewish law burdened Jews, distracting them from genuine love of God.

Greater sensitivity to Jews and Judaism can be found among some Christian rulers. Henry IV (1050–1106), Holy Roman Emperor and King of Germany (1056–1106), allowed baptised Jews to revert to Judaism after the massacres and forced conversions of the First Crusade in 1096, and asked the Bishop of Speyer to shelter survivors of the massacre. His ruling clashed with canon law which, notwithstanding its position against forced baptism, stipulated that anyone who had been baptised was a Christian.

Ferdinand II (1578–1637), Holy Roman Emperor from 1619 to 1637, introduced the institution of Court Jews, wealthy individual Jews who provided financial and commercial services to medieval princes, particularly in the sixteenth to eighteenth centuries. These were generally agents who arranged transfers of credit, rather than possessors of vast sums of capital in their own right. Soon afterwards, many Protestant and Catholic princes alike opened their courts to Jews who were accountable to the Royal Court. Although exempt from paying protection money (*Schutzgeld*), they were dependent upon the protection and whim of the ruler and liable to exploitation. When a new ruler came to power he often dismissed a Court Jew or brought him to court to remove existing financial obligations.

On the Jewish side, the rabbinic concept of the seven Noachide laws provided fertile ground for a more positive view of Gentiles. Non-Jews could be defined as monotheists if they adhered to basic social and religious values (establishing law-courts, refraining from blasphemy, idolatry, murder, theft and forbidden sexual relationships such as incest, and not performing vivisection) which would enable them to be regarded as 'the pious of the Gentile peoples'. In the Middle Ages, the concept was widely applied to Muslims but there were conflicting views about Christianity because of the Trinity.

Menahem Ha-Me'iri, Talmudist and defender of Maimonides, was one of the few Jewish scholars of the Middle Ages who maintained an openness and tolerance towards other religions. He amended the Talmudic conception of the *ger toshav*, the non-Jew who keeps the Noachide laws, and declared that Christians and Muslims, 'though they are, measured by our own faith, in some points mistaken', are nevertheless not idolaters but *ummot ha-gedurot be-darkhei ha-datot*, 'nations restricted by the ways of religion', and therefore stand between Jews and idolaters.

The Venetian Jewish scholar Leon of Modena (1571–1648) became well known in the Christian world as an interpreter of Judaism, where he was in demand as a consultant on Jewish learning. His book, *The history of the rites, customs, and manner of life, of the present Jews throughout the world*, composed for James I of England in 1637, explains Jewish ceremonies and customs and was designed explicitly for Christian readers.

The flowering of Jewish mysticism, first among the German Pietists and then with the emergence of Kabbalah in France and Spain (twelfth–thirteenth centuries), also presents some possible connections with Christianity, although these remain uncertain. Possible Christian influence on

Kabbalah has been a controversial subject for scholars; in recent years Peter Schafer (b. 1943) is one of a small number of scholars who have argued for Christian influence on some features of theosophical Kabbalah, noting, for example, the parallels between the Christian Marian cult and the emergence of the Shekhinah, which refers to the divine presence and the feminine aspect of God.

There is evidence of Christian influence on the twelfth-century Zohar, the classic text of medieval Jewish mysticism, demonstrated by the following:

When the Messiah hears of the great suffering of Israel in their dispersion, and of the wicked amongst them who seek not to know their Master, he weeps aloud on account of those wicked ones amongst them, as it is written, But he was wounded because of our transgression, crushed because of our iniquities (Isa. 53:5).

The use of Isaiah 53 is striking, for the normative medieval Jewish interpretation – to safeguard against the Christian use of this passage – was to insist that it did not refer to the Messiah but to a prophet in antiquity, or to the personification of the Jewish people. The passage continues:

The Messiah, on his part, enters a certain Hall in the Garden of Eden, called the Hall of the Afflicted. There he calls for all the diseases and pains and sufferings of Israel, bidding them settle on himself, which they do. And were it not that he thus eases the burden from Israel, taking it on himself, no one could endure the sufferings meted out to Israel in expiation on account of their neglect of the Torah. So Scripture says, surely our diseases he did bear (Isa. 53:4) . . . As long as Israel were in the Holy Land, by means of the Temple service and sacrifices they averted all evil diseases and afflictions from the world. Now it is the Messiah who is the means of averting them from mankind until the time when a man quits this world and receives his punishment. (Zohar 2, 212a)

Once again a proof-text from the 'suffering servant' passage in Isaiah 53 is cited and the 'vicarious atonement' doctrine is unmistakable. The Messiah takes upon himself the suffering deserved by Jews, thereby removing much of it from them although, unlike Jesus, his suffering occurs before he enters the world, not after. However, the insistence that it is part of the Messiah's role to suffer and thereby to remove affliction from the Jewish people is, like rabbinic interpretations of Genesis 22 discussed earlier, clearly influenced by Christian teaching.

To end this section on positive influences in the medieval Jewish–Christian encounter, we refer to an early fifteenth-century Spanish passage by Solomon Alami uncovered by the historian Marc Saperstein (b. 1944), which denounces the shortcomings of Jewish congregations and behaviour in the synagogue by making comparison with the commendable behaviour of Christian congregants:

Look what happens when a congregation [of Jews] gathers to hear words of Torah from a sage. Slumber weighs upon the eyes of the officers; others converse about trivial affairs. The preacher is dumbfounded by the talking of men and the chattering of women standing behind the synagogue. If he should reproach them because of their behaviour, they continue to sin, behaving corruptly, abominably. This is the opposite of the Christians. When their men and women gather to hear a preacher, they stand together in absolute silence, marvelling at his rebuke. Not one of them dozes as he pours out his words upon them. They await him as they do the rain, eager for the waters of his counsel. We have not learned properly from those around us. (Quoted by Saperstein in George W. E. Nickelsburg and George W. MacRae (eds.), *Christians Among Jews and Gentiles: Essays in Honor of Krister Stendahl on His Sixty-fifth Birthday*, Philadelphia: Fortress Press, 1986.)

SPAIN AND THE INQUISITION

In Spain in the early Middle Ages (from the tenth to the twelfth century), under Muslim rule there was a period of *Convivencia* (literally 'living together'), a term that describes the relatively easy coexistence of Jews, Christians and Muslims which allowed for sharing of concepts and common intellectual ideas about, for example, the nature of God and the purpose of creation. It is important not to idealise this relationship: non-Muslims were *dhimmis*, subject to restrictions such as heavier taxation; on the other hand, there was no attempt to insist on the full rigour of these restrictions and this period has commonly been called the 'Golden Age'.

Solomon Ibn Gabirol (*c.* 1020–*c.* 1057) was known in Arabic as Sulayman ibn Yahya ibn Gabirul, and in Latin as Avicebron. His philosophical and poetical writings were widely esteemed and medieval Christian readers generally assumed him to be a Muslim. Another important Jewish figure at this time was Judah ha-Levi, who was born in Tudela (Spain) and died in Egypt on his way to the Land of Israel. He was one of the most important Hebrew poets and philosophers of the Middle Ages whose most well-known work, *Sefer ha-Kuzari*, consists of a fictitious conversation between the King of the Khazars and representatives of Aristotelianism, Christianity, Islam and Judaism. The Khazars were a powerful state in Eastern Europe between the seventh and the tenth centuries, the rulers of which converted to Judaism. The *Kuzari* enables ha-Levi to demonstrate the superiority of Judaism as a prophetically mediated religion over other religions, in particular Christianity and Islam, to which he nevertheless grants a place as *praeparatio messianica* because they contain authentic Jewish elements.

Jewish and Christian life began to change for the worse in the late eleventh and twelfth centuries when Moroccan Berbers who had little experience of religious minorities began to rule. Many Jews and Christians migrated to Christian controlled areas of Spain – but these also became more intolerant. Jews were forced to listen to conversionist preaching and ecclesiastical legislation of the early Middle Ages was revived to exclude Jews from office. Ramon Llull (1232–1315/16) was a prolific author of conversionist tracts in Catalan and Latin, aimed at Jews (and Muslims); but, unusually at a time when preaching campaigns had become increasingly strident, he insisted on the need to show respect to his interlocutors.

Some Jews remained at court, such as Isaac Abravanel, but they became the object of bitter criticism. The age of *Convivencia* was dealt its death blow not by the expulsion of the Jews in 1492 but by the massacres of 1391, which resulted in mass conversions and the increased marginalisation of those Jews who remained; Islam, too, was suppressed and Spain rejoiced in its special reputation as the most Catholic of monarchies.

Hasdai Crescas (*c.* 1340–1410) represented the Jewish community at the court of the Kings of Aragon, and was considered one of the king's *familiares*, or close advisers. Crescas tried to rebuild the Jewish communities of Catalonia after 1391, but his success was limited. He defended Judaism in several books and aimed to refute Christian thinkers on their own terms by arguing that their positions were incoherent and would lead to self-contradiction if properly understood. Crescas presented Christianity as a faith opposed to reason, and his writings reveal considerable knowledge of Arab scholars such as al-Ghazzali (1058–1111) and Ibn Rushd (Averroes) (1126–98).

Public disputations also took place in Spain, the most famous of which involved Nahmanides and the Dominican convert Paul the Christian (thirteenth century, sometimes called Pablo Cristiani). Nahmanides was summoned by James I (1204–76), with whom he apparently had a warm relationship, to defend Judaism against the argument that the Messiah had already come. The disputation of 1263, held in the king's presence, is recorded in both the writings of Nahmanides and in a Christian version (which, perhaps not surprisingly, awards victory to Paul). What was distinctive was Paul's attempt to use the Talmud to demonstrate that the Messiah had come. Nahmanides argued that he was not obliged to believe as literal truth the aggadic material in the Talmud, but Paul mocked this position. Neither side 'won', in the sense that the king could not possibly declare that a Jew had been victorious.

The aim of the disputation had been to discredit Jewish belief and it marked a new intensification of attempts at the conversion of Jews in which attacks on the Talmud became increasingly intense, following the mass burning of the Talmud by Louis IX in France. After the disputation, Nahmanides was treated courteously by James I but the king made it plain that he would do well to leave Spain. In 1267 Nahmanides travelled to the Holy Land and became Rabbi of Acre.

Raymond Martini assisted Paul the Christian in the disputation and his anti-Jewish writings were utilised by later medieval polemicists and were also cited by Luther. Martini was well versed in Hebrew, and served as a censor to examine Jewish books for anti-Christian passages. His work *Pugio Fidei* ('The Dagger of Faith', *c.* 1280) cites quotations from rabbinic sources and although polemical nevertheless provides the only evidence of some rabbinic texts that were not otherwise preserved.

Around this time, the Inquisition (the 'Holy Office of the Inquisition') began, initially against heretical groups in southern France; it was to last off and on until the nineteenth century. In its beginnings it was not primarily concerned with Jews and Judaism *per se*, but it took particular interest from the 1391 riots onwards when Jews, known as the *conversos*, converted to Christianity, either by choice or under duress. These converted Jews and their offspring were a cause of suspicion and the Church wanted to ensure that their conversions were genuine.

Although there were also many Muslim *conversos*, by the mid-sixteenth century they were predominantly Jewish as a new wave of converts was created by the expulsion in 1492. The term *conversos* was used to distinguish recently converted Jews from 'Old Christians' – Christians by birth/blood with no Jewish affiliation. The *conversos* faced two major difficulties: the Inquisition which relentlessly pursued anyone who might be deemed a false convert, and popular opinion which increasingly marginalised those with Jewish blood, leading to their exclusion from universities and high office, on what can only be described as racial grounds.

The *conversos* are sometimes confused with the Marranos (literally 'swine' or one who damages Christian faith), which is a derogatory term. 'Marranos' refers to those Jews who converted to Christianity but continued to observe certain Jewish rituals (e.g., lighting of candles on Sabbath) and practices (e.g., keeping kosher). Another term used for this phenomenon is 'Crypto-Judaism', because of the underground or covert nature of the Jewish practice. Since they could not practise openly, Marranos are known to have developed elaborate ways of maintaining Sabbath and the Jewish holidays. They were a target of the inquisitors' investigation because the crime they were committing, apostasy, was considered by the Church to be worse than the sin of unbelief.

A problem for the Inquisition was the line of demarcation between *conversos* and the non-converted Jews. Although for the most part the Inquisition went after relapsing *conversos*, they also went after non-converted Jews because of the threat they posed to the *conversos* and their relapsing back into Judaism.

Solomon Molcho (*c.* 1500–32) is an example of a Portuguese Marrano, who was baptised by the name Diego Pires but subsequently returned to Judaism and was burned at the stake during the Inquisition. He led an unusual life because he was befriended by Pope Clement VII (r. 1265–8) who was convinced by his prophecies, many of which came true. In 1529, he preached the coming of the Messiah among Jews and Christians and travelled with David Reuveni (1490–1538), who claimed to be representative of the ten lost tribes of Israel. The Emperor Charles V (r. 1519–58) was less impressed and delivered them both to the Inquisition.

Breaking with the policies of previous Iberian rulers, Ferdinand the Catholic (1452–1516) and his cousin Isabella decreed the expulsion of all confessing Jews from their lands following their conquest of the last Muslim kingdom in Granada in 1492. The decree was seen as part of the recovery of Spain's Christian identity, and the king and queen hoped that many Jews would convert rather than depart, as many did. Ferdinand, mindful of the revenues they produced, did not expel the Muslims from Valencia and Aragon, even though Isabella thoroughly suppressed Islam in Castile. These expulsions represent the denouement of a lengthy process of the marginalisation of Jews, which had begun a century earlier, in 1391.

THE REFORMATION AND CHRISTIAN HEBRAISM

Initiated by Martin Luther, the Reformation was one of the greatest revolutions in the history of Western thought, breaking the religious monopoly of the Roman Catholic Church. Unfortunately, Luther's writings about Jews perpetuated the medieval view of Jews as God's enemy. They should not be seen as separate from his denunciations of the pope, false Christians and Muslims, all of whom he saw as the devil's legions. For Luther, Jews were unique deniers of Christ.

The older Luther's views cannot legitimately be divorced from the younger Luther's, though his later words were much more brutal. His

1523 work, *That Jesus Christ Was Born a Jew*, chastised the Church for its treatment of Jews and then expressed hope for the conversion of some Jews under a new approach. Luther argued:

If we wish to help them, we must practise on them not the papal law but rather the Christian law of love and accept them in a friendly fashion, allowing them to work and make a living, so that they gain the reason and the opportunity to be with and among us to see and to hear our Christian teaching and life.

After a call for increased contact and tolerance, he concludes: 'here I will let the matter rest for the present, until I see what I have accomplished'. This conclusion clarifies the aim of the treatise – it was a missionary epistle, aimed at Lutheran missionaries who sought to convert Jews. Luther was just starting to experience the incredible success of the early years of the Reformation and believed himself to be an instrument of God, destined to reveal the purified gospel. He believed that time was needed for the renewed gospel to do its work, and he called for patience and tolerance.

Using the Jew as a stick with which to beat the Catholic Church, in the same tract he wrote that 'if I had been a Jew and had seen such dolts and blockheads govern and teach the Christian faith, I would have become a hog rather than a Christian'.

For Luther himself, when the anticipated conversion of the Jews did not materialise and the Judaising tendencies of a number of reforming sects became more apparent, he became increasingly frustrated. He wrote a trilogy of anti-Jewish works, the most infamous being *On the Jews and Their Lies*. In this treatise of 1543 he called for forcible conversions and advised rulers to confiscate rabbinical texts, forbid the rabbis to teach and burn down synagogues along with Jews' homes. The older Luther was bitterly disappointed and indignant at how incompletely the newly cleansed gospel was received by Jews. Each opponent – Christian as well as Jew – was regarded as a manifestation of the devil. For Luther, as for virtually all others at the time, truth allowed no room for tolerance. He saw the evangelical proclamation of faith as the last chance for misguided Jews and Christians alike, since God was working in the Reformation to extricate all from the antichrist. The best strategy seemed to be that which Ferdinand and Isabella of Spain and Immanuel I of Portugal had done less than fifty years previously – say goodbye to Jews for ever.

Perhaps because of his criticism of the Roman Catholic Church, Josel von Rosheim (*c.* 1480–1554), leader of German Jews during the Reformation, initially showed sympathy to Luther and the early Reformers. However, within a few years he increasingly oriented his politics towards support of the Catholic emperor rather than the Protestant aristocracy, describing Luther with a play on words, *lo-tahar*, which means impure.

Compared with Luther, Calvin was more moderate, stressing the unity of the Hebrew Scriptures and the New Testament, the one covenant initiated by Abraham and permanently upheld by God, and the continuing importance of the 'Law' for Christians. Calvin insisted Christians must learn from Jews in order to understand the Hebrew Bible. Through the 'Law' people learned to know the will of God, were restrained from unacceptable behaviour and became aware of sin and their need for God's redemption.

Calvin was one of the very few voices speaking against supersessionism, the doctrine that the Church replaced the Jewish people as heir of the covenant. He stressed that the entire Reformation confession, *sola gratia* (by mercy alone), was rooted in God's covenant with Abraham and in promises to share Israel's blessing with all people. At times Calvin used 'Israelite' to mean both Jews and Gentiles elected by God as the remnant to be saved. In *Ad quaestiones et obiecta Iudaei cuiusdam Responsio* ('Response to Questions and Objections of a Certain Jew', *c.* 1597) he produced a sympathetic dialogue with a Jew, possibly based on meetings with Josel von Rosheim. Naturally the document affirmed the triumphant church position given that Calvin could not see Judaism as a viable alternative since 'only Christ is the sole means of salvation'. Yet Calvin was more tolerant of Jews (and Muslims) than Christian heretics although he still maintained many of the traditional *Adversus Iudaeos* views, such as the opinion that their sufferings are caused by the sin of rejecting Christ.

If the Reformation marked the end of the monopoly of the Roman Catholic Church, the Renaissance marked the beginning of the closure of the Middle Ages. It was an era in which the ancient world was rediscovered, as expressed in the humanist battle cry *ad fontes* (back to the original sources), which was reflected in the Christian theologians' rejection of scholasticism and the development of Hebrew scholarship. Initially, Christian Hebraists received instruction privately from Jewish teachers and began to take a serious interest in post-biblical Jewish literature.

The Renaissance saw the flowering of Christian Kabbalah in figures such as Giovanni Pico della Mirandola (1463–94) and his disciple Johannes Reuchlin (1455–1522), who believed that the Kabbalah confirmed Christian truth. His appreciation of post-biblical Jewish literature emerged in a bitter controversy with the Dominicans which raged for almost a decade. The Emperor Maximilian (1459–1519), at the instigation of the Dominicans, had ordered that all Hebrew books considered inimical to the Christian faith should be burned. Reuchlin came to the defence of Jewish literature.

His success in this 'battle of the books' was a victory for Jews and Christian humanists alike.

The missionary orders also regarded knowledge of Hebrew as essential. If Jews were to be won for Christ, their religion had to be understood and their interpretation of certain biblical passages refuted. Nicholas of Lyra, whose knowledge of Hebrew and of the work of Jewish exegetes such as Rashi is indisputable, is credited with securing a place for traditional Jewish exegesis in Christian thought. His *Postillae perpetuae*, a running commentary on the entire Bible, was widely used and emphasised the literal meaning of the text, grounded in the study of philology, grammar and history. Despite his extensive use of the Talmud, midrashic literature and rabbinic commentaries, his work is filled with anti-Jewish polemic.

In the Renaissance, Hebrew gained recognition as one of the historic languages of the West. By 1546 chairs of Hebrew had been established in the major European universities. Pico and Reuchlin stood at the forefront of this movement. Luther, though antagonistic to rabbinic exegesis, had a high regard for the Hebrew language and recognised its importance for understanding Scripture. Calvinist scholars became some of the leading Christian Hebraists and Christian Hebraism became a weapon in the disputes between Protestants and Catholics.

A Hebrew printing press was founded in Amsterdam in 1626, and the founder's son, Menasseh ben Israel (1604–57), appealed to Oliver Cromwell in 1655 for the right of Jews to return to England. Cromwell gave the London Marrano Company informal permission to establish a synagogue and a cemetery.

Cromwell (Lord Protector 1653–8) convened a conference in London to decide the issue. Those favouring readmission included millenarianists who argued that the messianic age would dawn once Jews were scattered to the four corners of the world, which necessitated entry to England. Cromwell himself was probably more influenced by the practical needs of the new Commonwealth and anticipated Jewish merchants playing an important economic role. Others, notably clergy, opposed readmission. When the conference failed to deliver a positive response, Cromwell dissolved it. Three months later a group of Marranos living in London and posing as Catholics openly professed their Jewish identity and petitioned Cromwell to allow them to establish a synagogue and cemetery. In giving his consent through a decision by the Council of State, Cromwell became the person most responsible for the readmission of Jews to England in 1656, following their expulsion in 1290. Menasseh ben Israel, however, died believing he had failed, as his proposal for a formal recall was not accepted. However, his efforts led to a *de facto* toleration of Jews living openly on British soil for the first time in over 350 years. In 2006, Queen Elizabeth II hosted a celebration at Buckingham Palace, marking three and a half centuries of Jewish life in the United Kingdom.

CHAPTER 7

Antisemitism and the Holocaust

The eighteenth-century European Age of Enlightenment, also called the Age of Reason, marked the beginning of modernity. It challenged the intellectual assumptions of the traditional religious and political role of the Church and religious authority in general. It witnessed not only the emancipation of Jews and the granting of equal rights, but also the denigration of Jews and Judaism, rooted in a new form of political and social thinking, called antisemitism.

Reaction to the Enlightenment was mixed as both Jews and Christians were struggling to come to terms with it, and in both camps there were radicals and conservatives. Some Jews, like Moses Mendelssohn, the Reformers and the Orthodox leader S. R. Hirsch, welcomed its political and intellectual achievements; others, including the Gaon of Vilna (1720–97) feared the potential of the new ideas to undermine Jewish religious tradition. Engaging in precisely the same battle, conservative Christians such as Pope Pius IX (1846–78) denounced the Enlightenment, condemning freedom of religion and applying the phrase 'synagogue of Satan' to describe the enemies of the Church. Pius IX's attitude towards Jews is demonstrated by the Mortara Affair, the forced removal in 1858 of six-year-old Edgardo Mortara (1851–1940) from the home of his Jewish parents because he had allegedly been baptised by a Christian servant as a sick infant. Pius, who took a personal interest in Edgardo, was aware of international outrage but was convinced he had acted in the boy's interests.

Mendelssohn, known as the father of the Jewish Enlightenment, (*Haskalah*) was an observant Jew who engaged with Christian thinkers, demonstrated by his open correspondence (1769–70) with the Zurich theologian Johann Kaspar Lavater, but who maintained the traditional Jewish view of Christianity. He argued that rationality was the criterion by which to assess religious claims, and regarded Christianity as deficient in comparison with Judaism. In *Jerusalem* (1783) he urged tolerance for other religious groups based upon a common humanity, and regarded the practice of religion as a private affair for the individual and for the community concerned.

On the political front, the Enlightenment led to the Jewish emancipation, that is, to Jews gaining civil rights on a more or less equal footing with other citizens of the countries in which they lived. On the intellectual front, humanist ideas were absorbed by the *Haskalah*, which also drew on earlier Jewish models from the Renaissance. It was assumed that there was one universal truth, attainable by reason, in which all might share, whether Christian or Jewish. Only the truths of reason, for instance in science, mathematics and ethics, were certain, and these were open to all.

France in 1791, the year of the emancipation act, was the birthplace of Jewish emancipation in Europe (although the Constitution of the United States of America was the first to grant Jews equality in 1789). Anti-Jewish laws began to be repealed in the 1780s, and the French Revolution granted Jews citizenship as individuals while depriving them of their group privileges. The emancipation of Jews was promoted alongside the emancipation of women, slaves and other religious minorities (Protestant groups in some countries, Catholics in England). However, the coming of the modern era resulted in political freedom for individual Jews, but not for the Jewish people as a community. So long as Jews identified themselves primarily as individual citizens they were accorded civil rights, but their communal identity was restricted.

The Emperor Napoleon (1769–1821) considered Jews 'a nation within a nation' and decided to create a Jewish communal structure sanctioned by the state. He also convened the Grand Sanhedrin which paved the way for the formation of the consistorial system, making Judaism a recognised religion under government control. There was much debate about whether Jews should be emancipated and a significant contribution was made by Count Clermont-Tonnerre (1757–92) in a speech to the Sanhedrin in December 1789. He argued for an inclusive interpretation of the declaration of rights, but rejected different legal status for Jews. In his view, citizens were citizens as individuals, not as members of a religion: 'we must refuse everything to the Jews as a nation and accord everything to Jews as individuals' (quoted in Paul Mendes-Flohr and Jehuda Reinharz (eds.), *The Jew in the Modern World*, pp. 325–6).

Underlying his words is a tension between religious and national identity, a tension that has existed from the rise of the modern nation state until today and can be illustrated with a brief discussion of the term 'Pole'. This has normally been used, not least among Poles themselves, as an everyday synonym for 'Catholic': it is not applied to Jews (or Protestants, who are also a small community in Poland). Yet are not Polish Jews, Poles? Is there no real identification of the Jewish community as part of the Polish nation? This tension, demonstrated by the inappropriate term 'Polish–Jewish relations', undermines a sense of one national community, holding Polish Catholics and Jews together, where there exists an overriding common interest shared by the whole community, transcending partisan interests. In this example, which is applicable well beyond the confines of Poland, it is sometimes difficult to acknowledge the common humanity of those who are excluded from our community, who live beyond its boundaries. This difficulty is easily transformed into hatred and can be viewed as a significant (although unappreciated) reason for the lack of opposition among Catholic Poles to outbreaks of antisemitic violence that were commonplace in Poland.

During the period of the Emancipation many expected Jews to assimilate or convert to Christianity, and significant numbers did indeed convert, amongst them the German Jewish poet Heinrich Heine, who abandoned Judaism only to return to it in later life. His famous remark that his baptismal certificate was an 'admission ticket to European culture' indicated something of the pressure under which Jews remained to conform, at least outwardly, to the dominant faith.

Voltaire exemplified the ambivalence of the Enlightenment. He called for religious tolerance and advocated universal human rights but was not free of the very anti-Jewish prejudices that he ridiculed, discussing Jews in ways that suggested they had innate negative qualities. Voltaire has been seen by some scholars as the father of antisemitism, thus associating antisemitism and the Holocaust with the emergence of modernity.

Wilhelm Marr (1819–1904) was the first to use the term 'antisemitism' in 1879 but it would be a mistake to differentiate it completely from its much older sister prejudice, anti-Judaism, which has a theological basis. Marr saw Jews as biologically different to model blue-eyed, fair-haired, white Teutons and asserted that Semites, darker skinned than and inferior to northern European peoples, could not be assimilated to the majority race and were a threat to them.

In France, an upsurge of antisemitism began in the late 1800s, and Jews were blamed for the collapse of the Union Générale, a leading Catholic bank. Although the Jewish community was one of the smallest and most assimilated groups in Europe (perhaps 100,000), Edouard Drumont (1844–1917) in his very popular *La France juive* (1886) argued that Jews had seized power in the Revolution of 1789 and were subverting French tradition and culture.

The Dreyfus Affair epitomised the disdain held for Jews in French society, particularly among Catholic nationalists. In 1894 Captain Albert Dreyfus (1859–1935) was arrested and tried for treason. He was the only Jewish member of the French General Staff, and was blamed when military secrets were passed to the German military attaché in Paris. In 1895, Dreyfus was publicly stripped of his rank before a crowd that shouted 'Death to the Jews!'; he was then sent to Devil's Island. When it was clear that the evidence was fabricated, Dreyfus was tried again in 1899 and found guilty by a military court. There was no chance that they would find him innocent, since that would, by implication, apportion guilt elsewhere and implicate high-ranking officers in the machinations against him. In the event, ten days later, Dreyfus was pardoned by the President of France.

Emile Zola (1840–1902) was convinced of his innocence and in *Le Figaro* in 1897 wrote the famous article, *J'accuse!*, attacking antisemitism; further articles warned of the danger of a military dictatorship in alliance with the Catholic Church. French Protestants tended to support Dreyfus and Catholics to oppose him, and Dreyfus become a symbol either of the denial of justice or of the eternal Jewish traitor. The publication of *J'accuse!* was followed by antisemitic riots in France, notably in Catholic strongholds. Synagogues were attacked in fifty towns, and Zola was put on trial and fled to England to avoid imprisonment.

The debate about Dreyfus split France. To the French nationalistic and religious right, Dreyfus the Jew symbolised all the liberal, alien and de-Christianising pressures on the traditional Christian order in the country. The Catholic Church through its media gave considerable support to the anti-Dreyfus sentiment sweeping France. The Dreyfus Affair had two major impacts: it motivated Theodor Herzl (1860–1904), a Viennese journalist who covered the trial, to write his book *The Jewish State* in 1896, and it also eventually led to the 1905 law separating church and state in France.

Perhaps influenced by Luther, many Protestant churches also shared in the antisemitic outlook on Jews and Judaism at this time and maintained the traditional *Adversus Iudaeos* position. Protestants emphasised the importance of the Old Testament (*sola scriptura*) with the aid of polarities such as promise/fulfilment, law/grace, old/new, judgement/love. The history of the Jewish people became viewed as a history of failure: God's 'old' covenant with Israel was broken and the 'new' covenant was made with Christians. This polarity easily led to a selective reading of Scripture, illustrated by the following passage by the Jewish scholar and Liberal leader Claude Montefiore (1858–1938), who criticised the approach of Harry Fosdick (1878–1969) to Scripture:

Theologians [should be] excessively careful of drawing beloved contrasts between the Old Testament and the New. We find even a liberal theologian, Dr. Fosdick, saying: 'From Sinai to Calvary – was ever a record of progressive revelation more plain or more convincing? The development begins with Jehovah disclosed in a thunderstorm on a desert mountain, and it ends with Christ saying: "God is Spirit: and they that worship Him must worship Him in spirit and truth"; it begins with a war-god leading his partisans to victory, and it ends with men saying, "God is love; and he that abideth in love abideth in God, and God abideth in him"; it begins with a provincial deity loving his tribe and hating its enemies, and it ends with the God of the whole earth worshipped "by a great multitude, which no man could number, out of every nation, and of all the tribes and peoples and tongues"; it begins with a God who commands the slaying of the Amalekites, "both man and woman, infant and suckling", and it ends with a Father whose will it is that not "one of these little ones should perish"; it begins with God's people standing afar off from his lightnings and praying that he might not speak to them lest they die and it ends with men going into their inner chambers, and, having shut the door, praying to their father who is in secret.' (*Christianity and Progress*, 1922, p. 209). Very good. No doubt such a series can be arranged. Let me now arrange a similar series. 'From the Old Testament to the New Testament – was there ever a record of retrogression more plain or more convincing? It begins with, "Have I any pleasure at all in the death of him that dieth?"; it ends with "Begone from me, ye doers of wickedness." It begins with, "The Lord is slow to anger and plenteous in mercy;" it ends with, "Fear Him who is able to destroy both body and soul in Gehenna." It begins with, "I will dwell with him that is of a contrite spirit to revive him"; it ends with, "Narrow is the way which leads to life, and few there be who find it." It begins with, "I will not contend for ever; I will not always be wrath;" it ends with, "Depart, ye cursed, into the everlasting fire." It begins with, "Should I not have pity on Nineveh, that great city?"; it ends with, "It will be more endurable for Sodom on the day of Judgement than for that town." It begins with, "The Lord is good to all who call upon Him"; it ends with, "Whoever speaks against the Holy Spirit, there is no forgiveness whether in this world or the next." It begins with, "The Lord will wipe away tears from off all faces; he will destroy death forever"; it ends with, "They will throw them into the furnace of fire; there is the weeping and the gnashing of teeth." ' And the one series would be as misleading as the other. (*The Synoptic Gospels*, edited with an introduction and commentary by C. G. Montefiore, London: Macmillan, 2nd edn 1927, vol. II, pp. 326–7)

Anti-Jewish presuppositions were common among Protestants, including eminent scholars such as Emil Schürer (1844–1910), who insisted that Judaism was doomed to fail because of its particularism. It is also possible to detect an anti-Jewish undercurrent in the writings of Julius Wellhausen (1844–1918), best known for *Prolegomena to the History of Israel* (1883) and his pursuit of Higher Criticism, which inquires into the authorship and dates of different books of the Bible; it was dubbed by Solomon Schechter (1847–1915) the 'Higher Antisemitism' because of its claim that the latest strata of the Pentateuch reflected a degeneration of spirituality into a compulsively legalistic fixation on the details of a sacrificial cult. An extreme example is Gerhard Kittel (1888–1948), editor of the influential *The Theological Dictionary of the New Testament*, who was also a Nazi, joining the party (1933) and its Reich Institute for the History of the New Germany (1936). He openly supported Nazi policies against Jews (whom he believed to be morally and racially degenerate), with the possible exception of genocide. 'Authentic Judaism', he wrote, 'abides by the symbol of the stranger wandering restless and homeless on the face of the earth' (*Die Judenfrage*, Stuttgart: Kolhammer, 1933, p. 73). In 1933 the Synod of Saxony stated (Article 13), 'we recognise [. . .] in the Old Testament the apostasy of the Jews from God, and therein their sin. This sin is made manifest throughout the world in the Crucifixion of Jesus. From thenceforth until the present day, the curse of God rests upon this people.'

Anti-Jewish prejudice can also be found in Protestant writings in the first decades after the Holocaust. If we turn to the prominent exegete Martin Noth, whose *History of Israel* has become a standard reference for students and academics alike, we find a description of Judaism as dying a slow agonising death in the first century. Eventually, 'Israel ceased to exist and the history of Israel came to an end' (*History of Israel*, London: A. & C. Black 1960, p. 400). Rudolf Bultmann offers a similar view. He stressed the antithesis between the teachings of Jesus and Rabbinic Judaism, and argued that by the end of the biblical period the Jewish God had become so transcendent and remote as to have been almost purified away. As for the Old Testament, 'To the Christian faith the Old Testament is no longer revelation as it has been and still is for the Jews. For the person who stands within the Church, the history of Israel is a closed chapter [. . .] To us the history of Israel is not a history of revelation.' ('The Significance of the Old Testament for the Christian Faith', in *The Old Testament and Christian Faith: A Theological Discussion*, ed. B. W. Anderson, New York: Harper & Row, 1963, p. 31). In *Theology of the New Testament* (London: SCM, 1952, pp. 12–13), perhaps his most influential work, Bultmann held to the view that a Jewish people cannot be said to exist with the emergence of Christianity.

In Orthodox Christianity, with its veneration of tradition, the *Adversus Iudaeos* tradition remained at the fore of its understanding of Jews and Judaism. Lengthy texts of Holy Week, included in the matins of Good

Friday, remained as anti-Jewish as the patristic and early medieval rhetoric that was employed to denigrate the 'perfidious Jews'.

There were serious outbreaks of antisemitism in Russia throughout the nineteenth and early twentieth centuries when no less than half the world's Jewish population was located within the Russian empire. In order to contain them, an extensive Pale of Settlement was established (1791), intended as a home from which Jews might move to other areas only with permission. Pogroms, a Russian word meaning 'devastation' and referring to violent attacks on Jews, regularly took place, the worst being in 1881, 1903 and 1905. While they might be prompted by social and economic factors, they were also coloured by religious ignorance dressed in the garb of zeal.

The most famous, or infamous, conspiracy document to condemn Jews was *The Protocols of the Elders of Zion*, which originated in Russia and appeared in the West in 1917. These purport to be a series of lectures given by an 'elder of Zion' to people to whom he could frankly and openly reveal the Jewish plot to take over the world by overthrowing its rulers. In 1921, *The Times'* correspondent in Istanbul demonstrated that the *Protocols* were based upon *Dialogue aux Enfers entre Montesquieu et Machiavel*, a satire by Maurice Joly (1829–78) on the grandiose ambitions of Napoleon III, Emperor of France from 1852 to 1870. All that the authors of the *Protocols* had done was to substitute 'the Elders of Zion' for Napoleon III, and to rearrange, somewhat clumsily, the material to suit their own purpose. The *Protocols* still occasionally come to public attention when they are used by antisemites to justify their hatred of Jews. For example, belief in the veracity of the *Protocols* and Holocaust denial were the main reasons why the proposed re-communication of the antisemitic Bishop Richard Williamson (b. 1940) by Pope Benedict XVI caused such controversy in 2009. The *Protocols* are sometimes portrayed as historically correct in a few Arab countries and in 2002 there was controversy over the broadcast of a TV drama series in Egypt based on the *Protocols*. However, in this case antisemitism is closely bound up with the political conflict involving Israel and the Arab states.

There were church leaders who condemned pogroms and antisemitism but it was rare for an Orthodox Christian to welcome Judaism as it stands. This was the achievement of Nikolai Ziorov (1850–1915), Russian Orthodox Archbishop of Warsaw, in 1912 and the most senior of Russian bishops, Antonii Vadkovskii (1846–1912), Metropolitan of St Petersburg. Another bishop, Platon Rozhdestvenskii (1866–1934), faced a mob in Kiev on his knees while endeavouring to still the pogrom of 1905.

Despite such individual exceptions, in the Age of the Enlightenment Christian anti-Judaism and its modern offspring, antisemitism, not only survived but thrived, gaining popularity both West and East. It could be found not only in theological and political writings but also in literary works, such as the books of English authors G. K. Chesterton (1874–1936, writer of many Christian works and the Father Brown detective stories), John Buchan (1875–1940, thriller writer, among whose works is *The Thirty-Nine Steps*) and Agatha Christie (1890–1976), 'the Queen of Crime'. In her *Three Act Tragedy*, first published in 1935, Mr Satterthwaite, an elderly snob yet an acute observer of the human condition, contemplates a young man named Oliver Manders:

A handsome young fellow, twenty-five at a guess. Something, perhaps, a little sleek about his good looks. Something else – something – was it foreign? Something unEnglish about him.

Egg Lytton Gore's voice rang out:

'Oliver, you slippery Shylock—'

'Of course,' thought Mr. Satterthwaite, 'that's it – not foreign – Jew!' (New edn, London: Pan in association with Collins, 1983, p. 28)

For further examples, including Buchan's frequent allusions to 'Judeo-Bolshevism' and Chesterton's description of 'the Jewish problem in Europe' in *The New Jerusalem* (1920) and elsewhere, see Bryan Cheyette's discussion of this topic in *Constructions of "the Jew" in English Literature and Society* (Cambridge: Cambridge University Press, 1993). The point is not that these authors were particularly virulent exponents of antisemitism, or even consciously anti-Jewish: indeed, Buchan had Jewish friends and Chesterton explicitly condemned Hitler's actions; rather, the casual comments illustrate the stereotypes and caricatures widespread in the society of their day.

THE ROAD TO AUSCHWITZ

For Adolf Hitler (1889–1945) and his Nazi party, race and not religion was the dominant motive for destroying Jews. He espoused a conspiracy view of history: Jews were responsible for Germany's defeat in the Great War of 1914–18. He regarded the German Weimar Republic, which rose from the ashes of the Great War and collapsed in the economic crisis of the early 1930s, as a racket run by Jews for their own benefit. Such an interpretation built on a foundation laid by others.

Jews, according to Hitler, were vile, even vermin. Yet if race provided the mythology and motivation for anti-Jewishness, secularised religious language provided the justification. In *Mein Kampf* (1925), Hitler did not hesitate to use overtly Christian language to appeal to a pious audience. He wrote that the Jews' 'whole existence is an embodied protest against the aesthetics of the Lord's image'. Thus he could piously affirm, 'I believe that I am acting in accordance with the will of the Almighty Creator: by defending myself against the Jew, I am fighting for the word of the Lord.'

Many Christians came to agree with him and many more stood by when the Nazis enacted policies that built on the racist and religious attitudes towards Jews in Europe that helped pave the way to Auschwitz.

- In 1933, book burnings began. Jewish scholars, members of the performing arts and others were forced from their posts.
- In 1935, liaisons between Jews and others were forbidden, designated as crimes against the state.
- In 1938, all Jews were forced to register their property, and Jewish communal bodies were put under the control of the secret police, the Gestapo.
- On the night of 9–10 November 1938, called *Kristallnacht*, a 'night of broken glass', over 300 synagogues were torched and many Jewish homes and businesses all over Germany were burned to the ground.

When Poland was occupied in September 1939, Jews were deprived of their belongings and forced into manual labour which Nazis called 'destruction through work'. After Hitler invaded Russia in 1941 Jews there were rounded up, taken to the outskirts of towns, shot and buried in mass graves. Between October and December 1941, perhaps 300,000 died in this way; and in 1942 a further 900,000. Special troops known as *Einsatzgruppen* were employed for this purpose. From 1941, death by gas was carried out and death camps were built: at Chełmno, Auschwitz, Majdanek, Sobibor, Treblinka and Belzec. After the Wannsee Conference in January 1942, the Nazis began the systematic deportation of Jews from all over Europe to these concentration camps which were designed to carry out genocide, known as the 'Final Solution', the extermination of all Jews. At the camps, the ill and the elderly were killed immediately, but the young and fit were put to manual work. At its greatest capacity, the camp at Auschwitz held 140,000. Its five ovens could burn 10,000 a day. Over 1.1 million people died at Auschwitz.

The Nazis aimed at identifying and murdering every single person they considered to be a Jew – without any exception. They included Jews who had converted to Christianity, such as Edith Stein (1891–1942), who converted to Catholicism in 1922 and became a Carmelite nun. She and her sister Rosa perished at Auschwitz. Controversy about Stein erupted with her canonisation in 1998, which whilst acknowledging her Jewishness recognised her as a Christian martyr. Stein herself interpreted her impending death as part of her 'Jewish fate', a joining of the 'sacrifice' of the Jewish people, and saw God's judgement enacted in the Holocaust and the persecution and murder of the Jewish people as the 'cross' of Christ. Although the Nazis certainly robbed Jews, Jewish property was not the motivation for the murder; rather, robbery was the 'natural' accompaniment of the desire, first, to expel Jews, and then, to murder them. The Nazi ideology was not based on economic, cost-effective calculations – the genocide was committed for purely ideological reasons.

When the war ended in 1945, so had a whole way of life for European Jews. Their numbers were catastrophically reduced – 6 million had perished. Of the pre-war Jewish populations of Poland, Latvia, Lithuania, Estonia, Germany and Austria, fewer than 10 per cent survived; and fewer than 30 per cent of Jews in occupied Russia, Ukraine, Belgium, Yugoslavia, Norway and Romania.

In the Holocaust, the morality of many Christians was tried and found wanting. Relatively few non-Jews helped their Jewish neighbours and even fewer Christian organisations – Zegota in Poland was a noteworthy exception – were established to rescue them. The Jewish people, not least at the Jerusalem memorial, Yad Vashem, honour names like Oskar Schindler (1908–74), a German industrialist, Raoul Wallenberg (1912–47?), a Swedish diplomat, Nicholas Winton (b. 1909), a British civil servant, Anna Shimaite, a Lithuanian librarian, Charles Lutz (1895–1975), a Swiss consul, and other individuals for their courageous acts. There, from the 1950s, trees were planted in their names in the Avenue of the Righteous of Nations. Many of these righteous Gentiles were Christians, but many were not.

CHRISTIANS AND THE HOLOCAUST

Few leaders of the Christian churches did much. Eugenio Pacelli, Pope Pius XII from 1939 to 1958, remains a controversial figure, with some claiming that he knew much and yet did nothing of importance to help Jews during the Holocaust, while others retort that he did what he could and encouraged others to do more. As Vatican Secretary of State, he signed a concordat with Hitler on 20 July 1935, which guaranteed the right of the Church 'to regulate her own affairs'. Hitler broke its terms almost immediately, but that never encouraged Pacelli to think he might do likewise.

The Third Reich neutralised the Protestant churches as effectively as the Roman Catholic Church. On 14 July 1933, the Reichstag proclaimed a new 'Reich Church', forcibly bringing together all Protestant churches.

The new Reich Bishop, Ludwig Mueller (1883–1945), was a friend of Hitler and an outspoken antisemite.

In 1999 a controversy broke out when it appeared that the Vatican intended to canonise Pius XII. At the same time, a critical book was published by a Cambridge University scholar, John Cornwell (b. 1940), entitled *Hitler's Pope: The Secret History of Pius XII*. In the same year there was controversy over limited access for scholars to the Vatican's archives even though the International Catholic–Jewish Historical Commission had been formally appointed to review the materials that had been released by Paul VI. However, when the Commission sought to review the Vatican's archives for the years 1939–45, they were blocked. In response they suspended their activities in 2001 amidst considerable acrimony, demonstrating both the deeply rooted sensitivities and the practical difficulties involved in such a process. Attempts to canonise Pius XII briefly gained momentum towards the end of 2007 when the fiftieth anniversary of his death was celebrated, but in 2008 Pope Benedict XVI announced a delay in the canonisation process to provide more time to study documents from World War II.

Until there is proper access to the archives for scholars, it will remain uncertain whether the Pope did all that he could and whether he did it soon enough. Pope Pius XII condemned the effects of the war on its innocent victims, but did not single out the persecution of Jews, either during or after the Holocaust. He certainly made some diplomatic interventions regarding Jewish safety but lived during a time, prior to Vatican II, when anti-Jewish prejudice was common in Christianity. The evidence released thus far does not satisfactorily demonstrate whether Pius XII acted soon enough and decisively enough. A more extensive study is still required, one that would draw in the best available scholars in the field to help achieve a scholarly consensus regarding his response to the Holocaust.

The impression we have of Vatican policy of the 1930s and 1940s, indeed, of the two popes of that time, Pius XI and Pius XII, is hardly a positive one. Individuals and institutions failed to demonstrate solidarity with their Jewish neighbours by condemning and actively opposing Nazi policies. Joint Catholic and Protestant protest against Nazi atrocity, however, proved successful in one notable instance: the almost complete cessation of the Euthanasia Programme, which had begun in 1940. The secret operation was code-named T4, in reference to the street address (Tiergartenstrasse 4) of the programme's coordinating office in Berlin. Six gassing installations for adults were established but the sudden death of thousands of institutionalised patients, whose death certificates listed strangely similar causes and places of death, raised suspicions. Hitler ordered a halt to the Euthanasia Programme in late August 1941, in view of widespread public and private protests concerning the killings, especially from members of the German clergy. Historians estimate that the Euthanasia Programme claimed the lives of 200,000 individuals. The success with which the Church contributed to the end of the T4 programme suggests that church opposition could be effective, the regime still being dependent on public support.

Yet, when reviewing this period, it is essential to differentiate between a failure by the churches to condemn Nazi antisemitic activities and explicit endorsement of, and active participation in, Nazi policies, whether by groups (e.g., the *Deutsche Christen*) or individuals (e.g., Jozef Tiso (1887–1947), a Catholic priest who, as leader of Slovakia, collaborated with Hitler). In Nazi-occupied countries other than Germany, the churches were often targeted themselves, and were thus preoccupied with protecting their own flocks rather than with the fate of Jews.

However, individual Christians did extend their support to Jews, facilitating escapes, offering places of hiding and participating in large and complex networks of rescue. There were also notable examples where church officials and leaders spoke out and acted on behalf of Jews. One of the most honourable was Angelo Giuseppe Roncalli (Pope John XXIII from 1958 to 1963) who, as Papal Nuncio for Turkey and Greece, made available baptismal certificates to thousands of Hungarian Jews in a bid to persuade Germans to leave them unmolested. The future Pope declared that he had no interest in whether any Jews actually were baptised or whether, when the war ended, any stayed in the Church. His sole aim was to save lives. Roncalli was instrumental in gaining papers for Jewish refugees seeking to enter Palestine, working closely with the Papal Nuncio for Hungary and other neutral diplomats to save tens of thousands of Jewish lives.

In Bulgaria, Catholic and Orthodox Christian representatives, along with secular authorities, protested against the deportation of Jews in 1943 which had been sanctioned by the Bulgarian government. Their protests succeeded and in the summer of 1943 the deportation of the majority of Jews living in Bulgaria, numbering approximately 50,000, was prevented.

In many Nazi-occupied countries, individual priests and lay people were active in their opposition to the Nazis' antisemitic policies and in rescuing Jews. Some monasteries and convents hid Jews – one of the most famous examples being the Carmel in Echt in Belgium, which sheltered both Edith Stein, then a nun, and her sister. Another example is part of the population of the largely Protestant village Le Chambon, in the south of France, who were motivated by their Huguenot heritage and organised the rescue of approximately 5,000 Jews during the war.

In one of the most spectacular rescue efforts, the majority of Jews from Denmark were saved in a secret transfer to Sweden. The churches and the population at large cooperated in this rescue activity, motivated by two concerns: first, a strong humanitarian rejection of Nazi inhumanity as a whole; and, second, a religious belief that Jews are significant for Christianity, if only because Jesus and the apostles had been Jews.

Rescuers often reported later that they were sometimes motivated by their Christian beliefs, and, at other times, simply by a humanitarianism which they felt to be Christian but which was also not confined to this religion. In many instances, it was possible for individuals to hold antisemitic beliefs and still engage in the rescue and assistance of Jews. One of the most striking examples is Dean Grüber (1924–75), a Protestant pastor in Berlin who was himself imprisoned in Sachsenhausen concentration camp for his activities on behalf of Jews. Yet, after the war, in a conversation with Richard Rubenstein, Grüber spoke about his belief that Jews were being punished in the Holocaust for their rejection of Christ, adding that he viewed Germans as God's agents in handing out this punishment. Since the actions of the Holocaust were clearly evil, Grüber thought that the Germans were being punished after the war by the division of Germany.

Is it possible to overstate Christian denigration of Jews and Jewishness? After all, the twentieth and twenty-first centuries have been an era of mass killings and genocide. As well as two world wars, the threat of global annihilation has continued to hang over our world. The Holocaust has been but one of a number of genocides and some play down its importance; a few have even argued that it never occurred. A British historian, David Irving (b. 1938), repudiated the reality of the gas chambers, and his views have reverberated in antisemitic circles in Europe, America and the Middle East. The Irving trial in the UK in 2000 brought this subject to public attention, although the impact of the verdict, which found Irving a Holocaust denier and flawed historian, has apparently not reduced the small number of Holocaust deniers.

Since the Holocaust occurred in the heart of Christian Europe, it remains an important issue for Europeans and especially Christians. Europeans today are expected to reflect on the fact that Nazism arose in the midst of a supposedly liberal, democratic and well-developed civilisation, in a country that had developed some of the most advanced ideas and achievements of modern culture. During the years 1933–45, the vast majority of Europeans looked on while their Jewish neighbours were taken away and murdered.

As far as Christianity is concerned, and most Europeans were of course at least nominally Christians, the problem is even more serious: some nineteen hundred years after the life of Jesus the Jew, his people were murdered by baptised pagans who, by their action and inaction, denied their baptism, while most other Christians, from the highest to the lowest, looked aside. For many Christians, the Holocaust remains as much a threat to Christian self-understanding today as it did at the end of World War II.

JEWISH RESPONSES TO THE HOLOCAUST

There are a number of different names used to describe the Holocaust. The Hebrew word 'Shoah', meaning destruction or desolation, is often used, especially by Jews. The word 'Holocaust', although the most popular term, is also the most contested because it is derived from the Greek translation of the Hebrew word *olah* ('whole burnt offering'). Hence, to some the term itself has become offensive, suggesting that victims of the Holocaust were a 'sacrifice' or 'offering'. Most people capitalise the word in order to emphasise that they are referring to the specific context of the murder of Jews during World War II. 'Shoah' is biblical in origin, but appears to avoid the references to God and sacrifice that have made the term 'Holocaust' appear problematic.

For twenty years, hardly anything was said or written about the Holocaust. It was almost too horrible to mention. Now, there is an enormous literature on the subject. Yet, although the Holocaust is of immense importance, it is misleading if it so dominates Christian–Jewish relations as to eclipse all other concerns.

Jewish responses to the Holocaust tend to fall into two categories. The first, represented by Emil Fackenheim and others such as Richard Rubenstein and Elie Wiesel (b. 1928), argues that the Shoah resulted in a rupture in the relationship between Jews and God. The second views the events as one would view persecution and oppression during other periods of extreme Jewish suffering. This view is represented by Jewish scholars such as Eliezer Berkovits, Eugene Borowitz (b. 1924) and Michael Wyschogrod (b. 1928). The latter makes their position clear when he states that 'the voices of the prophets speak more loudly than did Hitler' and that traditional approaches to Scripture provide the means by which to come to terms with the Holocaust.

Fackenheim urged a new commandment, to be added to the 613 biblical commandments (*mitzvoth*), that it was the duty of Jews to survive the trauma of the Shoah and not give Hitler posthumous victory by disappearing. He argued that the Holocaust has precipitated an unprecedented need in both Jewish and Christian theology to re-examine the nature of the relationship between man and God. 'So enormous are the events of recent Jewish history [...] that the Jewish Bible must be read by Jews today – read, listened to, struggled with if necessary – as though they had never read it before' (*The Jewish Bible after the Holocaust: A re-reading*, Manchester: Manchester University Press, 1990, pp. 16–17).

Emil Fackenheim calls for a struggle with the biblical text and, if need be, a fight against it. At the heart of his approach is an insistence that a traditional religious response is no longer appropriate in a post-Holocaust world because it fails to provide answers to the unique challenges posed by the Holocaust. He calls for a 'fraternal reading' of Scripture by Jews and Christians so that they can jointly face the challenges posed by the Holocaust and can give legitimacy and meaning to the post-Holocaust Jewish–Christian relationship.

As we shall see, the Holocaust not only caused Christianity to reassess its relationship with Judaism but also stirred greater Jewish interest in Christianity. Jonathan Sacks (b. 1948) spoke for many Jews when he stated in 1996 that Christians and Jews 'today meet and talk together because we must; because we have considered the alternative and seen where it ends and we are shocked to the core by what we have seen' (*Christian–Jewish Dialogue: A Reader*, Exeter: Exeter University Press, 1996, Foreword). His words echo those of Abraham Joshua Heschel who, in a speech to the Rabbinical Assembly Convention in the United States thirty years earlier, stated that 'Jews and Christians share the perils and fears; we stand on the abyss together.'

One radical response has been that of Richard Rubenstein. He holds that it is not possible to talk of the justice of God. Instead, Jews must hold on to a belief in the survival of the Jewish people and in the possibility of goodness as well as evil in humankind. In recent years, Rubenstein has become indebted to Buddhist and other Asian views of the Transcendence to establish his understanding of the divine Nothing. What is at issue here is how, if at all, God works in the world and Rubenstein rejects any notion of God acting in history. After Auschwitz only human beings can create value and meaning, and Judaism has a particular role in this renewal and reintegration.

Whilst Fackenheim has called for a re-reading of the Bible after the Holocaust, Elie Wiesel claimed that there is a need for a new Talmud and Primo Levi (1919–87) suggested that Holocaust testimonies could be considered as stories of a new Bible. Wiesel's response is narrated in his book *Night* which is characterised by a constant questioning and protest against God: 'man raises himself towards God by the questions he asks Him'.

Although he explores the biblical account of Job, it fails as an interpretative model for suffering after the Holocaust:

> I'll tell you, the problem I have with Job is, number one, the children. The ending of Job is superficially happy. He has children again. He gets everything he used to have in excess. He is saturated . . . I have often thought about this ending, and about the children lost at the beginning of the story. How does it speak to those of us who have experienced great loss and then find our lives again, those of us who survive? The only explanation I can find is in our generation's children. They saw them go away, never to return. ('Matter of Survival: A Conversation', in Tod Linafelt (ed.), *In Strange Fire: Reading the Hebrew Bible after the Holocaust*, New York: New York University Press, 2000, p. 30)

For Wiesel, Job's acceptance of the loss of his children is unsustainable when read in the context of the Holocaust. Furthermore, God ultimately reveals Himself to Job; there is no such revelation in Auschwitz. The Holocaust is a point of rupture in the relationship between man and God, made apparent by the absence of a responding voice from the whirlwind. In his autobiography, *All Rivers Run to the Sea*, Wiesel suggests that, even if this voice were made manifest, the rupture would not be healed. 'Nothing justifies Auschwitz,' he states, 'Were the Lord Himself to offer me a justification, I think I would reject it. Treblinka erases all justifications and all answers' (*All Rivers Run to the Sea: Memoirs*, volume I, 1928–69, London: HarperCollins, 1996, p. 103).

Irving Greenberg, an American orthodox rabbi, argues that the Shoah has resulted in a new voluntary covenant, according to which Jews are no longer commanded but choose to take on the continuity of Judaism. The crisis of the Holocaust requires a radical rethinking of the conditions under which the Jewish people commit to the covenant. In the Holocaust the covenant was endangered, but those Jews who survived responded with an ongoing commitment to remain Jewish, and this response is part of the new era of the covenant, the continuity of the covenant being a commitment the Jewish people make voluntarily.

In 2000, *Dabru Emet* ('Speak Truth'), a cross-denominational Jewish statement on Christians and Christianity, was issued and, commenting on the Holocaust, assessed Christian guilt while separating Christianity from Nazism:

> *Nazism was not a Christian phenomenon.* Without the long history of Christian anti Judaism and Christian violence against Jews, Nazi ideology could not have taken hold nor could it have been carried out . . . But Nazism itself was not an inevitable outcome of Christianity.

The statement generated much controversy and demonstrated how the Holocaust remains both central to and sensitive in the Jewish–Christian encounter. Some Jews criticised the statement as going too far, remaining convinced that Christians have not forsworn triumphalism; they point to the continuing targeted proselytism of Jews: others express concern that Christians might feel completely exonerated by the Jewish statement. For some Christians, it was troubling to learn that many Jews do view Nazism as the logical outcome of European Christian culture.

CHRISTIAN RESPONSES TO THE SHOAH

In 1947, soon after the end of the Second World War, the newly formed International Council of Christians and Jews (ICCJ, founded 1946) met in the Swiss town of Seelisberg. A declaration by the Christian participants was issued, known as *The Ten Points of Seelisberg: An Address to the Churches*, in which the Christians, in consultation with Jews, tackled the problem of Christian antisemitism. The *Ten Points* drew attention to the Jewishness of Jesus and of the early Christian community, and pointed out that Jews and Christians are bound by a common commandment to love God and one's neighbour. It proceeded to indicate what should be avoided in the presentation of Jews by Christians, including the misrepresentation of Jews as enemies of Jesus, portraying the Passion as if all Jews were responsible for Christ's death, or choosing critical passages from the New Testament without noting their universal application to humanity and not just to Jews. The *Ten Points* anticipated many later church statements in its understanding of Jesus and the early Church. In 2009, a revised and updated version of the *Ten Points* was issued by Jewish and Christian theologians under the auspices of the ICCJ.

In 1948 the World Council of Churches (WCC) held its first meeting in Amsterdam and in the introduction to its *Report on the Christian Approach to the Jews* it made reference to the fact that the conference was taking place 'within 5 years of the extermination of 6 million Jews'. The report marked a new stage in the attitude of the Protestant churches towards antisemitism, for the WCC not only acknowledged the existence of religious antisemitism but also accepted Christian involvement in it.

The report openly accepted that 'the churches in the past have helped to foster an image of the Jews as the sole enemies of Christ, which has contributed to antisemitism in the secular world'. It called upon 'all churches we represent to denounce antisemitism'. Consequently, awareness of the Christian contribution to antisemitism was placed firmly on the agenda of Christian–Jewish relations. The WCC report marked an admission that not only was Christian history linked to the history of antisemitism, but that it was one of the causes.

A few years later, in 1959, John XXIII changed the Good Friday liturgy during which Catholics said, 'Let us pray also for the perfidious Jews.' A year later, the Pope received wide attention for publicly greeting Jewish visitors with the words, 'I am Joseph your brother.' The Second Vatican Council devoted time to the question of relations with Judaism (and with other world faiths) through the publication of *Nostra Aetate* (1965), which marked the beginnings of a fresh approach to Judaism when the Roman Catholic Church 'came in from out of the cold'. The document was forceful in its condemnation of antisemitism and rejected the charge of Jewish responsibility for the death of Jesus, undermining the prevailing theology that Jews were divinely rejected and their punishment was that they were no longer to be in a covenant with God. According to Edward Flannery, it 'terminated in a stroke a millennial teaching of contempt of Jews and Judaism and unequivocally asserted the Church's debt to its Jewish heritage' ('Seminaries, Classrooms, Pulpits, Streets: Where We have to Go', in Roger Brooks, ed., *Unanswered Questions: Theological Views of Jewish–Catholic Relations*, Notre Dame: University of Notre Dame Press, 1988, pp. 128–9).

However, while condemning antisemitism, the Vatican avoided reflecting on the significance of the Holocaust. In 1987, however, in the wake of Jewish ire over the Pope's reception of the Austrian President Kurt Waldheim (1919–2007), who had been an active Nazi, the Vatican promised to issue a document that tackled the Holocaust, and the statement *We Remember: A Reflection on the Shoah* was published in 1998. It stressed the evils of antisemitism, concluding, 'we wish to turn awareness of past sins into a firm resolve to build a new future in which there will be no more anti-Judaism among Christians or anti-Christian sentiment among Jews but rather a shared mutual respect'. It incorporated much of Pope John Paul II's forceful criticism of antisemitism.

But its treatment of the Holocaust had some disappointing aspects for the Church did not make a formal apology, such as the *Declaration of Repentance* issued by the French bishops in 1997 in which they stated that 'it is important to admit the primary role played by the consistently repeated anti-Jewish stereotypes wrongly perpetuated by the Christians in the historical process that led to the Holocaust'. *We Remember* speaks of those Christians who helped the Jews and those who failed to do so, implying a balanced picture which was far from reality.

Two years later, in 2000, before his pilgrimage to Israel, John Paul II (r. 1978–2005) presided over a millennial liturgy of repentance which devoted one of its seven categories of major sins of the Church to repentance for Christian teaching against Jews and Judaism over the centuries and for the failures of the Church during the Shoah. In this the Roman Catholic Church was some years behind the Anglican Communion, which in 1988 had delivered a scathing denunciation of antisemitism and of the Christian teaching of contempt.

Through catechism, teaching of school children, and Christian preaching, the Jewish people have been misrepresented and caricatured . . . In order to combat centuries of anti-Jewish teaching and practice, Christians must develop programmes of teaching, preaching, and common social action which eradicate prejudice and promote dialogue and sharing among biblical peoples. (*Jews, Christians and Muslims: The Way of Dialogue*)

No document had so explicitly argued that there should be a fundamental change in the Christian approach to Judaism. It pointed the way forward and it is now common for statements from Protestant churches to acknowledge the legacy of the *Adversus Iudaeos* tradition and Christian antisemitism. For example, the Reformation Churches in Europe in 2001 issued *Church and Israel*, which states:

Irrespective of the particular responsibility of Germany and the Christians in Germany related to the National Socialist period – all the Christian churches in Europe share in the special history of European guilt towards Israel [the Jewish people], wherever they failed clearly to contradict antisemitism or even promoted it directly or indirectly. (2.6)

Unfortunately, the same is not true of the Orthodox churches. The changes that have taken place in what may be described as the Western churches find few parallels in the East. To some extent the uneasy relationship of the Orthodox churches with Judaism echoes the state of their involvement in the ecumenical movement too, and it is foolish to expect Orthodox Christians to be more forward in seeking reconciliation with Jews than with their own Christian brethren. Much has to be done before Orthodox Christianity abandons its repository of anti-Jewish and antisemitic polemic.

The shadow of the Shoah also lingered long among Christian biblical scholars who lived during and even under the Third Reich. Scholars as important as, for example, Günther Bornkamm (1905–90) and Joachim Jeremias tended to portray Judaism at the time of Jesus as 'late Judaism' (*Spätjudentum*) as if it had ended after 70 CE or should have done, as if nothing since had happened to the Jewish religion. This position was based on the conviction that post-exilic Judaism had ossified and betrayed the prophetic faith of Israel. Jesus stands outside such a hardened, legalistic religion, a stranger to it, condemning the scribes and the Pharisees (and, by implication, Rabbinic Judaism) who thus misled modern Judaism into perpetuating this sterile, legalistic religion.

In contrast, most Christian theologians began dramatically to change the theological understanding of Jews and Judaism. The American Lutheran scholars Alice and Roy Eckardt reflected on the impact of the Holocaust on Christianity through a dialectical interpretation of history, seeing the 'night' of the Holocaust followed by the 'day' of the establishment of the state of Israel. The Eckardts argue that the fact that the Nazis intended to murder every single Jew makes the Holocaust a 'uniquely unique' event with a quality that is rooted in the transcendent and thus lies partly outside of history.

Franklin Littell maintains that Christian teaching and the Holocaust are directly linked. He describes Jews as 'the suffering servant', mirroring Christ and as central to Christian thought as is Christ. Littell characterises the founding of the state of Israel as the 'resurrection' of the Jewish people. As much as Christ's resurrection is interpreted as a token 'proof' for the 'world to come', Jewish life itself becomes here a token of the 'truth' of God's existence, election and promises.

Some theologians such as Franklin Sherman (b. 1928) and John Pawlikowski have explored connections between the Holocaust and christological understanding. They argue that, if the notion of God and the divine–human relationship needs restatement in the light of the Holocaust experience, then our perspective on the Christ event also needs reconsideration, given its understanding as embodying the divine presence in a special way. Pawlikowski differs from Sherman in being reluctant to posit a direct link between Jesus' sufferings on the cross and the sufferings of the Jewish people because Jesus' sufferings have always been seen as voluntary and redemptive, which cannot be claimed for Jewish suffering, especially during the Holocaust.

European Christian theologians have also been profoundly influenced by the Holocaust, among them Jürgen Moltmann (b. 1926). He rejects Christian antisemitism on the ground that it is a form of Christian self-hatred. Through this, he rediscovers the Church's provisional nature alongside the Jewish people, argues against Christian triumphalism, and affirms that the Old Testament and Judaism continue to hold positive significance for the Church. He has explored the significance of the Jewish 'no' to Jesus, suggesting that Christians should postpone the question of who will be revealed as Messiah to the end of time, and learn from Jews what it means to live in the present in an unredeemed world. His view is mirrored in the 2001 statement by the Pontifical Biblical Commission, *The Jewish People and Their Sacred Scriptures in the Christian Bible*, that 'the Jewish messianic expectation is not in vain'.

The German Catholic theologian Johann-Baptist Metz (b. 1928) defines the question the Holocaust puts to Christianity by asking 'whether and how we Christians can and may speak of "God after Auschwitz" in a credible constellation'. Metz bases his response on the hermeneutical principle of the 'authority of those who suffer'. The restatement of the Church's relationship with the Jewish people requires a revision of Christian theology, for there are no easy answers that can evade the terror of the Holocaust:

> There is no truth for me, which I could defend with my back turned toward Auschwitz. There is no sense for me, which I could save with my back turned toward Auschwitz. And for me there is no God to whom I could pray with my back turned toward Auschwitz. ('The Holocaust as Interruption', *Concilium* 175 (1984), p. 28)

MEMORIALS AND OTHER RESPONSES TO THE HOLOCAUST

Many churches have now made a commitment to Holocaust education, often collaborating with Jewish institutions, publishing resources, sponsoring conferences and workshops for teachers, and designing curricula. They have encouraged rituals and prayers for Holocaust remembrance, particularly around *Yom HaShoah* (Day of Holocaust Remembrance) or around government-initiated days of remembrance (Holocaust Memorial Days).

According to Alice Eckardt, a Christian liturgy should include a confession of Christian failings and culpability and a willingness to share the suffering vicariously (as on Good Friday). However, there must be no attempt to 'Christianise' the Holocaust; rather, such a liturgy should lead participants to reflect on Christian failure to respond adequately to the needs of desperate people, to dedicate themselves to 'Never Again', and to consider the theological questions involved.

Some of the most creative responses to the Holocaust have been aesthetic and, as memories recede further into the past, memorials and museums are playing an increasingly crucial role, inserting the memory of the Holocaust into formal narratives of national collective memory. National memorials and museums shed light on the formation of post-war self-understandings as they demonstrate a nation's consciousness of the Holocaust as well as how it should be commemorated.

Germany understandably attracts particular attention for its efforts to commemorate the Holocaust. The design by Daniel Libeskind (b. 1946) for the extension to the Jewish Museum Berlin (2001) is in itself a struggle with the meaning of the Holocaust. The building is constructed from pieces which together form a Star of David. In the completed building this can only be seen from the architect's drawings. The building is centred on what Libeskind calls 'the void', a space that cuts through every level of the museum and which itself leads nowhere when entered at the lower ground level. This void is a representation of the Holocaust, around which Libeskind architecturally built the history of the Jewish community of Berlin and of Germany as a whole into the museum.

Israel, in some respects a country built on the memory of the Holocaust, constructed Yad Vashem as a national memorial. It highlights the heroism of armed resistance, in particular the fighters of the Warsaw Ghetto uprising. Both the museum and memorial centre, which every Israeli visits at least twice during his/her education, tell the story of suffering and redemption that happened to 'us', that is, the Jewish people.

In the United States, home to the largest Jewish community outside Israel, Holocaust museums and memorials have been established locally, mainly since the 1980s, and a national museum, the United States Holocaust Memorial Museum, was opened in 1993 with an accompanying research centre. The museum serves as a story-telling museum that not only tells the story of the Holocaust, but tells the story of the Holocaust to the American people.

While events and museums commemorating both world wars are well established, Britain has been comparatively slow in establishing museums and memorials that address the Holocaust. Britain's reluctance to engage in public acts of Holocaust remembrance may be due to the ambivalence in British society (including amongst British Jews) about their relationship to the Holocaust. The 1990s saw the inclusion of the Holocaust in the national curriculum for teaching children at secondary schools and the establishment of Beth Shalom in Nottinghamshire, a private Christian initiative to commemorate the Holocaust. In 2000, a permanent national Holocaust exhibition in the Imperial War Museum in Lambeth was opened by the Queen; it offers a British context for the experience of the Holocaust, including a focus on the *Kindertransport* and the Allied liberation of the camps. The exhibition emphasises Britain's role of a bystander to the

Holocaust and the consequences and responsibility that arise. However, some have criticised the lack of reflection on the more controversial aspects of Britain's role, such as the conscious decision not to bomb the railway lines leading to Auschwitz.

In the same year, at the Stockholm Forum on Holocaust Education, Remembrance and Research, European governments committed themselves to establishing an annual day dedicated to Holocaust education and remembrance. Several European countries now observe Holocaust Memorial Day on 27 January (the date Auschwitz was liberated), ensuring the Holocaust is remembered as part of a broader educational agenda promoting anti-racism, pluralism, multiculturalism and civil society. In the UK, for example, local, regional and national events take place, with particular attention paid to the participation of schools and representatives of each city's, region's and country's faith communities. Each year a theme is chosen such as Rwanda in 2004 (marking the tenth anniversary of the genocide of 1,000,000 Tutsis and some moderate Hutus, in 100 days in 1994) and 'Standing Up to Hatred' in 2009.

CHAPTER 8

Zionism and the state of Israel

Nowhere is the subject of peace and understanding – or, perhaps more realistically, violence and misunderstanding – more evident than in discussions among Christians and Jews about Israel and Palestine, whether they take place in the tea rooms of London and Washington or in the coffee parlours of Jerusalem and Tel Aviv, Ramallah and Bethlehem.

The apparently constant instability in Palestinian-controlled areas and anti-Israel attitudes of varying intensity in Arab countries, combined with the murder of Yitzhak Rabin by an Orthodox Jew in 1995 and threats from some Orthodox and ultra-Orthodox Jews against land for peace initiatives, are reminders of what seems to be an intractable conflict between Israel and the Palestinians. A story is told about an Israeli and a Palestinian leader meeting with God and asking whether there will ever be peace in the Middle East in their lifetime. 'Of course there will be peace,' God tells them. They look relieved. 'However,' God continues, 'not in My lifetime.' More than a century after the beginning of modern Zionism, a peaceful solution seems some distance away.

Yet the political and military conflict does not fully explain why Israel is such a controversial topic in Jewish–Christian relations. Any conversation between Jews and Christians on the significance of the Land and state of Israel brims with emotion and passion. Why?

For Jews, the centrality of the land of the Bible, as well as the survival of over a third of world Jewry, is at stake. Christians, for their part, not only disagree as to the place of Israel in Christian theology, but often, understandably, feel particular concern for Christians who live in Israel and in the future state of Palestine.

Israel is controversial because it cannot be viewed simply as a geographical and political entity whose emergence is like the establishment of any new state. Political, social, cultural and religious concerns all affect its place in the Jewish–Christian relationship. Indeed, the complexity and sensitivity surrounding Israel mean that it is not even easy to choose the appropriate words in discussions. Are we to use the term 'Holy Land', perhaps with a qualifier such as 'Christian', or, alternatively, 'the Promised Land'? Or must we seek ostensibly more neutral terms such as 'Israel' and 'Palestine'? Should we refer to 'Jerusalem', to 'Yerushalayim', or to 'Al-Quds'? Is Hebron, al-Khalil or Nablus, Shechem? How do we respond to terms such as 'the Zionist entity' rather than 'the state of Israel'?

As we have seen earlier in this book, there have been great changes in Christian teaching on Judaism and especially a tackling of the traditional 'teaching of contempt of Judaism'. Nevertheless, attitudes towards the Land and state of Israel continue to be difficult, making a Christian re-orientation to Israel problematic. Simply put, it has been easier for Christians to condemn antisemitism as a misunderstanding of Christian teaching than to come to terms with the re-establishment of the Jewish state. Alice Eckardt points out the contrast between Christian willingness to tackle antisemitism and reflect on the Shoah and Christian reticence on the subject of Zionism and the state of Israel. Christians are more likely to think about the Shoah than the state of Israel, she suggests, because the former accords with the traditional stereotype of Jews as a suffering and persecuted minority. Israel, however, challenges this assumption and transforms the victim into a victor.

Although Christians have always acknowledged that Jews feel a spiritual attachment to the Land of Israel, they have found it harder to accommodate the political consequences of the desire for and creation of a Jewish state, partly because of the separation of (or uneasy relationship between) church and state. For example, the Roman Catholic Church stated in its 1985 *Notes* that 'the existence of the State of Israel and its political options should be envisaged not in a perspective which is in itself religious, but in their reference to the common principles of international law'. However, Walter Brueggemann (b. 1933), the Baptist theologian and biblical scholar, has argued that the subject of land should move to the centre of Christian theology, suggesting that Christians cannot engage in serious dialogue with Jews unless they acknowledge land to be the central agenda.

THE LAND OF ISRAEL IN THE FIRST MILLENNIUM

The destruction of the Second Temple in 70 CE and the dispersion of Jews after 135 (when Hadrian built a temple devoted to Jupiter on the Temple ruins) were key moments in the formative period of Rabbinic Judaism and Christianity. The rabbis' response to dispossession and powerlessness consisted of the hope of divine restoration when exile would be followed by a time of messianic redemption for all peoples. They also developed the mystical idea that God was exiled with the Jewish people and that one purpose of this exile was to bring Torah to the nations of the world so that eventually they would recognise the one God.

During the rabbinic period, the Land of Israel was much changed from the biblical kingdom of David (*c.* 1000 BCE). The rabbis reflected on the nature of the biblical command to possess the land, the duty to live in the land, and the promise that after exile would come redemption and a return to the land. Yet the existence of the Diaspora in biblical times (which began at least in the seventh century BCE and remained in existence after the return of Nehemiah and Ezra to Jerusalem in the fourth century) hardly merited a mention. The focus was on the Land of Israel, even if the most famous rabbinic academies of the classical rabbinic period were located in Pumbedita and Sura, by the river Euphrates in Babylon, 1000 miles from the Land of Israel. Indeed, from the end of the biblical period to the present day, the majority of Jews have lived in the Diaspora, outside the Land of Israel.

The rabbinic writings illustrate how the Land of Israel is intimately related to Jewish self-understanding. For example, the covenant between the people of Israel and God could only be understood with reference to the land. In the Bible, possession of the Land of Israel is a key part of the promise given to Abraham by God:

And I will establish my covenant between me and thee and thy seed after thee in their generations for an everlasting covenant, to be a God unto thee, and to thy seed after thee. And I will give unto thee, and to thy seed after thee, the land wherein thou art a stranger, all the land of Canaan, for an everlasting possession; and I will be their God. (Gen. 17:7–8)

Consequently, the rabbis considered in detail the meaning of the promise for his descendants.

There was also a view that exile occurred as a result of divine punishment because of a failure to observe God's commands in Israel, for example, by fighting each other and failing to live peaceably together. Traditional Christian interpretation also emphasised divine punishment – in this case, for the Jewish rejection of Christ. This view underpinned the doctrine of replacement theology, the belief that Christians had replaced Jews as the people of God. Replacement theology, to be discussed in more detail in the next chapter, became dominant in Christian teaching about Judaism, contributing to anti-Judaism and antisemitism. The Church consistently pointed to the historical tragedies of the Jewish people as proof that God had rejected them definitively. For example, as we noted in chapter 3, John Chrysostom stated that as long as Jerusalem and the Temple lay in ruins, and Jews remained in exile, Christians could rightly claim Judaism had lost its legitimacy.

Christian interest in the Land of Israel began in earnest in the fourth century, after the conversion of Constantine in 312 CE. A decisive role was played by Helena (*c.* 250–330), Constantine's mother, who made a pilgrimage to the city of Jerusalem and journeyed throughout the land. According to folklore, she discovered the True Cross as well as the site of the tomb of Jesus at Golgotha. Large numbers of Christians followed her as they sought to trace the path of the life of Jesus through the year, from his birth in Bethlehem, through his ministry in Galilee, to Jerusalem at Holy Week, and her pilgrimage became a pattern for Christian pilgrims throughout the Middle Ages and even today.

The Holy Land was soon under Christian control and, although archae-ological records show continued coexistence with Jews through the fourth century, a large number of legal restrictions were enacted, implying that Jews lived on Christian land on sufferance. Helena launched a signifi-cant building programme, overseeing the construction of several churches including the Church of the Nativity in Bethlehem and the Church of the Holy Sepulchre (*Anastasis*) in Jerusalem, at the traditional site of Jesus' resurrection.

In spite of lavish attention, Palestine did not remain at the centre of imperial interests in the centuries that followed. Christian Palestine col-lapsed in the face of Persian and then Muslim invasion. Thrown into crisis, Palestinian Christianity became more divided than before, with the polemic against Jews being grafted into polemical literature used on all sides of the inner-Christian controversy.

The drive to wrest back control from Muslims gained great momentum, notably in the eleventh century in France and the Lowlands, and resulted in the Crusades. The First Crusade (1095) was, in part, an expression of the growing power of the Christian West, mobilised by the call of the Byzantine Emperor to defend Constantinople against the Turks. It led to the crusaders conquering Jerusalem in 1099 for a short period and establishing the Latin Kingdom of Jerusalem, extending across Syria to Armenia. Jerusalem was re-taken by Salah al-Din (Saladin, 1138–93) in 1187 and the last remaining city under Christian control, Acre, was destroyed by the Mamluks in 1291.

JEWISH DESIRE TO RETURN TO THE LAND OF ISRAEL

From the seventh century BCE onwards, significant numbers of the people of Israel lived in exile far away from the Land of Israel, under the authority of Gentile rulers. Their response to exile was to yield to outside power and accept the consequences (which sometimes included violence). This strategy not only contributed to Jewish survival but also enabled the flourishing of Judaism:

Thus saith the LORD of hosts, the God of Israel, unto all the captivity, whom I have caused to be carried away captive from Jerusalem unto Babylon: Build ye houses, and dwell in them, and plant gardens, and eat the fruit of them; take ye wives, and beget sons and daughters; and take wives for your sons, and give your daughters to husbands, that they may bear sons and daughters; and multiply ye there, and be not diminished. And seek the peace of the city whither I have caused you to be carried away captive, and pray unto the LORD for it; for in the peace thereof shall ye have peace. (Jer. 29:4–7)

By relinquishing desire for sovereignty, Jews were able to gain maximum autonomy in regulating their lives. Under the motto *dina d'malkuta dina* ('the law of the land is the law'), the Jewish community based its existence on the law of a particular host society. As a rabbinic saying has it, 'a person must be at all times yielding like a reed and not unbending like a cedar' (BT. Ta'anit 20a).

For over a thousand years, Jews accepted that they would suffer expulsions and pogroms, but believed that they could survive. With a few exceptions, they accepted the suffering passively, believing that they would live beyond such events. This survival technique is illustrated by the fact that even as the Jewish lights of Western Europe were extinguished one by one – expelled from England (1290), France (1306) and Spain (1492) – new Jewish centres were being established in Eastern Europe, Turkey and the Middle East.

Whether Jews survived in the Land of Israel or in exile, they perceived that they were on their own, that no one else shared their vision and that all outsiders were enemies. For many centuries, this reflected considerable truth. The mindset of isolation imbued Judaism, surrounded by Canaanites and later by Romans. It was reinforced by life in Christendom when they were forced to face anti-Jewish teaching and violence, inquisitions and pogroms, underpinned by a deep theological ambivalence about the continued existence of the Jewish people whose religious beliefs should have been long superseded by accepting Jesus Christ as the Messiah. In comparison the treatment of Jews under Islam has been considerably better, though not without destructive experiences under occasional fanatical regimes and the abuse of the gentler Muslim habit of treating Jews (and Christians) as second-class citizens (*dhimmis*). It is unsurprising that over the centuries a mentality permeated the minds of most Jews, which saw the Jewish community as being utterly engulfed by enemies. To a large extent this is understandable and its legacy exists today.

Jewish aspiration to return to the Land of Israel was noticed but dismissed in the *Adversus Iudaeos* writings, since much was made of the fact that the Temple had been destroyed, Jews expelled from Jerusalem and the land occupied by Romans. Yet Judaism did not change from remaining the religion of a particular people; two elements, ethnic identity and religious faith, continued to interact with each other in different ways in different periods.

Medieval writers, such as Judah ha-Levi, reflected on the future return of Jews to the Land of Israel. Ha-Levi, a representative of religious Zionism, portrays the 'longing for Zion' and expresses a belief in the imminent redemption of the land. In his poetry, Zion is the feminine allegory for the expression of religious passion, although the commandment to live in the land remained an unrealised ideal. Ha-Levi set off on a journey to the land towards the end of his life, making a concrete allegory for the steps that humanity was to make towards the messianic end-time. Around the same time, Joseph Kimhi (1100–70) in his *Book of the Covenant* promoted the restoration of Jewish self-government, rejecting Christian claims that identified Jewish loss of sovereignty as proof of the transfer of the promises to the Church.

Towards the end of the Middle Ages, leading Kabbalists broke with the passive tradition of waiting for the Messiah before returning to the Land of Israel and began to restore a religious-national existence, alongside small pockets of Jews who were already living there. For example, Isaac Luria (1534–72) moved to Safed in the Galilee, where he attempted to re-establish a Sanhedrin. This more active form of Zionism received further impetus from the belief that the suffering of Jews in exile merited the return to the land and the redemption of the whole world.

The will to survive in exile began to generate messianic hopes of redemption, which occasionally led to a high level of anticipation and the extraordinary claims of self-appointed Messiahs such as Shabbetai Zvi (1626–76). One of the common features of these times of messianic fervour was that the Land of Israel became a symbol of redress for all the wrongs that Jews had suffered.

When Shabbetai Zvi proclaimed himself Messiah, a movement grew around him that gained an enormous following among Jews, particularly in the Ottoman Empire, which at that time controlled the Land of Israel. He began preparations to travel to Jerusalem and some Christians saw him as a precursor to the return of Christ. His actions, such as appointing apostles to represent the twelve tribes of Israel, attracted the interest of Christian millenarians in England, the Netherlands and Germany. The rise in violence against Jews, particularly in Russia and Poland, also contributed to his success, as did the increase in popularity of Kabbalah, especially in its Laurianic form, which combined messianism with mysticism. Many Jewish communities made preparations or even left for the Land of Israel in messianic expectation. In 1666 Shabbetai Zvi was imprisoned by the Sultan and given the choice of converting to Islam or being put to death. He chose the former, as did thousands of his followers. Shabbeteanism continued to flourish after his death although most followers converted. The best known Shabbetean was Jacob Frank; although his followers later converted to Catholicism, remnants of the Catholic Frankists survived until the mid-twentieth century.

The religious fervour surrounding Shabbetai Zvi inspired a wealth of Chassidic literature on the land. (The *Chassidim* (Hebrew for 'pious') was a movement founded by the Baal Shem Tov (1698–1760) in eighteenth-century Poland.) Although relatively few sought to settle there, those who did formed a central component in the Jewish Yishuv (settlement), receiving support from religious Jews across the Ashkenazi and Sephardi worlds.

This period marks a significant shift, for Jews stopped waiting for a divine solution to their predicament and began to take their destiny into their own hands. This was a dramatic change from the earlier strategy of survival, which advocated endurance of the status quo as part of the covenant with God. By the time of the breakdown of Jewish life in Europe in the late nineteenth and early twentieth centuries, many Jews had concluded that a Jewish state offered them the best hope, not only for survival but also for fulfilment.

In 1862 Moses Hess (1812–75) wrote *Rome and Jerusalem*, which was the first modern proclamation of the Jewish national idea. He called for a Jewish national revival, based on the ideas of social justice, and was soon followed by Theodor Herzl. From the 1880s onwards, the Jewish goal for self-determination became a key objective. In 1897, the First Zionist Congress adopted Herzl's *Basle Programme* and declared that: 'Zionism seeks to secure for the Jewish people a publicly recognised, legally secured home in Palestine.' Herzl's book *The Jewish State* (1896) called for an independent Jewish state in response to antisemitism. Influenced by his experience of reporting as a journalist the Dreyfus Affair in 1895, he was convinced of the need for a political solution. Consequently, secular self-governance of the Land was given greater significance in the formation of Jewish identity. Geographical particularity, which had previously been only one aspect of Jewish self-understanding, provided an important (or, for some, the only) basis for Jewish identity.

At the same time, religious fervour also played an important role in the popularity and eventual success of the Zionist idea, notably in Eastern Europe where movements such as *Hovevei-Zion* ('Lovers of Zion') called for the re-establishment of 'the House of Jacob' in the Land of Israel. Thus, modern Zionism consists of both religious and secular ideologies and, though the state of Israel was ultimately the product of Herzl's secular-political vision, the contribution of religious Zionism was acknowledged in the *Proclamation of Independence* in 1948, which included spiritual phrases such as 'redemption of Israel' and 'trust in the Rock of Israel', although it did not explicitly mention God in its final publication.

However, not all Jews supported a Jewish state, particularly before the Holocaust, and the subject was the cause of vociferous disagreements within and between all Jewish groups, secular and religious, Reform and Orthodox. One aspect of the argument was whether Zionism encouraged antisemitism by confirming the view of antisemites that Jews were not committed to the national interests of the countries in which they lived. For their part, Reform Jews argued that Jewish nationalism undermined their emphasis on universal values and ethical monotheism; however, their view changed, like that of the vast majority of Jews, after the Holocaust. Today a small number of the most ultra-Orthodox Jews (ironically supported by a few radical Jewish socialist secularists) reject the creation of the Jewish state, arguing that Israel should be a divine and not a man-made creation. Relying on the traditional rabbinic teaching, they argue that eventually God will come, bring the Messiah, and so transform the world, enabling the Jewish people to return to the Land of Israel.

CHRISTIANS AND THE LAND SINCE 1900

The attitude of Roman Catholicism towards Zionism changed greatly in the course of the twentieth century. In 1904, Pope Pius X (1903–14) famously gave an audience to Theodor Herzl, who asked for support in his endeavour to bring Jews back to the Land of Israel. Herzl was told unequivocally by the Pope that because 'the Jews have not recognised our Lord, therefore we cannot recognise the Jewish people'.

However, the Roman Catholic Church has changed its attitude significantly since then, beginning with Vatican II and the 1965 document *Nostra*

Aetate which, while not explicitly mentioning Israel, began the process that eventually led to the Vatican's recognition of the state of Israel in 1994. Increasing awareness among Roman Catholics of the significance of Israel became more noticeable during the papacy of John Paul II and can be seen as early as 1984 when, in his Good Friday Apostolic Letter, he wrote: 'for the Jewish people who live in the State of Israel, and who preserve in that land such precious testimonies to their history and their faith, we must ask for the desired security and the due tranquillity that is the prerogative of every nation and condition of life and of progress for every society'.

Ten years later the state of Israel and the Holy See exchanged ambassadors, and the process begun in 1965 reached another significant landmark with the Pontiff's pilgrimage to Israel in 2000, and the iconic image of his visit to the Western Wall. Following Jewish tradition, the Pope placed a written prayer in a crevice of the Western Wall. The short typed prayer with an official seal read: 'God of our fathers, you chose Abraham and his descendants to bring your Name to the Nations. We are deeply saddened by the behaviour of those who in the course of history have caused these children of yours to suffer, and asking Your forgiveness we wish to commit ourselves to genuine brotherhood with the people of the Covenant.'

Although the papal visit carried theological import, the Vatican is careful to emphasise that its diplomatic policy is rooted in *realpolitik* rather than in theology. The fact that the Holy See signed an agreement with the Palestinian Authority in 2000 that is virtually the same as the one with Israel is one example. The secular diplomatic position is illustrated by the 1985 *Notes*, which states that 'the existence of the State of Israel and its political options should be envisaged not in a perspective which is in itself religious, but in their reference to the common principle of international law'. Nevertheless, the Vatican and the Chief Rabbis of Israel have annual meetings, alternately in Jerusalem and Rome, demonstrating an overlap between politics and theology.

In the first decade of the twenty-first century, relations between the Holy See and the state of Israel have become strained, epitomised by the lack of agreement over juridical and tax issues. Occasional bilateral talks have failed to produce agreement over 'the fundamental accord' that has been sought since 1993. The majority of the Holy See's religious communities own large properties purchased in the nineteenth century, when the properties were often deserted; today, they are generally surrounded by modern neighbourhoods. By virtue of a privilege granted by the Ottoman Empire, and then upheld throughout the British Mandate period, these communities were exempted from taxes. Today, there is disagreement about whether these communities should continue to benefit from this exemption or pay the taxes in the state of Israel.

In 2007, the Papal Nuncio, Archbishop Franco, threatened not to attend the annual Holocaust Memorial Day event at Yad Vashem, Israel's main Holocaust museum, stating that he would not attend unless the museum agreed to remove or re-write a caption about Pope Pius XII that he found offensive. The caption described the wartime pope as someone who refused to stand up to the Nazis, and who did not act to save Jewish lives during the Shoah. Although he changed his mind after the controversy became public, Archbishop Franco's action was a sign of a chill in the dialogue. The 2008 *Motu Proprio* of Pope Benedict XVI on the expanded use of the 1962 Latin Missal also raised concerns in Israel (to be discussed in the next chapter), and the controversy over the proposed re-communication of the Holocaust-denier Bishop Williamson in 2009 resulted in the Israeli Chief Rabbis temporarily breaking off formal ties with the Vatican. However, the Papal visit to Israel in the same year successfully passed without major incident and the Pope was generally well received. He called for reconciliation between Jews, Christians and Muslims and between Israelis and Palestinians.

Perhaps unsurprisingly, Protestantism is deeply divided on Zionism. While at one end there are some who make absolute moral demands on Israel and conclude, like Naim Ateek, that Zionism represents a profane corruption of Judaism's true prophetic mission, at the other, some Evangelicals (often called Christian Zionists) support Israel for a variety of reasons, political and moral as well as religious. Understanding the roots of the Church as the people of Israel, while the branches are a 'faithful remnant' from Israel, they adopt Jewish customs, notably relating to Sukkot, but still maintain a christological stance. Their support of Israel is rooted in Scripture, such as the promises to Abraham in Genesis 12, which describes God's covenant with Abraham and the blessings that will come to those who bless the Jewish people, and the New Testament letters of the Apostle Paul, which describe Judaism as the 'root' of Christianity and define the proper attitude of Gentile toward Jew as one of humility and love.

The origins of Christian Zionists can be traced to the Puritans of the seventeenth century and their desire to study Scriptures in their original texts. Puritan scholars, notably under the guidance of the rabbis of Amsterdam, not only mastered Hebrew but also developed a new understanding of covenant. They moved from a classical replacement theology to a position in which they believed that God's covenant with his people Israel was eternal. As this was a covenant of both land and people, they came to the conclusion that Palestine was the rightful home of the Jewish people and that God would eventually ensure that they returned to their homeland.

Christian Zionists grew in number in the nineteenth century, influenced by a dispensational eschatology, which viewed history as a series of epochs leading to the end-time, when Jesus will return (called the *parousia*). They believed that the rejection of Jesus by the majority of Jews only postponed all God's promises for Israel until his second coming. The *parousia* would bring in the millennial reign of Christ during which time all God's plans for Israel, which were thwarted at Christ's first coming, would come to fruition. The Anglican cleric William Hechler (1845–1931), who held this position, influenced Theodor Herzl and attended the first World Zionist Conference. Hechler encouraged Herzl in his quest to re-establish the homeland of the Jewish people in Palestine because it was part of God's plan, as prophesied in Scripture.

Hechler was also one of a number of influential Christians who influenced Balfour to make his Declaration in 1917 regarding the support of the British government for the establishment of a homeland for the Jewish people in Palestine. The Declaration consisted of a letter from Balfour as Foreign Secretary, which stated:

His Majesty's government view with favour the establishment in Palestine of a national home for the Jewish people and will use their best endeavours to facilitate the achievement of this object, it being clearly understood that nothing shall be done which may prejudice the civil and religious rights of existing non-Jewish communities in Palestine or the rights and political status enjoyed by Jews in any other country.

It would be simplistic to regard the Declaration in terms of religious agendas, but the intersection of religion and politics should not ignore an account of why Britain set aside the interests of the Arab inhabitants of the land, who made up around 90 per cent of the population (and 10 per cent of whom were Arab Christians), and how she sustained her commitment to a national home for the Jewish people throughout the difficult Mandate period.

Today, Christian Zionists such as The International Christian Embassy in Jerusalem and the International Fellowship of Christians and Jews in Chicago are the descendants of the early Christian Zionists. They are generally strong supporters of the state of Israel, basing their political and spiritual support on biblical prophecies such as Zechariah 14:16: 'And it shall come to pass, that every one that is left of all the nations which came against Jerusalem shall even go up from year to year to worship the King, the LORD of hosts, and to keep the feast of Tabernacles.' They argue that the modern state of Israel is intrinsically related to the Israel of biblical prophecy and a direct fulfilment of it.

Since the 1970s, Christian Zionism has been most evident in the American Protestant fundamentalist community, who make up a significant number of the Christian tourists who make a pilgrimage to Israel. In 2008, two and a half million tourists visited Israel, of whom a third came as part of a Christian pilgrimage, visiting major sites of Christian interest. A typical four-day pilgrimage today commonly includes two days in Jerusalem, including a journey into the Judean Desert, visiting Jericho and Masada; a third day includes a visit to Jaffa, the crusader city of Caesarea and a journey to the Galilee; a fourth day is spent visiting the Mount of Beatitudes, Capernaum, Bethsaida and Kibbutz Ginosar, which houses a wooden Galilee boat dating from the time of Jesus, before ending in Nazareth.

Conservative Christian Zionists' literal interpretation of biblical texts also tends to make them supportive of the more conservative elements in Israeli politics, as well as of the concept of a Greater Israel. For example, they refer to Luke 21:24 ff. which describes Jesus' apocalyptic predictions that include a restoration of Israel in the days preceding the end of the world. For these groups, support for the state of Israel is critical to its survival and ultimately, to the second coming of Jesus who will be acknowledged by the whole world. In this way, Jews have become pawns on the chessboard of history, used to fulfil this final predetermined game-plan.

However, significant problems are caused by arguing that what was once an interpretation about the nature of the biblical word and promise is now concretised in a contemporary event in the situation in Israel. The emphasis on the fulfilment of biblical prophecy (among some Christian Zionists and also fundamentalist Jews) brings particular challenges to Israel and to contemporary Jewish–Christian relations.

Here are some of the difficulties: what happened a hundred years ago is considered by some to be historically remote compared to biblical events, which are viewed as almost contemporary. The present becomes transformed into biblical language and geography, which leads to the danger of giving metaphysical meaning to geographical places. For example, ownership of the land is viewed in terms of a divine gift, transforming religious vocation into a dedication to the existence of the cosmic state. The return to the land is viewed as a fulfilment of the divine promise, but the biblical promises do not define the same borders, leading to the temptation of choosing the widest ones.

The more liberal, or 'mainline', Protestant denominations rarely use biblical proof-texts to provide a foundation for theological and political positions. The United Church of Christ's 1990 statement is typical:

We do not see consensus in the United Church of Christ or among our panel on the covenantal significance of the state of Israel. We appreciate the compelling moral argument for the creation of modern Israel as a vehicle for self-determination and as a haven for victimized people; we also recognize that this event has entailed the dispossession of Palestinians from their homes and the denial of human rights (Theological Panel on Jewish–Christian Relations)

Controversies between liberal Protestants and Jews often centre on Israel. For example, in response to Palestinian suffering, the Presbyterian Church (USA) voted in 2004 to initiate a process of phased, selective divestment from multinational companies operating in Israel that do harm to innocent people, whether Palestinian or Israeli. This prompted similar discussions within the Anglican Communion, and in 2005 the World Council of Churches' Central Committee voted to commend the Presbyterian action and to remind churches of the opportunity before them to use investment funds 'responsibly in support of peaceful solutions to conflict'. This remains a cause of consternation for many Jews because it seems that Israel is made solely responsible for a complex conflict.

When churches adopt divestment initiatives directed against Israel, a country whose policies they sometimes liken to the former apartheid regime in South Africa, many see these as attempts to delegitimise Israel's very existence. They recall the long-standing Arab boycott that was designed to undermine Israel's economy and existence, and that still prevails to no small extent. The fact that the churches do not act similarly regarding human rights abuses and state violence in many other places in the world adds to the strain.

Indeed, there are also dangers when Christians, in the name of dialogue and reconciliation, move from a position of commitment to the well-being of Palestinians to one of almost believing Israel can do no right. This is not an honest conversation firmly related to present realities, but is as unhelpful as that in which the Palestinians are the cause of all the ills in the Middle East.

Since the end of the twentieth century, the indigenous Christian population in the Middle East has been declining numerically. To a certain extent, the phenomenon has been provoked by the relative improvement in the situation of Arab Christians, whose education, economic position and international connections have often meant they are able to benefit more effectively from the birth of the global village. In the War of Independence, Arab Christians played a prominent role in Palestinian nationalist movements and were also prominent among those who fled in the 1948 war. Few ended up in refugee camps or fled to Jordan (which would have placed them in a state with even less experience of a Christian minority), so most left for more cosmopolitan destinations. Those that remained, or who returned, occupied an uncomfortable middle ground. A large part of the estimated 200,000 Christian population of Israel lives in the Galilee, which had been marked out to be part of the Arab state that was to have been created by the Partition Plan voted by the UN in November 1947, but not accepted by the surrounding Arab states.

Since 1948, a Palestinian theology of liberation has developed, influenced by traditional replacement theology as well as the everyday experiences of Palestinian Christians living in Israel. It is not too extreme to state that the Palestinian church has faced a major theological crisis since the establishment of Israel, partly due to a view that the Bible has been used as a political Zionist text. Naim Ateek, for example, has argued that, since the creation of the state, some Jewish and Christian interpreters have read the Old Testament largely as a Zionist text to such an extent that it has become almost repugnant to Palestinian Christians. In his view, this has resulted in a narrow concept of a nationalistic God; Zionism represents a retrogression of the Jewish community into the history of its very distant past, with its most elementary and primitive form of the concept of God. 'Zionism has succeeded in reanimating the nationalist tradition within Judaism,' he has argued (*Justice and Only Justice*, p. 101).

In 1964 Pope Paul VI visited Israel, the first pope in 150 years to leave Italy. He spent twelve hours visiting Christian holy sites in Israel but did not use the word 'Israel' during any of his public addresses, did not visit any Israeli monuments, and declined to meet with Israel's Chief Rabbis – largely because of differences over Israel's political statehood and a desire that the visit be seen as a purely religious act, avoiding any kind of political considerations. The visit also took place during Vatican II and before the publication of *Nostra Aetate*, making it a very sensitive topic. In its desire to avoid controversy, it was deliberately brief.

Shortly before the Pope's visit, the Brother Daniel affair took place (1962). Daniel Rufeisen (1922–98) was a Jewish convert to Christianity who immigrated to Israel under the Law of Return. He argued that his nationality was Jewish although his religion was Catholic. Complicating the issue was the fact that, according to *halakhah*, as the child of a Jewish mother Brother Daniel was indeed Jewish. The Chief Rabbinate ruled that he should be given citizenship as a Jew, regardless of his faith decisions. In 1962 the Supreme Court ruled that, despite this and the unusual circumstances (he had saved many Jews during the Holocaust), it was not possible to be both a Catholic priest and a Jew. While the national term 'Jew' did not necessarily imply the practice of religious Judaism, it could not be applied to someone who practised another faith. Although Brother Daniel lost his case, he was later naturalised as an Israeli citizen and lived in a Carmelite monastery in Haifa until his death in 1998.

Signs of a positive shift in Jewish Israeli attitudes to Christianity became noticeable after the Vatican's recognition of Israel in 1994, and especially in the wake of John Paul II's pilgrimage in 2000. To see the Pope at Yad Vashem, demonstrating solidarity, weeping at the suffering of the Jewish people, to learn that he had helped save Jews during the Holocaust and that subsequently, as a priest, he had returned Jewish children adopted by Christians to their Jewish families, to see the head of the Catholic Church placing a prayer of atonement for the sins of Christians against Jews between the stones of the Western Wall – all of these scenes had a profound effect on many Israelis.

This is reinforced by a survey of attitudes to Christianity (carried out by the Jerusalem Institute for Israel Studies and the Jerusalem Center for Jewish–Christian Relations) in 2009, which showed that 75 per cent of Israeli Jews do not see Christians as missionaries, and are not bothered by encountering a Christian wearing a cross. Furthermore, 41 per cent stated that Christianity is the closest religion to Judaism, with Islam coming second at 32 per cent.

In 1999, a Center for the Study of Christianity was founded at the Hebrew University in Jerusalem. This ensured that the pioneering work of Israeli scholars such as David Flusser (1917–2000), who examined the relationship between early Christianity and Rabbinic Judaism, could be secured for the long term, thus influencing future generations of students. The study of Christianity at the Hebrew University is now consciously geared to a scholarly Jewish–Christian dialogue and to the wider inter-religious dialogue. A wind of change has also begun to sweep into the religious-nationalist (Modern Orthodox) Bar Ilan University, where scholars have established a collaborative project with Christian theologians from Leuven (Belgium) focusing on 'Antisemitism in the Gospel of John'.

The opening of interreligious dialogues via bodies such as the Hartman Institute and the Elijah School has also broadened out from a Jewish–Christian basis. Even some in the religious settler movement have been motivated to engage in dialogue with Christians, which occasionally moves towards a dialogue with Muslims, as Christians appear to be potential mediators in the struggle between the spiritual children of Isaac and those of Ishmael; this illustrates the view of Michel Sabbah (b. 1933), Latin Patriach from 2000 to 2008, that Christians in Israel 'are called to be leaven contributing positive resolution of the crises we are passing through' (*Reflections on the Presence of the Church in the Holy Land*, Theological Commission of the Latin Patriarchate, 2003). One example is the initiative of Shlomo Riskin (b. 1940), Chief Rabbi of Efrat, who in 2008 founded the Center for Jewish–Christian Understanding and Cooperation, which is primarily aimed at Evangelical Christians.

Sabbah took part in a Synod that started in 1995 involving the Catholic Churches of the Holy Land, comprising not only the Roman Catholic Church but also the Oriental churches. It lasted five years and reflected on the changes since *Nostra Aetate*. The Synod document was entitled 'Relations with believers of other religions' and contains two sections, the first dedicated to Muslims and the second to Jews. The document makes clear that the local church does not have the same starting point as its European counterparts, for it sees itself as free of antisemitic practice and policy and the responsibility for the fate of European Jewry.

David Neuhaus (b. 1959), a Jesuit living in Jerusalem who is active in Jewish–Christian dialogue in Israel, explains further:

Christians live as a minority face to face with a Jewish majority (those in Israel), under Israeli military occupation (those in the West Bank) or confronting a regional economic and military power (those in Jordan and Gaza). This is an absolutely unique historical situation. Nowhere else in the world do Christians experience directly the sovereignty and power of a Jewish polity and never in history have Christians experienced Jewish sovereignty and power (these only having been reestablished in 1948 with the creation of the State of Israel). This unique situation must inform dialogue that takes place in this land between local Christians and Jews, predominantly in Israel. For many of the Holy Land faithful, unfortunately, the Jew is often first and foremost a policeman, a soldier or a settler. (David Neuhaus and Jamal Khader, 'A Holy Land Context for *Nostra aetate*', *Studies in Christian – Jewish Relations* (e-journal), 2005)

Thus, a key factor to reckon with is Christian status as a minority in the Middle East as a whole. Not only are Christians a minority within the state of Israel – approximately 2 per cent of the Israeli population are Christian – they are also a minority within the Arab minority. Purely on the psychological level, their church representatives feel under pressure. Yet the Christian Arab and the Muslim Arab, whatever their religious differences might be, live in one society, speak one language and share one culture.

Dialogue with Muslims is sometimes a priority for Christians and in some dioceses it is only the dialogue with Muslims that is real, for example in Jordan and Gaza (where there are no Jews).

In addition, there have been occasional violent attacks on Christians and Christian properties by ultra-Orthodox Jews. In the 1970s the attacks were linked to the extremist right-wing party of Meir Kahane (1932–90), 'Kach', which was banned by the government for its overt racism. In 2004, a controversy erupted when some yeshiva students spat at Nourhan Manougian, the Armenian Archbishop of Jerusalem, to protest against 'idol worship', demonstrating the antagonism felt by some Jews towards Christians. Tensions also occasionally rise for what seem to be minor reasons, such as dress. For example, in 2008 leaders of Ireland's main Christian churches were barred from praying at the Western Wall because they refused to remove the large crosses they were wearing. The security guards at the Kotel who prevented the delegation from reaching the area were supported by the Rabbi of the Kotel, Shmuel Rabinovitch, who argued that the display of large crosses was provocative to Jews. While for Christians the cross is a reminder of the triumph of Jesus over death, the love of God as manifested in Jesus and God's presence revealed in suffering, the disagreement showed that for some Jews it still symbolises oppression and domination.

For Christians, however, the relationship with Jews exists within a framework of a larger dialogue that includes Muslims. This may explain why Palestinian liberation theologians are accused of being politically partisan, hostile to Jews and Judaism and naive about the possibilities of dialogue with increasingly militant Arab Islam. At the outset of the First Intifada in 1987, Christian Arab congregations pressed their hierarchies to demonstrate more solidarity with the Palestinian cause, and in addition to begin to advance Palestinian Christians to positions of leadership. Although integrated in Palestine, Christian Palestinians are clearly concerned at the prospect of the gradual Islamisation of the nascent state and of a time when Hamas and other Islamist parties might take over completely.

The significant reduction in the Christian population elsewhere in the Middle East adds to feelings of insecurity. Nablus, a city that once had a sizeable Christian population, now has almost none. In the areas controlled by the Palestinian National Authority, Christians mostly live in the Bethlehem area, and their situation is even more subject to scrutiny. Evangelical Christian Arabs have encountered special problems against which they are to some extent shielded in Israel.

Divisions between Christians sometimes spill over into acts of violence. For example, fights between Catholic and Greek Orthodox priests at Easter 2005 and between Greeks and Armenians at Easter 2008 at the Church of the Holy Sepulchre illustrate an intra-Christian conflict that has marked the history of Christianity in the region since its earliest days. The intervention of the state may formally be decried, but the reluctance of Christian representatives to dialogue amongst themselves on the difficulties means that Israeli intervention is also quietly welcomed.

Finally, some Christians are actively involved in dialogue programmes between Israelis and Palestinians. For example, *Neve Shalom* ('Oasis of Peace') was founded in 1972 by Bruno Hussar (1911–96), a Dominican friar, with the aim of peaceful reconciliation between Jews, Muslims and Christians. Another example is Tantur Ecumenical Institute, located on the border between south Jerusalem and the West Bank. Proposed by the Vatican initially as a centre for Catholic–Orthodox dialogue, the institute, under the guidance of both Protestant and Roman Catholic rectors, now focuses on the relations among the three Abrahamic faiths and the promotion of ecumenical and interfaith dialogue through study and research. The previous Latin Patriarch, Michel Sabbah, hosted a monthly dialogue with local Jews until his retirement in 2008, which may seem an unremarkable event in the West but in the context of Israel is a noteworthy initiative.

JEWISH LITERATURE

The dramatic impact of Zionism on the religious, political and social spheres of Jewish–Christian relations in the nineteenth and twentieth centuries was also mirrored in Jewish literature, notably Hebrew and Yiddish literature. We have already mentioned the writings of authors such as George Eliot, and their influence on Christian views about the Jewish desire to reclaim sovereignty in the Land of Israel; Jewish authors from the same period also wrote influential literary works not only about Zionism but in addition about Christianity.

One of the most well known, Asher Ginsberg (1856–1927), better known by his pen name Ahad Ha'am ('One of the People'), provided a literary counterpoint to Herzl's political Zionism. While Herzl focused on the plight of Jews alone, Ahad Ha'am was also interested in the plight of Judaism, which could no longer be contained within the limits of traditional religion. His solution was cultural Zionism, the revival of Jewish culture based on a metaphysical attachment to the Land and a renewed

Hebrew renaissance. In his writings he suggested that any rapprochement with Christianity implied the abandonment of Jewishness and the denial of the national dimension of Jewish identity. In contrast, Joseph Klausner (1874–1958), who like Ahad Ha'am made Aliyah to Palestine, cherished the ethical teachings of Jesus and viewed both Jesus and Paul as important figures in the history of Palestine. Martin Buber also famously commended Jesus' individual religiosity, calling Jesus his 'elder brother', and by linking his empathy for Christianity to his own Jewish identity he earned the respect of many Christians.

Yiddish literature also provides some positive views of Jesus, such as the expressionist poetry of Uri Zvi Greenberg (1894–1981) in which he compared himself to Jesus and also referred to him as 'my brother'. In this, Jesus symbolised universal human suffering, emptied of his humanity by 2,000 years of distance from his native land, and was still being crucified by the Christians. On the other hand, Scholem Aleichem (1859–1916), in his serial *Tevye the Milkman* (published from 1895 on, later filmed as *Fiddler on the Roof*), was concerned about Jews deserting Judaism (for the sake of love). This was also the focus of Isaac Bashevis-Singer (1904–91), who portrayed sexual relations between Jews and Christians as a tragedy.

Antisemitism, a key factor in the success of political Zionism, was also a common theme in Jewish literature. Following the Kishinev pogrom in 1903, H. N. Bialik (1873–1934), one of the most important modern Hebrew poets, composed a short poem, 'On the Slaughter', and a long poem, 'In the City of Slaughter'. His description of the cowardice of the victims led to the formation of Jewish self-defence units. Some writers, such as Greenberg, were convinced that Europe was a Jewish graveyard created by fanatical Christians, but others wrote wistfully of a bygone Jewish life in Europe, portraying the interactions between Jews and Christians in a softer light.

Jesus remained of interest to Jews, together with modern antisemitism. Y. H. Brenner (1881–1921) wrote: 'We sometimes see in the story of Jesus a world tragedy and our heart goes to him, the tortured prophet [. . .] and sometimes we see in the whole business of prophecy a ridiculous and comic matter, and in his disciples fools who deviated from the way of the world' (H. Bar-Yosef, 'Jewish–Christian Relations in Modern Hebrew and Yiddish Literature: A Preliminary Sketch', in E. Kessler and M. Wright, eds., *Themes in Jewish–Christian Relations*, p. 131).

In 'On Behalf of Jesus the Nazarene: How My Hair Grew White in One Night', Avigdor Ha-Me'iri (1890–1970), who during the First World War was a soldier in the Austro-Hungarian army, describes the fate of his

Jewish comrade, who together with him was taken captive by Russian soldiers. He states that his friend was forced to drink human blood, crucified and buried alive by a Russian commander. Aharon Kabak's (1883–1944) novel *Narrow Path: The Man of Nazareth* (1936, English 1968) portrays Jesus sympathetically, seeing him as the founder of one of the many sects into which Judaism was split at his time. The purity of Jesus is distinguished from the heathen Christianity of his apostles and he speaks in postbiblical Hebrew mixed with Aramaic, making him part of contemporary Judaism.

After the Shoah and the creation of the state of Israel, a new wave of Israeli writing on Jewish–Christian relations appears, such as the work of Aharon Appelfeld (b. 1932), who described love between Jews and Christians and was influenced by the stories of M. Y. Berdychevsky (1865–1921) and the writings of H. N. Bialik. For example, in Bialik's *Behind the Fence* a Romeo and Juliet theme is transposed to a provincial Russian town. In Appelfeld's novels *Katarina* (1989, English 1990) and *Railroad* (1991), the author warns against the sexual attraction of Jews to Christian women and against the seduction of proselytism for the sake of social success. Appelfeld's deterministic world view denies the chances of reconciliation between Jews and non-Jews. Amos Oz's (b. 1939) short historical novel *Unto Death* (1971, English 1992) is a diagnosis of the pathological Christian attitude to Jews, depicted against the historical background of the Crusades. 'My historical account with Christian Europe is bitter and more frightening than the quarrel with the Arabs and Islam, which is just an episode,' said the writer in 1991.

The interest in Christianity in Israeli literature in recent years can be partly explained by a society almost free from the trauma of Christian antisemitism; but still the subject is less commonly discussed than in the literature of Western Europe and North America. In Israel it is Arabs, not Christians, who are conceived of as the dangerous 'Other'.

JERUSALEM

Before David made it his capital, Jerusalem was just one centre of Israelite worship, alongside Shechem, Beth-El and others. In subsequent Jewish literature, however, Jerusalem was portrayed as chosen by God and the shock of its destruction in 587 BCE was a major feature of the lamentations of the Israelite exiles. Its importance continued after the destruction of the Second Temple in 70 CE and the city was central to the religious vision of the rabbis. Indeed, they maintained faith in the imminent prospect of a rebuilt Temple, and the association between Jews around the world and the physical city of Jerusalem has persisted over millennia. After the Muslim conquest of Palestine, Jewish pilgrimages to Jerusalem became a common occurrence. In the gaonic period (sixth–tenth centuries), major festivals, particularly Sukkot, saw Jews from across the region assembling to pray on the Mount of Olives.

Jerusalem appears not to have had central religious significance for the writers of the New Testament texts, though it was the subject of much comment, particularly in Paul and Acts (which wanted to make Rome the central city). New Testament references suggest that the earthly Jerusalem was a reflection of the heavenly Jerusalem, indicating a spiritualisation of the city (reflected in the practice of naming cities after Jerusalem by using names such as 'Zion' and 'Salem'). Interestingly, there are similarities with the rabbinic use of a heavenly Jerusalem paralleling the earthly Jerusalem, but for the rabbis the earthly Jerusalem was the model for the heavenly Jerusalem and not vice versa.

With the development of Christian pilgrimage to the Holy Land in the fourth century, the earthly Jerusalem again took on a central significance for Christians. Helena, mother of Constantine, sought to refound the Church on the earthly Jerusalem, through the building of numerous churches, which contrasted with the ruined Temple. Accounts of the pilgrimages of a fourth-century woman called Egeria and others inspired an influx of pilgrims and a corresponding outflow of relics that linked Christianity with the Holy Land.

For Muslims, Jerusalem (called Al-Quds) is the third most holy site, after Mecca and Medina. According to tradition, Muhammad made the miraculous journey from Mecca to the Western Wall, tethered his horse, al-Buruqa (the name by which the Wall is known in Islam), and ascended from Al-Aqsa to the heavens where he met with Musa (Moses), Isa (Jesus) and with the divine countenance itself.

Caliph 'Umar (r. 634–44) refused to enter the Holy Sepulchre on the grounds that Muslims would one day appropriate the site if he did. To this day, a Palestinian Muslim family is the official doorkeeper and holds the keys to the Holy Sepulchre and the Church of the Ascension on the Mount of Olives. At the present time, Wajeeh Nuseibeh ceremoniously opens the buildings once a year in a demonstration that this tolerance is a gift from the Muslim community. Al-Quds has not been the capital of any Muslim kingdom – but its religious history has made it of great importance, notably to the Sufi orders. This makes even more striking the symbolism of Anwar Sadat (1918–81), President of Egypt, praying in Jerusalem together with the head of the Al Azhar College, the oldest university in the world (founded in 972), on their visit to Israel in 1977.

In 1099, the crusaders stormed Jerusalem. The Dome of the Rock was converted into a church and the Al-Aqsa mosque, renamed the Temple of Solomon, became the residence of the king. Jerusalem became the capital of the Latin Kingdom: the crusaders' building and street planning can be seen in basic form in the Old City of Jerusalem preserved today. Non-Jews were forbidden to live in Jerusalem until Salah al-Din (Saladin) re-took the city in 1187; from then until it fell in 1291, the crusaders ruled their kingdom from Acre. From the time of Salah al-Din, Jews were increasingly encouraged to settle in the new Jewish quarter, though they also remained in property in other parts of the city as well.

The fierce competition over Jerusalem among Christian rulers provided a primary cause for the Crimean War, and was a persistent cause of division from the time of the conquest of Jerusalem in 1917, in spite of Allenby's tactical entry into the city accompanied by a Catholic. With increasing numbers of non-Arab Protestant and Orthodox churches represented in Jerusalem, the pressure for Britain and then their Israeli successors to make changes in recognising the respective rights of the churches under previous agreements has often exacerbated tensions on the ground.

Though it was mentioned, there is no evidence that the Western Wall, an outer wall of the Second Temple, was an important site of prayer for Jews until about 1520 when the Spanish exiles came to the Turkish empire. The Wall became more popular as the Jewish world turned its attention to Palestine in the nineteenth century. During the Mandate period, Zionists imbued the Wall with a national significance that prompted the Jerusalem Mufti, Haj Amin al-Huseini (1897–1974), to believe that Jews were aiming to seize the Wall; his response was to proclaim it a sacred Muslim site. An International Committee of Inquiry conducted the 'trial of the Wall' in 1930, concluding that Muslims had absolute ownership of the Wall and Jews had an uncontested right to worship and to place seats in the street, but that they were not to blow the shofar there. The *waqf* objected, while on the Jewish side the nationalists would blow the shofar every Yom Kippur, leading to the intervention of the British police. From 1947, after bloody clashes, Jews were no longer able to approach the Wall; after the capitulation of the Jewish Quarter in May 1948, Jews were expelled from the Old City.

At the time of the reunification of Jerusalem in 1967, the houses and religious foundations in the area of the Western Wall were quickly cleared, making the Wall one of the main sites of Israeli and Diaspora Jewish religious activity in the world. Up until the 1940s, the Vatican opposed Jewish control of the holy sites and supported the internationalisation of the city as a whole. After 1967, however, it dropped this position in favour of the internationalisation of the Old City alone and, when the peace process began, called for a special regime for the Old City that would guarantee the equality of rights of the three major religions. In 1994 the Vatican promoted international guarantees rather than shared sovereignty.

Since the assassination of Yitzhak Rabin in 1995, the prospects of a negotiated settlement over which part of Jerusalem would become the Palestinian capital have been steadily reduced. The collapse of trust between Israel and the Palestinians and the Israeli building programme designed to ring-fence Jerusalem with suburban developments for Jews have made this possibility even less likely. However, as details of the failed agreement (2000) between Ehud Barak (b. 1942) and Yassir Arafat (1929–2004) emerged, it has become clear that the Old City of Jerusalem was envisaged to be the capital of the future state of Palestine as well as remaining the existing capital of Israel. Jerusalem remains an unresolved issue in the Israeli–Palestinian peace process.

Much of the contemporary dialogue between Israelis and Palestinians since then has bypassed religious issues, consisting of secular and inter-cultural efforts at understanding, designed to underline how much Arabs and Jews have in common. However, the Alexandria Declaration (2002), which consisted of senior Christians, Jews and Muslims pledging them-selves to work together for a just and lasting peace, ensured that religious figures remained involved in the dialogue. There are Palestinian clerics, both Christian and Muslim, who, during the Second Intifada, have been willing to risk their lives to talk with Jews. They have successfully worked with rabbis from groups like Rabbis for Human Rights.

Perhaps it is best to end this chapter with a story from David Flusser, the eminent Israeli scholar of first-century Judaism, who once described an encounter with a group of evangelical Christians visiting Jerusalem:

'Why should we quarrel?' I asked. 'You believe in the coming of the Messiah – so do we. So let us both work for it and pray for it. Only, when he arrives, allow me to ask him one question first, "Excuse me sir, but is this your first visit to Jerusalem?"'

CHAPTER 9

Covenant, mission and dialogue

This chapter deals with three interconnected subjects that have been touched on in previous chapters but need more detailed consideration because they have been and continue to be central to the Jewish–Christian encounter. Covenant, mission and dialogue illustrate both the extent of the common ground between Jews and Christians and also many of the difficulties that still need to be addressed. The challenge they bring is demonstrated by *Nostra Aetate*, perhaps the most influential of the recent church documents on Jewish–Christian relations. On the one hand, the document states that 'the church is the new people of God' and, on the other, that 'the Jews remain most dear to God because of their fathers, for He does not repent of the gifts He makes nor of the calls He issues (cf. Rom. 11:28–29)'. The tension between the two statements is caused by continuing divergence of opinion over the identity of the people of God – both Jews and Christians have claimed to be *Verus Israel*, the True Israel. This claim is regarded by Jews as the very core of their self-understanding, yet for nearly two millennia the Church also saw itself as the True Israel and the heir of all the biblical promises towards Israel.

COVENANT

Covenant (Hebrew *berith*), a central concept in both Judaism and Christianity, is a subject that has been receiving serious attention from theologians in recent years. It refers to God initiating a covenant with a community of people, and that community accepting certain obligations and responsibilities as covenant partners. A covenant is not, as is sometimes mistakenly assumed, a contract or a transaction but is an agreement dependent upon a relationship. Some exegetes hold to the view that *berith* is better translated by 'obligation' because it expresses the sovereign power of God, who imposes his will on his people Israel: God promises in a solemn oath to fulfil his word to his people Israel, who are expected to respond by faithfulness and obedience. Jonathan Sacks explained this in his address to 600 Anglican bishops at the 2008 Lambeth diennial meeting of the Anglican Communion Conference when he said:

[I]n a covenant, two or more individuals, each respecting the dignity and integrity of the other, come together in a bond of love and trust, to share their interests, sometimes even to share their lives, by pledging our faithfulness to one another, to do together what neither of us can do alone . . . a contract is about interests but a covenant is about identity. And that is why contracts benefit, but covenants transform.

In the New Testament, the Old Testament covenant is reinterpreted through the experiences of the early Christian community and after the death and resurrection of Jesus is seen as a new phase in the story of Israel. The change in emphasis marked by the translation of *berith* into the Greek *diathēkē* ('decree') in the Septuagint developed still further in the New Testament, where the concept acquired the meaning of a definitive 'last will and testament' on the part of God. The Vulgate translation used the word *testamentum*, which became the official designation of both parts of the Christian Bible – the Old Testament and the New Testament – with its inescapable implication of supersessionism.

From the rabbinic perspective, no change took place in Israel's covenantal relationship with God, as described in the Hebrew Bible. Jews remained a community of faith, although there was a change in emphasis. The Sinai covenant became seen as the most important of the biblical covenants and there was an increased emphasis on the mutuality of the covenantal relationship between God and His People. This is summarised in a midrash, in which God was depicted as travelling around the world asking various peoples to accept His Torah. None was willing to accept its yoke until God came to Israel and the Israelites answered (Exod. 24:7) in one voice: 'All that the Lord has spoken we will do, and we will be obedient' (*Mechilta BaChodesh* 5.74a).

As far as Christianity was concerned, however, a radical break had occurred. Christianity had introduced a new covenant, or, at the very least, a radical transformation of the old covenant. According to the New Testament, the relationship between God and His people was mediated decisively through His Son, Jesus Christ. The early Church, focusing on the Epistle to the Hebrews, regarded the old covenant of Israel as definitely abrogated. The text on the new covenant in Jeremiah 31:31–34 was explained as pointing not only to fulfilment in Christ but also the replacement of Judaism:

For finding fault with them, he saith, "Behold, the days come, saith the Lord, when I will make a new covenant with the house of Israel and with the house of Judah: Not according to the covenant that I made with their fathers in the day when I took them by the hand to lead them out of the land of Egypt; because they continued not in my covenant, and I regarded them not, saith the Lord. For this is the covenant that I will make with the house of Israel after those days, saith the Lord; I will put my laws into their mind, and write them in their hearts: and I will be to them a God, and they shall be to me a people: And they shall not teach every man his neighbour, and every man his brother, saying, 'Know the Lord': for all shall know me, from the least to the greatest. For I will be merciful to their unrighteousness, and their sins and their iniquities will I remember no more." In that he saith, 'A new covenant', he hath made the first old. Now that which decayeth and waxeth old is ready to vanish away. (Heb. 8:8–13)

The question that has been absorbing the attention of Christian theologians engaged in Jewish–Christian dialogue in recent years concerns the role of the Jewish people after the appearance of Christianity. The traditional Christian teaching is that with the coming of Jesus Christ the Church has taken the place of the Jewish people as God's elect community – this is known as replacement theology (sometimes called supersessionism), which implies the abrogation (or obsolescence) of God's covenant with the Jewish people.

Beginning in the first half of the twentieth century, but especially after the Holocaust, many Christians became aware of the inadequacy of replacement theology, which was perceived to have formed the linchpin of the teaching of contempt. Accordingly, the identification, analysis and repudiation of replacement theology have occupied a prominent place among Christian theologians seeking to put the Church's relationship to the Jewish people on a new theological footing. However, there is less agreement among Christians about what replaces replacement theology.

Clearly, the rejection of replacement theology entails some affirmation of the continuing validity of God's covenant with the Jewish people and the fact that Christians must regard Jews as continuing in a covenantal relationship with God, however the Church might eventually interpret the meaning of the Christ event. But Christian theologians continue to differ about the implications of the rejection of replacement theology for central Christian doctrines, notably Christology and the Church's mission. It is for this reason that, in 2006, Boston College, Catholic University of Leuven, Catholic Theological Union and the Gregorian University in Rome, with the endorsement of the Pontifical Commission for Religious Relations with the Jews, initiated an ecumenical Christian group whose purpose was to explore the relationship between the Church and the Jewish people on the assumption that Christologies that revolve around the notion that through the Christ event Christianity totally fulfilled and replaced Judaism can no longer be sustained. Although the 1947 Seelisberg statement began the modern process of rethinking Christology, constructing a new theology of the Church and the Jewish people in the light of the Christ event remains an unresolved and formidable undertaking, perhaps because, as Johann-Baptist Metz argued, the restatement of the Church's relationship with the Jewish people is a fundamental revision of Christian theology.

The German scholar Friedrich-Wilhelm Marquardt (1928–2002) viewed covenant as the most constructive biblical concept to explain Christian–Jewish relations and help develop a positive Christian identity. The Church can only hope to become partners in a covenantal relationship with the people of Israel if they are willing to accept the burden of Israel in sanctifying the Name of God in the world, if they join in the calling of Israel to restore the world, and if they are ready to embark with the people of Israel on its journey to the 'new covenant' with God, which lies ahead.

There seem to be at least three possible ways in which Christians may understand the relation between the 'old' and 'new' peoples:
- Only one (the newer) is truly the 'people of God'.
- There are two peoples of God, the Jewish and the Christian.
- The two peoples are really one people of God – identical in some respects and different in others.

The first position identifies Christians as the people of God. In this case, Jews need to convert to Christianity and those who remain as Jews are a remnant destined to suffer, whose lowly position gives witness to the truth of Christ. This Augustinian position, called the witness doctrine, dominated Christian thought until it began to be questioned during and after the Enlightenment.

The second position argues that there are two peoples of God, the Jewish and the Christian. This view is espoused by theologians such as the Jewish writer Franz Rosenzweig, who suggests that both Jews and Christians participate in God's revelation and both are (in different ways) intended by God. Only for God is the truth one and earthly truth remains divided. Rosenzweig was influenced by Jacob Emden (1697–1776), who viewed Christianity as a legitimate religion for Gentiles. In *Seder Olam Rabbah Vezuta* (1757) he wrote positively about Jesus and Paul, utilising the New Testament in his argument that they had not sought to denigrate Judaism and that their teachings were primarily concerned to communicate the Noachide laws to Gentiles. 'The Nazarene and his apostles [. . .] observed the Torah fully,' he wrote. Emden's views are remarkably similar to those of the Italian Renaissance figure Abraham Farissol of Ferrara (1451–1528), who in his work *Magen Avraham* (Shield of Abraham) argued that the messiah had come for the Gentiles because Jesus eliminated idol worship and idolatry. Like Emden, he believed that Jesus and his disciples were faithful observers of the Torah.

James Parkes also took the two-covenant position and suggested that the Sinai and Calvary experiences provided humanity with two complementary revelations. In his view the Sinai revelation emphasised the aspect of community while Calvary focused on the individual. Parkes remained convinced that the revelation in Christ did not replace the covenant at Sinai but that Judaism and Christianity were inextricably linked together. Although there are variations in the views of theologians who follow the two peoples of God (or two-covenant) approach, they share the view that the revelation in Christ was a unique event and resulted in a new sense of intimacy between God and humanity. John Pawlikowski has suggested that the two-covenant approach is particularly close to the New Testament teachings because it emphasises that as a result of the Christ event, humanity has achieved a deeper understanding of the God–humankind relationship. The difficulty of this approach from the perspective of Jewish–Christian relations is how – after having proclaimed this uniqueness – a special role can be maintained for Judaism in the salvation process.

As for contemporary Jewish supporters of the two-covenant theory, it is an approach shared by the author of this work as well as the Israeli scholar David Hartman (b. 1931). For Hartman, a covenant between people and God is predicated on a belief in human adequacy and dignity. Other religions, especially Christianity and Islam, have their own covenants with God and are called to celebrate their dignity and particularity.

The third position posits that Jews and Christians represent one people of God who are identical in some respects and different in others. Although they differ substantially they nevertheless share sufficient common ground to make it possible for the same covenant to be applied to both. Christians favouring the one-people (or one-covenant) approach sometimes refer to Ephesians 2:12 which states that to be separate from Christ is to be strangers to the community of Israel. The Roman Catholic Church favours a single covenant model as does the German Rhineland Synod, which in *Towards a Renewal of the Relationship of Christians and Jews* (1980) declared: 'We believe in the permanent election of the Jewish People as the People of God and realize that through Jesus Christ the Church is taken into the covenant of God with His People.'

Similarly, the Catholic scholar Monika Hellwig (1929–2005) argues that Judaism and Christianity both point towards a common goal – the same eschatological event. As a result, Christian claims that Jesus had totally fulfilled Jewish messianic expectations must be set aside. In her view, there still remains an unfulfilled dimension awaiting completion. Her words, published in an article in 1970, foreshadowed the Pontifical Biblical Commission's 2001 declaration *The Jewish People and Their Sacred Scriptures in the Christian Bible*, which stated that the 'Jewish messianic expectation is not in vain'. In a striking passage which deals with eschatological expectations the document also stated that Jews, alongside Christians, keep alive the messianic expectation. The difference is that, for Christians, 'the One who is to come will have the traits of the Jesus who has already come and is already present and active among us'. What Christians believe to have been accomplished in Christ 'has yet to be accomplished in us and in the world'.

The most comprehensive theological study among Protestant theologians is found in the three-volume work by Paul van Buren entitled *A Theology of the Jewish–Christian Reality* (1980–7), which argues that the people 'Israel' should be recognised as two connected but distinct branches. The Christian Church represents the Gentile believers drawn together by the God of the Jewish people in order to make God's love known throughout the world. Through Jesus, Gentiles were summoned by God for the first time as full participants in God's ongoing salvation of humanity. However, the Gentiles went beyond God's eternal covenant with the Jewish people and attempted, unsuccessfully, to annul the original covenant. Van Buren argues that both branches must grow together rather than in isolation and that in time they will draw closer whilst retaining their distinctiveness.

The evangelical scholar David Holwerda (b. 1932), however, argues that Christians are in danger of minimising the differences between Judaism and Christianity and in so doing producing a theology that is not true to the New Testament message. Although he recognises the importance of the Christians' re-acquaintance with the Jewish Jesus, Christianity still has an implicit argument with Judaism on several key issues. However, 'the category of election still applies to the Jewish people, even those who do not now believe in Jesus'. Basing himself on Romans 9–11, he suggests that the Church is the New Israel but the Old Israel remains elect and in God's faithfulness still has a future.

Although there are significant differences between proponents of the single-covenant thesis, they all share a number of key features:

- Gentiles can ultimately be saved only through a linkage with the Jewish covenant, something made possible in and through Christ.
- The uniqueness of Christianity consists far more in modes of expression than in content.
- Jews and Christians share equally and integrally in the ongoing process of humanity's salvation.

It is much debated whether the concept of covenant, in its one- or two-covenant versions, could function as a bridge between Judaism and Christianity. It has certainly become a common subject for discussion in activist and scholarly circles. Numerous official ecclesiastical statements have in the last few decades declared that the covenant of God with His People was never abrogated, illustrated by the 1985 Vatican *Notes* and the 1992 catechism which stated that the biblical covenant had not been revoked and that 'Israel is the priestly people of God [. . .] the older brothers and sisters of all who share the faith of Abraham' (para. 63; note the use of the present tense with reference to the Jewish people).

In recent years a number of scholars have become somewhat dissatisfied with the single and double covenant options. These scholars, both Jewish and Christian, have begun to suggest new images of the relationship such as that of 'siblings' (Hayim Perelmuter (1915–2001)), 'fraternal twins' (Mary Boys) and 'co-emergence' (Daniel Boyarin). These images stress both linkage and distinctiveness between Christianity and Judaism, tending to emphasise the 'parallel' rather than 'linear', correctly indicating that both Christianity and Judaism, as we know them today, emerged out of a religious revolution in Second Temple Judaism.

Discussion of covenantal models has also influenced contemporary Jewish thinkers. Irving Greenberg, for example, proposes that Jews have to be open to the idea that God speaks in different ways to different people. Because Christianity grew out of Judaism, it could be viewed as God's way of speaking to Gentiles and entering into a covenant with them, without replacing Judaism. Indeed, for Greenberg the logic behind Christian doctrines such as incarnation and resurrection are part of a shared value system.

Jonathan Sacks regularly discusses ways for Judaism and Christianity (and other faiths and cultures) to live together. In the past, the principles of religious tolerance or separation of church and state worked well inside the boundaries of a nation state, but today everything affects everything else and in response difference should not be viewed as a difficulty to be overcome, but as the very essence of life. Sacks applies the biblical story of the Tower of Babel, when God splits up humanity into a multiplicity of cultures and a diversity of languages, to suggest that God commands humanity to be different and to teach the dignity of difference. Instead of the familiar notion of one God, one truth, one way, Sacks is claiming divine approval for human variety.

Although both Greenberg and Sacks have been criticised by ultra-Orthodox Jews for blurring distinctions between Judaism and other religions, and in particular for expressing the sense that God has spoken to people of all religions, they represent contemporary Jewish covenantal thinking that, in an interconnected world, it is essential to learn to feel enlarged, not threatened, by difference.

Re-reading Paul

It is clear from the above that Paul's writings, notably Romans 9–11, are central to Christian reconsideration about the role of covenant in the Christian encounter with Jews and Judaism. Paul's comments on the identity of the people of Israel and their relationship with God are complex and sometimes hard to follow and it is unfortunate that they are commonly and misleadingly simplified. He is generally viewed as arguing that membership of the True Israel is not determined simply on physical descent from Abraham, but rather on the spiritual affinity to Abraham's trusting relationship with God. In other words, Israel is composed of a combination of Jews and Gentiles. The former, due to their spiritual past, include those who have extended their trust in God to a dependence upon Jesus as Lord; the latter includes those Gentiles who have entered into the covenantal relationship with God by their acceptance of Jesus. This, however, is a facile interpretation of Paul's assessment for it simply imputes to him the view that the old becomes new. As we saw in the opening chapter, Paul is the New Testament writer *par excellence* who struggles deeply with the meaning of the covenant of Israel and the election of the Church.

A significant re-reading of Paul's writings in modern times began in 1977 when the Lutheran scholar Krister Stendahl published *Paul among Jews and Gentiles*. Stendahl showed that Paul could not accept the idea that Jews as a people and religion are totally and for ever outside the people of God. According to Stendahl, Paul suggests that both Israel and the Church are elect and both participate in the covenant of God. Paul affirmed that the Jewish people, despite their disobedience toward Christ, are still the elect people of God and that Christian Gentiles are honorary citizens grafted on to the rich tree of Jewish heritage. While Paul argued that unbelieving Jews are in a state of disobedience regarding Christ, nevertheless, he unreservedly affirmed their continued election.

In his letter to the Romans, Paul asked a controversial question: what of the ongoing validity of God's covenant with his Jewish people? Did the Church, as the New Israel, simply replace the Old as inheritors of God's promises? If so, does this mean that God reneges on his word? If God has done so with regard to Jews, what guarantee is there for the churches that he won't do so again, to Christians this time?

One might argue against Paul by saying that, if Jews have not kept faith with God, then God has a perfect right to cast them off. It is interesting that Christians who argue this way have not often drawn the same deduction about Christian faithfulness, which has not been a notable and consistent characteristic of the last two millennia. Actually, God seems to have had a remarkable ability to keep faith with both Christians and Jews when they have not kept faith with God, a point of which Paul is profoundly aware in Romans 9–11. He goes out of his way to deny claims that God has rejected the chosen people, and asserts that their stumbling does not lead to their fall. He also offers a severe warning that Gentile Christians should not be haughty or boastful toward unbelieving Jews – much less cultivate evil intent and engage in persecution against them. This critical warning remained almost totally forgotten by Christians, who tended to remember Jews as 'enemies' but not as 'beloved' of God and have taken to heart Paul's criticisms and used them against Jews while forgetting Paul's love for Jews and Judaism.

In Paul's view it was impossible for God to elect the Jewish people as a whole and then later displace them. If that were the case, God could easily do the same with Christians. In his view, the hardening took place so that the Gentiles would receive the opportunity to join the people of God. The Church's election, therefore, derives from that of Israel but this does not imply that God's covenant with Israel is broken. Rather, it remains unbroken – irrevocably (Rom. 11:29).

The American Greek Orthodox writer Theodore Stylianopolous (b. 1937) explained this as follows: regardless of whether Israel is disobedient (as Christians have been disobedient over the centuries) the faithfulness of God remains. 'As a father to His children, who has deep and unbreakable faithfulness to His children, the election does continue for Jews in the present day as well.' (*Immanuel* 26/27 (1994), p. 156).

Similarly, the 1980 Rhineland Synod referred to the continuing existence of the Jewish people, its return to the Land of promise and the creation of the state of Israel as 'signs of the faithfulness of God towards His people'. In the same year, John Paul II's Easter Letter referred to 'the people of God of the Old Covenant, which has never been revoked'. As the 1985 *Notes* stated:

The permanence of Israel (while so many ancient peoples have disappeared without trace) is a historic fact and a sign to be interpreted within God's design. We must in any case rid ourselves of the traditional idea of a people *punished*, preserved as a *living argument* for Christian apologetic. It remains a chosen people, 'the pure olive on which were grafted the branches of the wild olive which are the gentiles. (John Paul II, 6 March 1982, alluding to Rom. 11:17–24)

MISSION

It is of course a mistake to equate mission to proselytism; mission is a complicated concept and refers to the sending out of someone to fulfil a particular task, and both Judaism and Christianity have a missionary vocation in the sense that their adherents carry out a specific witness in the world. Christian missionary activity has traditionally been understood as converting non-Christians to belief in Christ, and that has included Jews.

Generally, Jews have not understood their mission as converting others to Judaism but as faithfulness to Torah and the covenantal obligations, sometimes described in terms of 'being a light to the nations' (Isa. 42:6) or attempting to perfect the world. Non-Jews are not targets for conversion, partly because of the rabbinic teaching (developed in more detail in the later medieval period) that the righteous of all nations will have a share in the world to come if they keep the Noachide laws. It is also disputed whether Judaism was ever proselytising, and in 438 the Theodosian Code officially made conversion to Judaism illegal.

Of course, there has always been ambiguity in the Church's understanding of mission and Jews: on the one hand it sought to bring as many Jews as possible into the fold, at times by force; on the other, it had respect for the tradition that was at the root of the Christian faith. The Church sought to preserve the identity of the Jewish people because Jews were the recipients of God's providential care as the chosen people and eschatologically they had a role in the final act of redemption. This raised a tension between belief that the conversion of Jews was an essential part of Christian mission and not wanting to thwart God's final salvific plan.

This tension remains, as demonstrated by those who seek the conversion of all Jews because there is no exemption from the need for salvation in Christ; others who witness to faith in Christ, without targeting Jews specifically, becauses they believe in sharing the Christian faith with all people (including Jews); and, finally, those who have no conversionary outlook towards Jews, where mission is understood as mutual influence and a joint ethical witness in an unredeemed world (sometimes called 'critical solidarity' or 'mutual witness').

The issue of mission is in many ways more difficult for the Church to resolve in its relationship with Judaism than, for example, Christian antisemitism. This is because it is relatively easy to condemn antisemitism as a misunderstanding of Christian teaching, whereas mission (in the sense of making converts) has been and still is central to the Christian faith – the legacy of the command found in Matthew 28:19. Initially, the Christian message was preached by Jews to Jews (cf. Acts 2:14 ff.) until Paul raised the issue of preaching to the Gentiles. The Gospels themselves reflect early controversies over the inclusion of Gentiles in Christianity's missionary activity. Mark 7:27 says in this context, 'let the children first be fed, for it is not right to take the children's bread and throw it to the dogs'; and similarly in Matthew 10:6 the instruction to 'go nowhere among the Gentiles, and enter no town of the Samaritans, but go rather to the lost sheep of the house of Israel' is ascribed to Jesus. Both verses express the view that the proclamation of Jesus as the Messiah should be expressed primarily to Jews. The conclusion of the New Testament authors, however, contradicts this, shown not only by Matthew 28:19 ('Go ye therefore, and teach all nations, baptizing them in the name of the Father, and of the Son, and of the Holy Ghost') but also by Acts 28:28, which argues that the 'good news' should also be transmitted to Gentiles: 'let it be known to you then that this salvation of God has been sent to the Gentiles'. Indeed, the author argues the Gentiles, unlike Jews, 'will listen'.

For Jews, Christian mission is contentious because it conjures up images of centuries of persecution by the Church in response to the Jewish 'no' to Jesus. Some Jews view Christian missionary activity as no different from Hitler's policies because for centuries the Church had tried to do spiritually what Hitler had sought to do physically: to wipe out Jews and Judaism. Indeed, the 1948 meeting of the World Council of Churches (WCC) in Amsterdam called for a redoubling of efforts to convert Jews. Whilst acknowledging the 6 million Jews who perished under the Nazis, the WCC report nevertheless recommended that the churches should 'seek to recover the universality of our Lord's commission by including the Jewish people in their evangelistic work'. The conclusion of the WCC was that, in the light of the Holocaust, an even greater effort should be made to convert Jews.

Much missionary theology rests on Christian claims that salvation is only possible through Christ. The exclusive understanding of salvation, demonstrated by the traditional teaching, *extra ecclesiam nulla salus* (outside the Church there is no salvation), is being challenged by many Christian theologians today. John Pawlikowski strongly argues that *Nostra Aetate* necessitates a rethinking of Christology, Christian identity, covenant and mission.

The 2002 document *A Sacred Obligation*, a statement from an ecumenical American Christian Scholars Group on Christian–Jewish Relations, argues that with the recent recognition within the Church of the permanency of God's covenant with the Jewish people there automatically comes the realisation that the redemptive power of God is at work within Judaism. So, if Jews who do not share the Christian faith are indeed in such a saving relationship with God, then Christians require new ways of understanding the universal significance of Christ. This has been the subject of fierce debate among Christians, particularly in the United States, and remains highly contested.

Despite (or perhaps because of) the recognition of Christian theologians that the repudiation of the *Adversus Iudaeos* tradition has profound implications for Christology, major problems remain. The Vatican document *Dominus Iesus* (2000) reiterated that all salvation ultimately comes through Christ and that those that do not acknowledge him stand in considerable peril in terms of their redemption. Cardinal Walter Kasper (b. 1933), head of the Holy See's Commission for Religious Relations with the Jews (2002–10), has advanced the notion that Jews are an exception to the rule in terms of the universality of salvation in Christ because they are the only non-Christian religious community to have authentic revelation from the Christian perspective. Hence Torah is sufficient for Jewish salvation. This thesis remains in its infancy but seems marginal under the papacy of Benedict XVI, as the 2008 controversy over the revised Tridentine Rite Good Friday Prayer demonstrates. The reason the Tridentine Rite touched a raw nerve in Jewish–Christian relations is that the prayer deals with mission to Jews and expressly looks towards their conversion.

Since 1965 and until 2008, official Catholic teaching was clear for, according to the *Catechism of the Catholic Church, no. 839*, 'the Jewish faith, unlike other non-Christian religions, is already a response to God's revelation'. The one prayer for Jews in Catholic liturgy was called the Good Friday Prayer for the Perfidious Jews, which in the 1962 Latin missal (from which the phrase 'perfidious Jews' had already been deleted in 1961), read:

Let us pray also for the Jews:
that almighty God may remove the veil from their hearts;
so that they too may acknowledge Jesus Christ our Lord.
[. . .]
Almighty and eternal God, who dost not exclude from thy mercy the Jews:
hear our prayers, which we offer for the blindness of that people;
that acknowledging the light of thy Truth, which is Christ,
they may be delivered from their darkness.

In the 1970 English missal, it was transformed into a prayer that Jews will be deepened in the faith given to them by God. The 1970 version reads:

Let us pray for the Jewish people, the first to hear the word of God,
that they may continue to grow in the love of his name
and in faithfulness to his covenant.
Almighty and eternal God,
long ago you gave your promise to Abraham and his posterity.
Listen to your church as we pray that the people you first made your own
may arrive at the fullness of redemption.

The 2008 Tridentine Rite prayer, which retains the pre-Vatican II heading 'Prayer for the Conversion of the Jews', has been reformulated as follows:

We pray for the Jews.
That our God and Lord enlighten their hearts
so that they recognize Jesus Christ, the Saviour of all mankind.
[. . .]
Eternal God Almighty, you want all people to be saved
and to arrive at the knowledge of the Truth,
graciously grant that by the entry
of the abundance of all people into your Church,
Israel will be saved. Through Christ our Lord.

With the publication of the prayer, the Roman Catholic Church now holds two contradictory positions because the new prayer challenges the teaching that accepts the irrevocable nature of the covenantal relationship between the Jewish people and God. Indeed, since its promulgation in 2007 a small number of conservative Catholic groups have begun to voice more loudly their desire to seek Jewish converts, raising a fundamental question: if the Church accepts that the covenant in some way still belongs to the Jewish people, surely there is a less pressing need to convert Jews to Christianity? The revised rite indicates a growing tension within the Church, which no longer has a clear consensus in this area. For their part, many Jews expect that if they dialogue with Christians there should be no hidden missionary agenda or secret desire for their conversion.

At the Second Vatican Council, Cardinal Patrick O'Boyle (1896–1987) expressed concern if conversion came on to the agenda of Catholic–Jewish relations. 'The word "conversion" awakens in the hearts of Jews memories of persecutions, sufferings [. . .] If we express our hope for the eschatological union in words that give the impression we are guided by the definite and conscious intention of working for their conversion, we set up a new and high wall of division, which makes any fruitful dialogue impossible.' His words still echo today.

Since 1945, the place of mission has been a significant item on the agenda of the Protestant churches, particularly in terms of interfaith issues, but a rather lower priority for the Roman Catholic Church and the Orthodox Church. On the one hand, it has been argued that the Church alone is the theological continuation of Israel as the people of God and mission to the Jewish people is necessary, as illustrated by missionary organisations such as the Christian Mission to the Jewish People; on the other, Jews were still the elect of God, demonstrated by the Leuenberg document (2001) which rejected the need to actively seek the conversion of Jews.

Put slightly differently, if the main emphasis is put on the concept of the Church as the Body of Christ, the Jewish people are seen as being outside. The Christian attitude to them would be in principle the same as to adherents of other faiths, and the mission of the Church is to bring them either individually or corporately to the acceptance of Christ so that they become members of this body. However, if the Church is primarily seen as the people of God, it is possible to regard the Church and the Jewish people together as forming the one people of God, separated from one another for the time being, yet with the promise that they will ultimately become one. Consequently, the Church's attitude towards Jews is different from the attitude she has to all others who do not believe in Christ. Mission is therefore understood more in terms of ecumenical engagement, in order to heal the breach, than of seeking conversion.

Thomas Stransky, rector of the Tantur Institute near Jerusalem between 1987 and 1999, explained the problem of mission slightly differently, and his words raise new questions. He argues that Christians should always avoid proselytism (in the pejorative sense). They should shun all conversionary attitudes and practices, which do *not* conform to the ways a free God draws free people to Himself in response to His calls to serve Him in spirit and in truth: 'In the case of the Jewish people, what is Christian proselytism in practice? And what is "evangelization" – the Church's everlasting proclamation of Jesus Christ, "the Way, the Truth and the Life"? Is open dialogue a betrayal of Christian mission? Or is mission a betrayal of dialogue?' ('The History of *Nostra Aetate*', in Roger Brooks (ed.), *Unanswered Questions: Theological Views of Jewish–Catholic Relations*, Notre Dame: University of Notre Dame Press, 1988, p. 68). His description of the tension between mission and dialogue will be discussed in more detail shortly.

The 1988 Anglican Communion at Lambeth was the first Anglican conference to reflect on the issue of Christian mission and Judaism. It explained mission, not in terms of the conversion of Jews, but rather of a *common mission*. In the light of Christian–Jewish and Christian–Muslim relations, proselytism was to be rejected and the Conference called for 'mutual witness to God between equal partners'. It stated that, although there are a variety of attitudes towards Judaism within Christianity,

All these approaches, however, share a common concern to be sensitive to Judaism, to reject all proselytizing, that is, aggressive and manipulative attempts to convert, and of course, any hint of antisemitism. Further, Jews, Muslims and Christians have a common mission. They share a mission to the world that God's name may be honoured. (*Jews, Christians and Muslims: The way of dialogue*)

In contrast, some, evangelical Christian leaders firmly believe that it is the divinely mandated mission of the Church to preach the gospel to Jews, as well as to everyone else. Alongside the missionary activity, it is also suggested that Christians should re-examine their relationship with Judaism by increasing their understanding of the Jewish roots of Christianity. This has led to some intriguing social and political alliances between evangelical organisations and Orthodox Jewish groups, particularly in the USA, such as a joint opposition to abortion.

According to this view, embraced by many Southern Baptist churches in the United States, Christians would be false to their faith if they failed to try to bring Jews into Christian fellowship. The 1996 Southern Baptist Convention reaffirmed the need to direct 'energies and resources towards the proclamation of the gospel to the Jewish people', and the Jews for Jesus movement also exemplifies active mission towards Jews. Its charter states that 'we believe in the lost condition of every human being, whether Jew or Gentile, who does not accept salvation by faith in Jesus Christ, and therefore in the necessity of presenting the gospel to the Jews'. As part of its evangelical activity Jews for Jesus seeks to generate publicity by, among other things, controversial advertising such as the full-page advert that appeared in the UK press on Holocaust Memorial Day in 2004 featuring a Holocaust survivor who came to Jesus.

Such groups also organise Jewish Bible studies and use Jewish prayers in worship in order to rediscover Jewish roots of their faith. For evangelicals in particular, the question of Christian mission to Jews is not a practical problem as to whether Christians should witness their faith to Jews; rather, it is how Christians should witness their faith to Jews. At the heart of the tension between evangelism and dialogue lies conversion and conversation. An evangelical Anglican, Roger Hooker (1934–99), argued that evangelism – in other words, conversion – and dialogue – in other words, conversation – 'have to walk together but always as uneasy partners'.

If they are not walking together, there can be no tension between them. If there is no tension, then the proponents of each caricature the other in order to enjoy the phony security of always being right. When that happens we stop asking questions and so no longer grow. ('Christian Faith and Other Faiths: The Tension Between Dialogue and Evangelism', *Common Ground* 3, 1997)

DIALOGUE

The word 'dialogue' (and the nature of dialogue activity) is often both misconstrued and ill defined. A casual conversation between Jews and Christians that may add up to no more than a loose restatement of entrenched theological positions is sometimes claimed to be dialogue. Equally, any communication between persons of two differing religious points of view (e.g., by phone or email) may be on occasion described loosely as dialogue. However, dialogue is not simply synonymous with 'communication'. For dialogue to take place, there must be a genuine hearing of 'the Other'.

In addition to distinguishing dialogue from communication it is also important not to confuse dialogue with the host of related activities that provide an essential framework for, but are not the same as, dialogue. For example, some adopt the term 'Jewish–Christian relations' as synonymous with 'Jewish–Christian dialogue'. You can after all have good or bad relations (as is often the case with relatives!), but relations in themselves are not the equivalent of dialogue. Nor is the comparative study of religions, which is also taken by some as a synonym for dialogue. Of course, dialogue does involve the pursuit of knowledge, the serious study of the religion of others and minimum levels of faith literacy before dialogue can take place. However, dialogue is not equivalent to knowledge and consists of more, for example, than an ability to identify the major festivals and rites of passage in Judaism and Christianity.

In reality, dialogue consists of a direct meeting of two people and involves a reciprocal exposing of the full religious consciousness of the one to the 'Other'. Dialogue speaks to the Other with a full respect of what the Other is and has to say. This is never less than personal but can develop in such a way as to be extended to a group and even to communities. However, it begins with the individual and not with the community.

Such a quest is never easy because it is not merely about the Other, nor where the Other differs from us. The thoughts and experience of dialogue are perhaps best expressed in the letters of Franz Rosenzweig and Eugen Rosenstock-Huessy (1888–1973), which passed between the trenches of the First World War. Rosenstock-Huessy, a friend of Rosenzweig, was born to Jewish parents and baptised at the age of sixteen. A strong advocate of revelation, he urged Rosenzweig as a representative of philosophy to abandon his faith in reason and be baptised; Rosenzweig, accepting his Jewishness as a cultural reality, found his way to the Judaism of faith instead. This exchange became the topic of an uncompromising correspondence in which Rosenzweig emphasised not the subject matter that connects the speaker with the listener but the 'I' confronting the 'Thou'. The word is not only an expression of reality but also a means by which to express it.

Speech for Rosenzweig consisted of articulating an awareness and comprehension in living contact with another person, which he called *Sprach-denken*. Thus the use of words in a live encounter was for him more than just talking – something is not only said but something happens. This means that dialogue is dependent upon the presence of another person. It is not difficult to see how Rosenzweig became one of the main sources out of which Martin Buber developed his 'I and Thou' formula.

Buber in his exposition of the I–Thou relationship maintained that a personal relationship with God is only truly personal when not only is there awe and respect on the human side but we are not overcome and overwhelmed in our relationship with God. This has implications for Jewish–Christian dialogue – it means that Christians and Jews must meet as two valid centres of interest. Thus one should approach the Other with respect and restraint so that the validity of the Other is in no sense belittled. Further, not only is the essential being of the Other respected but the world of 'faith' is also treated as valid and genuine; not an 'it' to be carelessly set aside but a distinctive value of belief. An I–Thou relationship is a meeting not of religions but of religious people.

Emmanuel Levinas (1906–95) was greatly influenced by Buber and argued that the relationship with the Other is not an idyllic relationship of communion, or a sympathy through which we put ourselves in the Other's place; the Other resembles us, but is exterior to us. For Levinas, the face of the Other necessitates an ethical commitment. According to Levinas, when people look at each other, they see not only another face but also the faces of other people, the face of humanity. The relationship becomes less 'I–thou' and more 'we–thou' entailing an ethical commitment to and responsibility for the other person of faith. The responsibility for the other is linked to the human approach to the Divine, for

there can be no 'knowledge' of God separated from the relationship with human beings. The Other is the very focus of metaphysical truth and is indispensable for my relation with God. He does not play the role of a mediator. The Other is not the incarnation of God, but precisely by His face, in which he is disincarnated, is the manifestation of the height in which God is revealed. (*Totality and Infinity*, Pittsburgh: Duquesne University Press, 1979, p. 78)

Dialogue therefore involves a respect that takes the Other as seriously as one demands to be taken oneself. This is an immensely difficult and costly exercise. We find it all too easy to relate to others in a casual way with a lack of concentration on the reality and good of the Other. It is far easier to compare the facts and features of each other's religion than to engage with our dialogue partner on a quest, for example, to seek the nature and meaning of God's purpose for humanity.

In a letter to Rudolph Ehrenberg in 1913 Rosenzweig writes about the saying of Jesus in the Gospel of John (14:6) that 'no man cometh unto the Father, but by me'. Rosenzweig does not condemn this saying but asserts that it is true, particularly when one remembers the millions who have been led to God through Jesus Christ. However, he continues, 'The situation is quite different for one who does not have to reach the Father because he is already with him. Shall I, he asks, become converted, I who have been chosen? Does the alternative of conversion even exist for me?' (Franz Rosenzweig, *Der Mensch und sein Werk: Gesammelte Schriften I–IV*, The Hague and Dordrecht: Martinus Nijhoff, 1976–84, vol. I, pp. 132ff.).

In these few sentences Rosenzweig introduces us to the crucial question of Jewish–Christian dialogue – can Christians view Judaism as a valid religion in its own terms (and vice versa)? Directly related to this is the need, from a Christian perspective, for reflection on the survival of the Jewish people, the vitality of Judaism over 2000 years and the significance of what Paul called 'the mystery of Israel'. Questions also need to be considered from the Jewish perspective. What was the purpose behind the creation of

Christianity? Does the fact that Jesus was a Jew have any implications for Jews?

Before dialogue could begin with Judaism, Christianity shifted from what was, for the most part, an inherent need to condemn Judaism to one of a condemnation of Christian anti-Judaism. This process has not led to a separation from all things Jewish but, in fact, to a closer relationship with the 'elder brother'.

It is possible to trace the emergence of this insight in the primary church documents. So, for instance, the 1975 Roman Catholic *Guidelines* states: 'Christians must therefore strive to acquire a better knowledge of the basic components of the religious tradition of Judaism: They must strive to learn by what essential traits the Jews define themselves in the light of their own religious experience.' Similar statements can be seen in WCC documents such as the 1967 Bristol Document, *The Church and the Jewish People*, one of the most important early Protestant statements on this topic:

For a real encounter with the Jews we consider it imperative to have knowledge and genuine understanding of their thinking and their problems both in the secular and in the religious realm. We should always remain aware that we are dealing with actual, living people in all their variety, and not with an abstract concept of our own.

All we have said above can be summarily stated as a demonstrable shift from a Christian monologue about Jews to an instructive (and sometimes difficult) dialogue with Jews. A monologue, which generally fails to exhibit an understanding of the reality of the Other, is therefore replaced by a dialogue. This begins with respect for the Other as it understands itself.

Changing attitudes and a more accurate understanding of the other faith are also required among Jews. The need for an understanding and respect for the self-definition of the other must also apply to Jews involved in dialogue with Christians, for Jews may also be criticised for triumphalist attitudes. For example, whilst Judaism does not desire the conversion of all, it does teach that eventually all nations will acknowledge the sovereignty of the God of Israel. *Dabru Emet* remains the first tentative step towards the reassessment of Christianity but only a small minority of Jews are aware of the document; a new understanding of Christianity has yet to filter into the pews of the synagogues.

In 1979 the WCC issued the *Guidelines on Dialogue with People of Living Faiths and Ideologies*. This major statement, translated into scores of languages, sets out four principles of dialogue:

(1) 'dialogue should proceed in terms of people of other faith, rather than of theoretical impersonal systems';
(2) 'dialogue can be welcomed as a way of obedience to the commandment of the Decalogue: "You shall not bear false witness against your neighbour"';
(3) 'dialogue [. . .] is a fundamental part of Christian service within community';
(4) 'the relationship of dialogue gives opportunity for authentic witness [. . .] [W]e feel able with integrity to commend the way of dialogue as one in which Jesus Christ can be confessed in our world today' and 'to assure our partners in dialogue that we come not as manipulators but as genuine fellow-pilgrims'.

This set of principles has formed the basis for commitment by member churches of the WCC to interfaith activity since 1979. The thinking behind these four principles of dialogue owes much to the Canadian scholar of religion Wilfred Cantwell Smith (1916–2000). Smith insisted that 'religions' were not to be reified as 'impersonal theoretical systems' that could be juxtaposed and compared. 'Ask not what religion a person belongs to but ask rather what religion belongs to that person' lies behind the first principle. Accordingly, authentic Jewish–Christian conversation must include the Christians' commitment to Jesus Christ, but equally Jews must testify to the truths of their own tradition.

This might be described as holding on to 'particularities of faith', whilst engaging in dialogue. This term can be defined as referring to those points which Christians and Jews regard as being of fundamental significance and, in a sense, non-negotiable elements of their relation to the Divine. From a Jewish perspective they include, for example, an emphasis on Torah, the conviction that Israel's covenant with God remains and that the Jewish attachment to the Land of Israel has divine sanction. From the Christian perspective, they include the Christian conviction that in the life, death and resurrection of Jesus God acted decisively for all humanity. Christianity combines a claim to be universal in scope with the demand of exclusiveness in belief: Christ is Lord of all and the Saviour of all.

Although these will always provide a bridge, ensuring that dialogue is not simply limited to areas of common ground, the 'particularities of faith' are central to their understanding of God's purpose and all such convictions are strictly irreducible. Both Judaism and Christianity contain features which, although shared in principle, can divide in practice, as, for example, the issue of the identity of the people of Israel.

Although from the outside the particularities of faith might seem narrowly possessive, from within they reflect an experience and a tradition that cannot be denied or ignored, otherwise it would be seen as a denial of faith. Dialogue is not prevented by the acknowledgement of these 'particularities of faith' and the assumption of each partner in dialogue that the ultimate and deepest insight into God's purpose lies on its side. It takes a high degree of maturity to let opposites coexist without pretending that they can be made compatible. At the same time, it takes the same degree of maturity to respect an opinion that conflicts with one's own without attempting to achieve a naive accommodation.

CHAPTER 10

Jewish–Christian relations and the wider interfaith encounter

THE ENCOUNTER WITH ISLAM

In one sense, Islam's influence upon Jewish–Christian relations can be dealt with under the familiar theme of supersessionism, since Muslims believe that Islam was the final religion revealed by God through the Prophet Muhammad (*c.* 570–632). Islam sees itself as perfecting the two monotheistic religions and the Qur'an calls both Jews and Christians *Ahl al-Kitab* (People of the Book). One consequence of Islamic supersessionism on Jewish–Christian relations is that it provides Christians with an insight into the difficulties raised by traditional Christian supersessionism of Judaism and what is sometimes called replacement theology.

Muhammad's religious practice at first owed much to Arabian Christians and especially Jews: Muslims faced Jerusalem in prayer and fasted during the Day of Atonement.

Surely those who believe, and those who are Jews, and the Christians, and the Sabians, whoever believes in God and the Last day and does good, they shall have their reward from their Lord, and there is no fear for them, nor shall they grieve. (Q2:62)

But after Muhammad failed to gain the support of both other groups, his became a separate religion, claiming to be the fulfilment and reformer of all previous revelations, not just Judaism and Christianity. He expelled two Jewish groups from Medina; finally, a third group was severely treated, the men being killed and the women and children sold into slavery. Muhammad showed a similar though less violent ambivalence towards Christians: the Qur'an describes them as 'nearest in love' to the believers (5:82), yet condemns their christological and Trinitarian beliefs.

Muhammad's ambivalent attitude towards Judaism and Christianity continued into later history. On the one hand, as we saw in medieval times, Jews and Christians were often (though not always) well treated under Muslim rule: they were regarded (unlike polytheists and atheists) as *dhimmis*, 'protected people', who were, on payment of a tax, allowed to practise their faith and participate in political and social life, but not seek converts. The concept of *dhimmitude* was created by Caliph 'Umar, as Islam grew rapidly and came to rule over numerous peoples who were not Muslims. For Jews, life under Islamic rule was far easier than for those living in Christendom. Even so, this attitude was one that regarded Jews and Christians as believers who had not understood the logic of their faith as pointing to the finality of Islam; it treated them as second-class citizens, rather than as equals.

In their contemporary encounter with Muslims, Jews and Christians have much to discuss. Theologically, it is commonly argued that Islam is more similar to Judaism than Christianity since both have problems with Christian Trinitarian theology, stress religious law and the centrality of monotheism, and have no priesthood. The 2008 Muslim Letter to the Jewish Community (*Call to Dialogue*), initiated by Muslim scholars at the Centre for the Study of Muslim–Jewish Relations in Cambridge, is an example of a contemporary attempt to demonstrate the commonality between these two faiths. However, the rise of modern political Zionism, the creation of the state of Israel and the Israeli–Palestinian conflict have become major sources of tension between Jews and Muslims, not just in the Middle East but throughout the world.

There are also important similarities between Islam and Christianity since both have a strong sense of mission to people of other religions. Also, Jesus is revered by Muslims as a prophet. The 2007 letter from Muslim scholars to the Christian world (*A Common Word*) outlines the similarities between the two faiths. Tensions also exist, demonstrated by outbursts of violence between Muslims and Christians in Africa (for example, Nigeria's *sharia* riots in 2006 and 2008 in which hundreds of Muslims and Christians died) and the fall-out from Pope Benedict XVI's controversial Regensburg address (2006), in which he was accused of fermenting anti-Muslim feeling. Anti-Christian violence followed in parts of the Muslim world.

Similarities and dissimilarities could provide the substance for fruitful and respectful debates. There are problems with this scenario, however, partly because the three faiths, particularly Islam, have difficulty with their fundamentalists. For example, Islam's Wahabi sect, which has a following among many Muslims, including among Diaspora communities in the West, seeks to return to an idealised form of certain early Islamic values, and strongly condemns many other forms of Islam, as well as other religions.

Christian and Jewish fundamentalism also exists and is growing (alongside similar movements in Hinduism and other world religions). Jewish fundamentalists, sometimes called the *haredim* (literally 'the trembling ones'), generally focus on issues related to the Land and state of Israel and some take hardline political positions. In recent years they have emerged as a significant political and religious force within Israel as well as in the Diaspora. The *haredim* not only affirm the literal truth of the Bible, but seek to impose many biblical and Talmudic laws and ordinances upon the state of Israel. Some, both within and outside Israel, have joined with Christian fundamentalists in calling for the building of a third Temple in Jerusalem. While they are largely secluded from mainstream society, following a tightly regulated lifestyle, *haredi* beliefs and moral understanding of the world have similarities to those of some evangelical communities. Christian allies of Jewish fundamentalists believe the creation of the Jewish state in 1948 and the yet-to-be-built Third Temple are theological prerequisites for the second coming of Jesus. Some of these same fundamentalists also actively seek the conversion of Jews to Christianity.

Both Jewish and Christian fundamentalists reject modern scriptural criticism, particularly the documentary theory of biblical scholarship. They also reject the Darwinian concept of human evolution and are profoundly opposed to abortion and euthanasia. In America in recent years, Christian and Jewish fundamentalist leaders have sometimes worked together, advocating a broad public policy agenda that opposes the strict separation of church and state and 'secular humanism', a pejorative term used to describe opponents of fundamentalism. Often, fundamentalists have a special loathing of co-religionists whose views do not fit their own: for example, the al-Qaeda movement(s) has been quite as prepared to kill other Muslims as it has Jews and Christians, Americans and British, and other perceived enemies.

Once belittled by modernists, Protestant fundamentalism remains a major force within Christianity, especially among newly emerging Christian communities in Asia and Africa. The encounter between Jews and Christians in Asia brings its own challenges, including the encounter with Islam. Christianity is a minority religion in Asia, with the exception of the Philippines, and is primarily concerned with its relationship to the major Asian religions rather than with Jewish–Christian relations. However, both Judaism and Christianity share minority status.

For some Asian theologians, like the Sri Lankan S. Wesley Ariarajah (b. 1941), the relationship with Judaism is no different from the Christian relationship with any other faith tradition and Judaism has no role to play in the Church's theological understanding of Jesus' ministry. Ariarajah has described the effort to return Jesus to his Jewish context as a 'futile attempt' to create Christian faith expression in a non-European context.

He acknowledges Jesus' connections with the Jewish community of his day, but in his view these carry no theological significance. Other Asian thinkers, however, such as the Vietnamese-American scholar Peter Phan (b. 1951), explore the contextualisation of Christian theology in differing cultural settings and maintain that Jesus' Jewish context remains indispensable for an accurate understanding of his basic teachings. Scholars such as Phan, while developing a theology suitable for an Asian context, argue that this cannot succeed without an effort to understand the original message of the New Testament, and that this in turn is impossible without a deep appreciation of Jewish religious thought at the time of Jesus and of the composition of the New Testament. Phan's position, which is representative of the Roman Catholic Church and mainstream Protestantism, is important because it suggests that the encounter with Jews and Judaism is significant for Christians, regardless of whether Jews are present in their midst or not. This position lies behind the preamble of the 1975 Roman Catholic *Guidelines*, which states that the formation of Christian identity is intrinsically linked to relations with Judaism, and perhaps for this reason the Vatican defines relations with Jews under the portfolio of ecumenical rather than interfaith relations.

As we saw in the chapter on Zionism, the creation of the state of Israel in 1948 has been a cause of controversy not only between Jews and Christians but also with Muslims. For Jews, the establishment of the state of Israel in the wake of Shoah was considered a miracle. However, for the Arab Palestinians, the vast majority of whom are Muslim, this marks the beginning of their *Naqba*, 'the catastrophe', in which approximately two-thirds of their population became refugees and lost control and ownership over the majority of the land they inhabited prior to the War of Independence. In addition to the political conflict between Israelis and Palestinians, Israel occupies the third holiest Muslim site, the al-Aqsa Mosque, located on the Haram al-Sharif, known to Jews as the Temple Mount, in the Old City of Jerusalem. These holy places are at the centre of both religious ideology and rhetoric as well as being the focus of much global attention (and contention). Their symbolic value to Christians, Muslims and Jews worldwide cannot be overestimated.

The positive developments in Jewish–Christian relations, in the last fifty years in particular, are viewed with distrust by some Muslims who see them as an attempt to marginalise and disempower them. The recent creation of interfaith structures, which include Muslims alongside Jews and Christians and other faith communities, such as the Three Faiths Forum and the Interfaith Network in the UK, may help to change this negative point of view. At the same time, more positive contemporary Muslim relations with Jews and Christians are also dependent upon intra-Islamic discussions that would admit more internal diversity, and articulate and apply more generous attitudes towards other religions than the noisiest ones that emanate from some parts of Islam.

For Christians, intra-faith conversation and relations (ecumenism) is also a relatively recent movement, beginning in the early twentieth century but gaining momentum after 1948, the year the World Council of Churches (WCC) was founded. In 1961 the Orthodox churches joined the WCC, but the Roman Catholic Church sends only observers to WCC Assemblies.

Originally the ecumenical Christian movement paid significant attention to Jews only as the objects of mission, but two factors caused a profound change of heart. First, the Swiss theologian Karl Barth insisted that Jews were *verus Israel*, the True Israel, and that it was appropriate to speak of 'the Church *and* Israel'. Then in 1965 *Nostra Aetate* affirmed 'the sacred spiritual bond linking the people of the new covenant with Abraham's stock'. The Faith and Order Commission of the WCC expressed its conviction in the same year that the Jewish people still have theological significance of their own for the Church; and in 1982 *Ecumenical Considerations on Jewish–Christian Dialogue* was published. It argued that the Jewish people were full partners in dialogue: 'The spirit of dialogue is to be fully present to one another in full openness and human vulnerability.' Yet mission to the Jewish people was not repudiated, in an effort to reflect the many different views held by WCC member churches.

For Jews, intra-Jewish conversations about Christianity have been much more limited and Claude Montefiore's call for a Jewish theology of Christianity, in his book *The Old Testament and After* published in 1923, has yet to be fully realised. *Dabru Emet* ('Speak Truth'), the cross-denominational Jewish statement on Christians and Christianity published in 2000, begins the process of reflecting on the place of Christianity in contemporary Jewish thought. It stresses that it is time for Jews to reflect on what Judaism may now say about Christianity and asserts eight points:

- Jews and Christians worship the same God;
- Jews and Christians seek authority from the same book (the Bible);
- Christians can respect the claim of the Jewish people upon the Land of Israel;
- Jews and Christians accept the moral principles of Torah;
- Nazism was not a Christian phenomenon;
- the humanly irreconcilable differences between Jews and Christians will not be settled until God redeems the world;

- a new relationship between Jews and Christians will not weaken Jewish practice;
- Jews and Christians must work together for justice and peace.

Dabru Emet represents a positive affirmation of Christianity and has been well received by the churches but was the cause of controversy within the Jewish community, notably because of two statements affirming that Christians worship the God of Israel and that Nazism was not a Christian phenomenon. For example, an American academic, Jon Levenson (b. 1949), criticised the statement because he was opposed to reciprocity as a justification for Jewish engagement with Christians and to what he saw as the over-riding concern for self-affirmation by the supporters of *Dabru Emet* which only serves to blur the distinctions between Judaism and Christianity.

Contemporary Muslim communities are also grappling with the place of Judaism and Christianity in Islamic thought, particularly minority communities who now live in significant numbers in the United States and Europe. More Muslims are playing an important role in the wider interfaith community, building on the pioneering work of leading figures such as Prince Hassan (b. 1947) of Jordan and the American-based Pakistani academic, Akbar Ahmed (b. 1942), both of whom have devoted their lives to the interfaith endeavour. There are signs that they are no longer alone, as demonstrated by the action of King Abdullah (b. 1924) of Saudi Arabia, the Custodian of the Two Holy Places, who opened a World Conference on Dialogue in 2008 and called for dialogue between Muslims and non-Muslims, in the face of criticism from some senior clerics in Saudi Arabia. Yet it is too early to predict what results these events will have.

Despite the challenge to search for a common language and potential symbiosis, there are major doctrinal and psychological barriers to a trialogue with the three monotheistic religions and collective memories prevent uninhibited dialogue: for example, many Jews think of Christianity in terms of suffering and persecution; while many Muslims have not forgotten the Crusades, and see in Western aspirations for world hegemony the old crusader mentality in a new guise. All three religions have wide experience in polemics and apologetics, but interfaith dialogue remains limited to a minority.

ABRAHAM

Abraham is often regarded as a symbol of hope in the Jewish–Christian–Muslim encounter and acclaimed as a spiritual mentor and guide. For example, Karl-Josef Kuschel (b. 1948) calls for 'an Abrahamic ecumenism', in which Jews, Christians and Muslims work together in mutual respect and for the common good. The first decade of the twentieth-first century has witnessed a number of interfaith initiatives adopting the term 'Abrahamic' in their title, such as the Woolf Institute of Abrahamic Faiths in Cambridge and the Children of Abraham in New York. Since Judaism, Christianity and Islam all trace their spiritual ancestry to Abraham, viewing him as a paradigm of the human–divine relationship, there is an attempt to depict him as a figure who can help reconcile three related but divided religions, the 'Abrahamic faiths'.

Whilst Abraham is certainly an important figure to the three faiths, it is just as possible that his significance to each can be interpreted as undermining his importance to the others because they have not interpreted him appropriately. For example, for Jews the Bible's descriptions of Abraham's encounters with God are viewed most commonly in terms of God's promises concerning continuity of family and inheritance of the Land of Israel. Jewish claims to be the inheritors of the Land of Israel through the promises of Abraham have been and remain a source of controversy among Jews, Christians and Muslims.

The New Testament reveals both continuities and discontinuities with the patriarch. Jesus descends from the seed of Abraham, but ancestry from Abraham is not sufficient to avoid the divine wrath and Paul's assessment of Abraham, discussed earlier, has been a significant point of contention in Jewish–Christian relations. Narratives of the early Church reinforce the division between those who believe in Christ and are spiritual, and Jews who adhere to Torah. The Qur'an describes Abraham as the *hanif*, the God-seeker *par excellence*. Muslims revere Abraham as a holy figure, and trace their lineage back to his son Ishmael. Muslim traditions elaborate the biblical narratives, understanding, for example, the object of Abraham's sacrifice narrated in Genesis 22 to be Ishmael rather than Isaac. For Jews and Christians, the child of the promise is Isaac: it is through Isaac that Abraham becomes the father of the people of Israel and of the nations.

The Qur'an designates Islam as 'the religious community of Abraham' (*millat Ibrahim*) and portrays Muhammad as a follower of the monotheistic faith of Abraham (16:123). According to a common translation, the Qur'an affirms that:

Abraham was not a Jew nor yet a Christian; but he was true in Faith, and bowed his will to Allah's (Which is Islam), and he joined not gods with Allah. Without doubt, among men, the nearest of kin to Abraham, are those who follow him, as are also this Messenger and those who believe: And Allah is the Protector of those who have faith. (Q3.67f.) www.islamicity.com/Mosque/QURAN/3.htm

The translator's interpretative gloss, 'Which is Islam', shows how Abraham is interpreted as a Muslim possession, the father of those who truly submit in

faith to God, and do not associate other gods with him; namely, Muslims.
Note the difference with a more recent translation of the Qur'an published
by Oxford University Press in 2008:

*Abraham was neither a Jew nor a Christian. He was upright and devoted to God,
never an idolator, and the people who are closest to him are those who truly follow
his ways, this Prophet and [true] believers – God is close to [true] believers.* (M. A. S.
Abdel Haleem, *The Qur'an*, Oxford: Oxford University Press, 2008)

Each tradition, therefore, hearkens back to the biblical Abraham, who
becomes the basis upon which Jews, Christians and Muslims may seek
reconciliation of their differences. The resolution of their theological and
communal differences will depend upon how carefully they negotiate the
virtues of Abraham that belong to all three traditions and appreciate the
particular claims made by each of them. Clearly, Abraham can be a model
of faith for the three but the point at issue is whether each one of these
religions can allow him to be a model for members of the other two
(or, conceivably, for members of one of them but not the other). Even if
Abraham is not as promising a figure as many assume or press him to be,
the long history of suspicion and bloodshed between Jews, Christians and
Muslims surely motivates them to search for common ground.

MEMORY AND IDENTITY

Religious identities, based on key sacred events, have usually occurred
much further in the past than most national events. Yet they possess contemporary significance. For example, Muslims find meaning in the *hijra*,
the emigration from Mecca to Medina of Muhammad and his followers
in 622 CE; likewise, Jews view the exodus from Egypt which took place in
1200 BCE as of contemporary significance, as Christians view the death and
resurrection of Jesus, nearly 2000 years ago.

Taking Passover as an example, how these events are celebrated or commemorated sheds light on Jewish–Christian relations. For Jews, Passover is
connected to the historical commemoration of the exodus from Egypt and
the Torah commands the Israelites to recall this event (Deut. 16:2, 6–7).
Deuteronomy 16:3 refers to unleavened bread as 'the bread of affliction',
remembering the Egyptian oppression. Christians for their part associate
the festival with the death of Jesus. The eucharistic liturgy during the Easter
season includes the words: 'Christ our Passover is sacrificed for us. Therefore let us keep the feast.' These words derive from Paul's theology as found
in his first letter to the Corinthians (5:7–8), where he compares clearing out
the bad elements of their lives with getting rid of the old yeast or leaven.

For Jews, Christians and Muslims, the inheritance of the past is important to their religious identity and their encounter, but so too is the continuing relevance of this past. Learning from the past does not require us to live there, but there are some believers who wish to restore the past, by force if necessary.

Thus says the LORD, who makes a way in the sea, a path in the mighty waters, who brings forth chariot and horse, army and warrior; they lie down, they cannot rise, they are extinguished, quenched like a wick: 'Remember not the former things, nor consider the things of old. Behold, I am doing a new thing; now it springs forth, do you not perceive it?' (Isa. 43:16–19a)

So spoke Isaiah, prophet of the Exile to his people, encouraging the Israelites to believe that there was the hope that they would return to the Land of Israel. Strikingly, the prophet speaks in terms of forgetting the past, for the sake of the future. To what extent we should forget the past clearly has an impact on memory and on identity.

There are those religious believers who are not prepared to forget about the past, just as there are those who prefer to forget. For the latter, the baggage of the past makes no sense. They hold, for example, that the search for simple certainties is mistaken and unethical and that theological and ideological questions, such as seeking truth, serve (at best) to confuse and (at worst) to abuse memory and identity. Of course, it may well be that their view is correct, but it does not necessarily follow that passing over the past is a constructive way to form memory and identity.

Commemorations of past events relate the collective memory of a historical community to an inaugural moment or a founding act. By repetition they help preserve a sense of historical continuity, identity and even social integration. Collective memory contains a strong conservative force, furnishing a community with a sense of historical continuity. By re-enacting these founding moments, the inspiration of the heroic or founding event is preserved and reinforced.

However, a preoccupation (some might call obsession) with the past may be harmful. The memory of a founding event that is recollected and re-enacted may become a danger if it results in a negative identity and self-understanding, especially if it becomes the only or primary lens through which reality and the changing world is viewed. For example, the legacy of being a victim has left an enduring mark on the Jewish psyche and impacts on the Jewish encounter with Christians and Muslims. A history of being surrounded by oppressive nations has become a feature of Jewish memory, leading to a sense of victimisation. Taking to heart the Bible's command to the Children of Israel to remember (*zachor*), because 'you were slaves in the land of Egypt', Jews are reminded at Passover, not only to remember that

God took them out of the land of Egypt, but to remember the suffering of Israel in Egypt; the Torah also reminds them not only to treat the stranger with care but to remember the violence committed against the Israelites by the surrounding nations.

A modern example of a focus upon victimisation is the 614th commandment proposed by Emil Fackenheim, in his reflection on the Holocaust. One dangerous consequence of demanding Jewish continuity, so as not to give Hitler a posthumous victory, is that Jewish identity can easily became Shoah-centred as can relations between Jews and Christians. The Holocaust reinforced a mentality in the Jewish world that Jews are a small minority and that the Jewish people, even Jews in Israel, are surrounded by hostile non-Jews. Consequently, a young Jew will easily construct a negative Jewish identity which, without the positive side of Judaism, will not be of value to be handed down over the generations. A young Christian will come away with an exclusive picture of the Jew as victim, without an awareness of the positive aspects of Jewish culture. If the Jew disappears from the historical horizons from the death of Jesus in 33 CE, and only reappears when Hitler came to power in 1933, not only will a negative identity be formed but Jewish–Christian relations will also be based on a victim–perpetrator relationship.

Like Jews, Muslims can also view the outside world as a threat. This may lead to a preoccupation with a memory of suffering, which impacts on relations with Jews and Christians. Akbar Ahmed's study of the views of Muslims in Islamic countries in the twenty-first century (*Journey into Islam*, Washington, DC: Brookings, 2007) lists numerous examples of Muslims feeling 'under attack by the West and modernity', which are viewed as a 'Judeo-Christian' creation.

When modernity was first brought into the Muslim world by Napoleon Bonaparte and subsequent colonial powers, Muslims experienced it as Christian aggression. Nevertheless, there have been attempts by Muslims to bring modernity into an Islamic setting and create an 'authentic' modernity with an Islamic identity in an attempt to relocate modernity in the ambit of the sacred. For example, during the colonial wars of liberation, many Muslims advocated an Islamic state despite the fact that the modern nation state lacks a precedent in Muslim history. By merely 'Islamicising' the modern nation state through the imposition of Islamic law or *sharia*, Muslim political movements believed themselves to be re-sacralising the Western secular nation state. However, the process of 'Islamicising' did not address the deeper social, cultural and political changes brought by modernity but has only served to contribute to a besieged or victim mentality.

MEMORIA FUTURI — MEMORY FOR THE FUTURE

One way to disarm an obsession with the past is to adopt a critical approach to it in order not to be become victims of an ideological 'vindication' of the past that is nostalgic, dogmatic, and sometimes irrational. If the past is approached critically, it can reveal new interpretations and understandings of the world that can be liberating and constructive.

For example, although reflection on and reaction to the Shoah are essential for an understanding of Jewish–Christian relations, positive relations cannot be built solely on responses to antisemitism and Christian feelings of guilt. Certainly, the past must be remembered and memories have to find a way to be reconciled so that horrors are not forgotten. Otherwise, as George Santayana (1863–1952) said, 'those who cannot remember the past are condemned to repeat it'. However, no healthy and enduring relationship between people is built on guilt. If recent Christian soul-searching in the aftermath of the destruction of European Jewry leads to a new approach and a revision of traditional anti-Jewish teaching, so much the better. However, the future relationship cannot be built on the foundations of guilt. The sense of guilt is transient and does not pass to the next generation; moreover, it is unstable, inherently prone to sudden and drastic reversal. So it is necessary for Jews and Christians to negotiate a better stance towards a compromised past in order to look forward to a more hopeful future. Indeed, redeeming a compromised past offers grounds for hope in Jewish–Christian relations but also in relations with Muslims and other faith communities.

Walter Kasper, President of the Pontifical Commission for Religious Relations with the Jews (2002–10), has called for a renewed emphasis on *memoria futuri* and for Jews and Christians to reflect on the more positive aspects of memory. Religious remembrance, he argued, is not an act of nostalgia, but one that empowers in the present. For example, in their liturgy, Jews and Christians remember not only what God has done for them in the past, but remember that God's people continue to have a role today.

Christianity has recognised that past practices about and traditional views of Jews are wholly unacceptable and many Christians have worked to create a new relationship. The tackling of Christian triumphalism and overcoming the *Adversus Iudaeos* tradition illustrates a shift from what was, for the most part, an inherent need to condemn Judaism to one of a condemnation of Christian anti-Judaism. It has also led to a closer relationship with 'the elder brother' and not, as some have feared, to the undermining of Christian teaching. The rediscovery of a positive relationship with Judaism facilitates a positive formation of Christian identity and memory.

For Jews, *memoria futuri* may help Jews view Diaspora life not primarily in negative terms (as an anti-Jewish environment and exemplifying a continuous history of oppression) but in positive terms (as a fruitful environment facilitating vigorous Jewish existence and dynamic development). Traditionally, Diaspora has been understood as *galut*, 'exile', implying that life outside of Israel is an undesirable situation. Indeed, the rabbis understood *galut* as a divine punishment. Diaspora, on the other hand, is a Greek word meaning 'dispersion' (a voluntary situation desirable to the individual), which can be a positive experience for the Jewish people living among the nations of the world, leading to constructive interaction.

The host communities, both Christian and Islamic, had a significant impact upon Jews (and Christians or Muslims) in the Diaspora, who often adopted the languages, dress, customs, names and even religious styles of the majority population. Examples include the *haredim* who today wear distinctive clothing similar to that of eighteenth-century Polish gentry, Yiddish, the language of Ashkenazi Jews, which is a mixture of Hebrew with medieval German and Polish, and the Ladino of Sephardic Jews, a mixture of Hebrew and Spanish.

As a minority, Jews have thrived, having lived in a Diaspora community since at least the fall of the First Temple in the sixth century BCE. After 70 CE, Jews had to create a sense of religious identity without the possession of Jerusalem or the Temple and, arguably, Rabbinic Judaism survived and flourished precisely because it had not been so attached to the rites of the Temple as the Sadducees.

Traditionally, the social interaction inherent in Diaspora communities was frowned upon because it could easily lead to assimilation and interfaith marriages. The absorption of a person or group into a surrounding culture has long been viewed, particularly by critics of Jewish–Christian dialogue, as a dangerous consequence of modern Jewish–Christian relations. The fear of Jewish assimilation into Christian society has often led Orthodox Jewish leaders to discourage the possibility of close contact between members of the two faiths. Church leaders have also worried that their flock may be influenced by Jews in their midst, resulting in a lessening of faith and the introduction of heretical ideas. This fear lay behind the fact that the entry of Roman Catholicism into dialogue with Jews and Judaism was delayed until the 1965 publication of *Nostra Aetate*.

Jews and Christians, like any other community, religious or secular, are in a continual process of change, affected not only by assimilation but also by differences in, for example, gender, age, language and converts. They are also affected by change in the wider society. In the UK, for example, change in recent decades is one result of immigration, especially from the former colonies, and the changing social and economic conditions of ethnic groups. This leads to a change in an individual's identity or the now more common notion of hybrid identity, when one's identity is constituted by a multiplicity of different identities – cultural, religious, ethnic, linguistic, national – that were once considered distinct.

This is a relatively new development in Europe but has a longer history and is more common in the USA. An example of hybrid identity is that of an American-born citizen of Israeli origins. With the increased communication and ease of travel today, many American citizens of Israeli origin can participate in the cultural and religious world of Israel while simultaneously participating in the cultural and linguistic world of the USA. If asked about his or her identity, this person would most probably reply with a hyphenated response such as 'American-Israeli'. Pushed further, one might find out even deeper layers of identity such as 'American-Israeli-Sephardi'.

A consequence of hybrid identities is that people regularly cross boundaries that divide insider from outsider, thus blurring identity boundaries that were previously more clearly defined. The impact of Jewish–Christian relations is obvious because shifts in identity boundaries result in boundaries being remade, redefined and re-imagined, thus creating new identities, new cultures, and new relations. In the process of such changes collective identities of groups change and their collective historical memories are reinterpreted.

In times of change, when people have to readjust and redefine who they are, identities can be quite fragile. It is no easy task to redefine one's identity, the fragility of which can lead to prejudice as a defensive mechanism. The reaction against rapidly shifting boundaries of identity, especially when one or more identity is perceived to be under threat, inevitably leads to an over-rootedness in one's identity and a subsequent decrease in a desire to engage in dialogue with the 'Others'. This is one of the challenges of living in multicultural society.

One positive example of the changing historical situation can be seen in changes in immigrant areas, such as East London, a highly populated immigrant area. The Brick Lane Jamme Masjid (mosque) presently serves local Bangladeshi Muslims. It was originally built in 1743 as a French Protestant church, made into a Methodist chapel in 1819, converted into the Spitalfields Great Synagogue in 1898, and finally became the Brick Lane Jamme Masjid in 1976. When the Christian and later the Jewish community decided to sell the building, they wanted it to continue being a house of worship. Therefore, they sold the building to the Bengali Muslim community for a low price, thus ensuring that the church would become a synagogue and the synagogue would become a mosque. As a relic of the interfaith and communal past, there remains a sign in Hebrew commemorating some of its former Jewish community members.

Another change affecting relations can be seen in the growth of secularism, a challenge that has brought Jews and Christians (and those of other faiths) together. Alongside changing Christian attitudes towards and increasing appreciation of Judaism, and the growth of Jewish–Christian dialogue, the secular challenge has led some to call for a 'common mission' and for Christian and Jewish leaders to see each other as allies opposing religious indifference, which is understood as a greater threat than religious differences. This may lessen the sense of rivalry that characterised past relations and pave the way for joint approaches on issues of common interest, both at national leadership level and in local areas. An example is the way in which Jewish, Christian and other faith communities demonstrated together in the jubilee year (2000) against poverty and for the relief of third world debt. This led to further joint interfaith action such as the 200,000 people who travelled to Edinburgh during a meeting of the G8 leaders in 2005 to support the 'Make Poverty History' campaign.

On the other hand, practitioners of interfaith dialogue are apt to overlook the fact that some of their colleagues in this enterprise are attached to their religion not because of faith in God but for community reasons, or because they like its artistic and aesthetic values. For example, a number of Christians go to church because of its liturgical and musical excellence or for cultural or other reasons. Likewise, many Jews are secular but retain their identity as Jews in terms of culture. Secular Jews may have a rather tenuous connection with Judaism but are as likely to be involved in interreligious conversation as observant Jews. Indeed, proponents of dialogue may be convinced of its ability to bring together and reconcile members of antagonistic religious faiths, but lack any great degree of personal faith themselves. The assumption that a strong, personal faith is at the heart of religion is often a Protestant Christian emphasis. Equally, however, outsiders often assume that Christians possess or at least declare such a faith when many, in fact, do not.

SOURCES OF REVELATION

There are many sources of revelation and holy books are one form. The oral transmission of stories can powerfully focus the divine presence for devotees. It is therefore important not to overburden texts and their interpretations, as many people do, with too great an importance as revealers of truth: they may reveal ultimate reality, but no religion believes that they exhaust it; all, at least in some of their branches, suppose that revelation breaks through in other ways.

Oral traditions also play an important role. Primal faiths – those of the First Peoples of Africa, for example, and many other parts of the world – often have no written texts and so oral stories function rather as Scripture does, to point to the will of God (or gods), as the British scholar of religion Geoffrey Parrinder (1910–2005) has shown. Furthermore, since many cultures have been illiterate, Scriptures have usually been received by the devotee in spoken rather than written form. In Africa, Christians appear at first glance to demonstrate little awareness of Judaism. However, upon further study it is clear that the African emphasis on the Old Testament, such as the biblical understanding of creation, the life cycle, and the family and community – expressed, for example, in African sacrifices at births, weddings, funerals and other religious ceremonies, hand-washing ceremonies and the rite of circumcision – provides a natural link between Judaism and Christianity. Western missionaries were in fact reluctant to use the Old Testament in the instruction of converts, fearing that its atmosphere would be too close to indigenous African culture and converts might feel that there was no need to proceed to the New Testament.

The World Council of Churches organised a small number of meetings between Christians and Jews, which have pointed to a number of 'convergences' in African theology and Judaism, other than the centrality of the biblical text and story. These included the similarities between the concept of shalom and *Ubuntu* (humaneness or humanity), the role of the word and of *palaver* (discussion, consensus-formation), and the idea of *tikkun* (repair) and the theology of reconstruction. African theology is unhindered by many of the concerns underlying Jewish–Christian dialogue in Europe. An example is the topic of memory, since Jews and Africans have experienced a similar history of exclusion, exploitation and violence (from antisemitism and the Shoah to the slave trade, apartheid and the Rwandan genocide) as well as of survival. In this context, the biblical account of the Exodus and the journey from bondage to freedom plays a central role in African as well as in Jewish theology.

In Jewish and Christian Scripture, God speaks and so his people would do well to listen and obey. The focus of revelation is God. It is God who calls forth creation by speaking his word (Genesis 1), who reveals his will on Mount Sinai (Exodus 34); and who, Christians teach, speaks his final word in his son, Jesus (John 1). Since there is a great emphasis on the word of God (in Islam, as well as Judaism and Christianity), it is hardly surprising that sacred writings are so important to all three.

In talking with Muslims, a dialogue partner may refer to Q2:256: 'There is no compulsion in religion; truly the right way has become clearly distinct from error; therefore, whoever disbelieves in the Shaitan [Satan] and believes in Allah he indeed has laid hold on the firmest handle, which shall not break off, and Allah is Hearing, Knowing.' Less helpfully (at least, at first glance) is a quotation from Q3:85: 'And whoever desires a religion other than Islam, it shall not be accepted from him, and in the hereafter he shall be one of the losers.' Looking at another's sacred writings may help us to see the paradoxes therein that we can fail to locate in our own. It may also teach us the importance of interpretation. In this case, for example, if the first text were revealed before the second, the second may have abrogated its meaning. Or else, one might reflect that not being compelled into the truth does not make falsehood acceptable. Or one could make a case that *islam* is used in the lower-case sense of 'submission to God', and that, for example, a Christian is submissive to God within his Christian faith, just as a Muslim is within hers.

The very process of discussing sacred texts together has proved helpful to many people, particularly in the Abrahamic faiths, as they have gained an insight into their own faith as well as others. They may also come to realise that serious differences, intra-faith as well as interfaith, are seriously held.

As we have seen, one of the achievements of Jewish–Christian dialogue has been the realisation that texts have a history; and a compromised history at that. It is impossible to read the Passion narratives of the Gospels without recognising the antisemitic uses to which past readings of them have been put. When Matthew wrote: 'And all the people answered, "His blood be on us and on our children!"' (27:25), how are we to read them from our perspective, not his? Sometimes, then, we have to deal with (meaning, in practice: reject) long-held readings that have been death-dealing, not life-giving.

The choices we make can be crucial for living harmoniously together in a religiously diverse world. Jews, Christians and Muslims can choose to prioritise and act on more inclusive or more exclusive readings. The person who reflects upon Q2:62, and takes it to heart, would have positive things to say about Jews (and others): 'Surely those who believe, and those who are Jews, and the Christians, and the Sabians, whoever believes in Allah and the Last day and does good, they shall have their reward from their Lord, and there is no fear for them, nor shall they grieve.' Not so, if she were to read Q5:51: 'O you who believe! do not take the Jews and the Christians for friends; they are friends of each other; and whoever amongst you takes them for a friend, then surely he is one of them; surely Allah does not guide the unjust people.'

It is often an exclusive reading of selected texts that has marginalised the other. Examples abound in Jewish and Christian texts, notably violent passages such as Deuteronomy 20, which deals with fighting a war and the ethics of warfare and begins with a remarkably democratic and morally topical message:

When thou goest forth to battle against thine enemies, and seest horses, and chariots, and a people more than thou, thou shalt not be afraid of them; for the Lord thy God is with thee, who brought thee up out of the land of Egypt. And it shall be, when ye draw nigh unto the battle, that the priest shall approach and speak unto the people, and shall say unto them: 'Hear, O Israel, ye draw nigh this day unto battle against your enemies; let not your heart faint; fear not, nor be alarmed, neither be ye affrighted at them; for the Lord your God is He that goeth with you, to fight for you against your enemies, to save you.' And the officers shall speak unto the people, saying: 'What man is there that hath built a new house, and hath not dedicated it? Let him go and return to his house, lest he die in the battle, and another man dedicate it. And what man is there that hath planted a vineyard, and hath not used the fruit thereof? Let him go and return unto his house, lest he die in the battle, and another man use the fruit thereof. And what man is there that hath betrothed a wife, and hath not taken her? Let him go and return unto his house, lest he die in the battle, and another man take her.' And the officers shall speak further unto the people, and they shall say: 'What man is there that is fearful and faint-hearted? Let him go and return unto his house, lest his brethren's heart melt as his heart.' And it shall be, when the officers have made an end of speaking unto the people, that captains of hosts shall be appointed at the head of the people. (Deut. 20:1–9)

The text proposes a volunteer army and suggests that many groups of people should not be expected to fight in a war, particularly those who have:
- recently moved into a new home
- planted a vineyard but not yet reaped its fruits
- become engaged and are shortly to be married
- fear of war.

The passage goes on to explain that the city to be attacked should first be offered terms for a peaceful surrender, but, if it refuses, should be besieged.

Upon victory its women and children should not be harmed. So far, so good, but verses 16–18 are problematic:

Howbeit of the cities of these peoples, that the Lord thy God giveth thee for an inheritance, thou shalt save alive nothing that breatheth, but thou shalt utterly destroy them: the Hittite, and the Amorite, the Canaanite, and the Perizzite, the Hivite, and the Jebusite; as the Lord thy God hath commanded thee; that they teach you not to do after all their abominations, which they have done unto their gods, and so ye sin against the Lord your God.

The Hebrew Bible commands that the cities of the Hittites, Amorites, Canaanites, Perizzites, Hivites and Jebusites should be destroyed and that every man, woman and child (and animal) should be killed. Although these cities, from the perspective of Scripture, may symbolise the Nazis of their time, how should such verses be interpreted, particularly in today's violent world?

Interestingly, the rabbis decreed that military power should no longer be used. They did this by evading, nullifying, and otherwise interpreting away the genocidal commands against the Canaanites and other idolatrous people. Instead of extrapolating from these commands that it was right – even obligatory – to wipe out a people that rejected the one true God, the rabbis went in the opposite direction, ruling that the Canaanite example was null and void. Since the Canaanite peoples no longer existed – the rabbis explained that the Assyrians had scattered them as well as the ten lost tribes of Israel in 721 BCE – the rabbis ruled that the commands to use military action against the Canaanites were a dead letter (M. Yadayim 4.4). If military action against the Canaanites was no longer necessary, then military action itself was no longer commanded.

The rabbis could have understood the six nations as symbols for ongoing dangers to be dealt with militarily but chose instead to annul the genocidal meaning of the text and even rejected the command to execute a rebellious Israelite child or wipe out a rebellious Israelite city. This was an ethical decision not to carry out literally the command of Torah. One could argue that to a certain extent the rabbis were simply being pragmatic, given the power of the Roman and Byzantine empires; but these rulings also point to an ethical rejection of the use of violence.

For Jews, the Rabbinic Bible, the *Mikraot Gedolot*, with its commentaries spanning the centuries ranged around the biblical text, is regarded as a celebration of the enduring nature of the debate about meaning. The rabbis tend to see a multitude of different possible meanings, in marked contrast to the single 'authentic' meaning backed by clerical or scholarly authority. This approach may be described as exegetical pluralism and is explained by the rabbis as follows:

In the School of Rabbi Ishmael it is taught: 'See, My word is like fire, an oracle of the Eternal, and like a hammer that shatters a rock' (Jer. 23:29). Just as a hammer divides into several sparks so too every scriptural verse yields several meanings. (BT. *Sanhedrin* 34a)

A similar approach can also be found in classical Christian exegesis, illustrated by the fourth-century church father, Ephrem:

The facets of God's word are more numerous than the facets of those who learn from it. God depicted His word with many beauties, so that each of those who learn from it can examine that aspect of it which he likes. And God had hidden within his word all sorts of treasures, so that each of us can be enriched by it from whatever aspect he meditates on. For God's word is the Tree of Life which proffers to you on all sides blessed fruits; it is like the Rock which was struck in the Wilderness, which became a spiritual drink for everyone on all sides: 'They ate the food of the Spirit and they drank the draught of the Spirit'. (*Commentary on the Diatessaron* 1:18–19)

Thus, both the rabbis and the church fathers recognise that texts have more than one meaning. Origen argued that Scripture has three meanings, literal, moral and spiritual. As mentioned previously, the rabbis tended to follow a four-fold method: simple or straightforward, allusion, homiletical or drawn-out and mystical; one midrash states that 'the Torah can be interpreted in forty nine ways' (*Pesikta Rabbati* 14:20). Among modern scholars, however, it remains a temptation to seek the one and only correct meaning of a text, rather than offering a critical examination of different readings, each in its own context, each with its own nuances and associations, each worthy of careful consideration in its own right.

The existence of exegetical pluralism means traditional interpretations of Scripture allow for a breadth and plurality of viewpoint. Both the Jewish and the Christian exegetical traditions provide a means by which to deal with texts which run contrary to what we regard as the fundamental values of our tradition, or which may be read as a licence for violence or bigotry. This approach is based on a hermeneutical principle shared by Christians and Jews and reinforced by responses to the Holocaust: humanity should live by the commandments and not die by their observance. This means that, in the light of the Shoah, the Bible needs to be examined for any potential damage it may cause (or the real damage it has caused). The rabbis coined the term *Pikuah nefesh*, referring to the duty to preserve life as taking precedence over the commandment: simply put, when human life is at stake the biblical text needs reinterpretation.

In a lecture to Quakers in 1938, Abraham Joshua Heschel told the story of a band of inexperienced mountain climbers. Without guides, they struck recklessly into the wilderness. Suddenly a rocky ledge gave way beneath their feet and they were tumbled headlong into a dismal pit. In the darkness of the pit they recovered from their shock, only to find themselves set upon by a swarm of angry snakes. Every crevice became alive with fanged, hissing things. For each snake the desperate men slew, ten more seemed to lash out in its place. Strangely enough, one man seemed to stand aside from the fight. When the indignant voices of his struggling companions reproached him for not fighting, he called back: 'If we remain here, we shall be dead before the snakes. I am searching for a way of escape from the pit for all of us.' Heschel uses the analogy to show that killing snakes may provide security for a brief moment but not for long. This applies also to handling violent texts shared by Judaism and Christianity.

The recognition of more than one valid meaning in the biblical text may help. Exegetical pluralism may leave the interpreter with an uncomfortable tension owing to the presence of a number of interpretations arising out of a single biblical passage. These may be disconcerting to some, but their existence illustrates the variety of interpretations that can be applied to Scripture. The application of exegetical pluralism is dependent upon one criterion: rejection of interpretations that promote hatred, discrimination or superiority of one group over another. For example, the literal application of a biblical text for the purpose of the subjugation of women to men, black to white, Jew to Christian, and so on, should be considered invalid, requiring reinterpretation.

The ambiguity of the biblical text is seen in Job 13:15, demonstrated by the following translations:
• Behold, he will slay me; I have no hope (Revised Standard Version).
• Though he slay me, yet will I trust in him (King James Version).
The difference between the RSV and KJV is the result of a variation in the read and spoken versions. The Masoretic vocalisation (spoken reading) indicates that Job has hope, while the consonantal text (written text) offers the view that Job has no hope. The Mishnah acknowledges the ambiguous meaning of the biblical text and has recognised that both translations are possible: 'the matter is undecided – do I trust in Him or not trust?' (M. Sotah 5:5) The contradiction is meaningful as it expresses the tension of one who is torn between hope and doubt: the very tension that inhabits

our mind when we read the Bible today. Job pronounces two words that signify simultaneously hope and hopelessness.

Using this verse from Job as a hermeneutical springboard results in an uncomfortable reading of Scripture, for it leaves the reader with unresolved tension and contradiction. Nevertheless, the two opposed readings of Job do offer a realistic approach to the text. For Job's hope and (at the same time) his lack of hope provide an insight into the divine–human relationship by demonstrating human failing in the encounter with God. Awareness of the prevalence of ambiguity in Scripture can be liberating for Christians and Jews because it indicates that the plain, obvious and literal interpretation is not the final meaning of the text. In other words, more than one interpretation is not only acceptable but also to be expected.

In addition, by applying the rabbinic principle of *kal v'homer* (from minor to major) the reader notices that the tension that arises from the interpretation of this one verse illustrates the tension that exists within the Jewish–Christian encounter as a whole: like the Bible and its interpretations, the Jewish–Christian relationship is full of ambiguity, demanding more than one approach, just as texts and stories shared by Judaism and Christianity demand more than one interpretation. Exegetical pluralism, which is ultimately rooted in the sort of ambiguity found in Job 13:15, suggests that biblical exegetes should approach the text with a jointly owned hermeneutic of ambiguity.

Moreover, a successful re-reading of the biblical text is more likely to be achieved through partnership than in isolation. Jews and Christians share many of the same texts as well as some of the same textual difficulties which these texts raise. They also have similar tools within their exegetical traditions with which to tackle these problems. Exegetical pluralism and a hermeneutic of ambiguity demonstrate that Jews and Christians can learn from and help one another. This may generate the space to create a theology about each other, one that will lead them beyond simple tolerance, or even acceptance, to mutual affirmation.

Further reading

BIBLE

Bieringer, Reimund *et al.*, *Anti-Judaism and the Fourth Gospel* (Louisville: Westminster John Knox Press, 2001)

Boyarin, Daniel, *A Radical Jew: Paul and the Politics of Identity* (Berkeley and London: University of California Press, 1997)

Brooks, Roger and Collins, John J. (eds.), *Hebrew Bible or Old Testament?: Studying the Bible in Judaism and Christianity* (Notre Dame, IN: University of Notre Dame Press, 1990)

Charlesworth, James H. (ed.), *Jesus' Jewishness: Exploring the Place of Jesus in Early Judaism* (Philadelphia: American Interfaith Institute and New York: Crossroad, 1991)

Chilton, Bruce, *Judaic Approaches to the Gospels*, University of South Florida International Studies in Formative Christianity and Judaism 2 (Atlanta: Scholars Press, 1994)

Cunningham, Philip A., *Sharing the Scriptures* (New York/Mahwah: Paulist Press/Stimulus Books, 2003)

Davies, W. D., *Paul and Rabbinic Judaism* (London: SPCK, 1948)

Efroymson, David P., Fisher, Eugene J. and Klenicki, Leon, eds., *Within Context: Essays on Jews and Judaism in the New Testament* (Collegeville, MN: Liturgical Press, 1993)

Flusser, David, *Jesus* (Jerusalem: Magnes Press, Hebrew edn 2001; first publ. in English in 1969)

Fredriksen, Paula, *Jesus of Nazareth, King of the Jews: A Jewish life and the emergence of Christianity* (London: Macmillan, 2000)

Hall, S. G., *Christian Anti-Semitism and Paul's Theology* (Minneapolis: Fortress Press, 1993)

Janowski, Bernd, and Stuhlmacher, Peter (eds.), *The Suffering Servant: Isaiah 53 in Jewish and Christian Sources*, trans. Daniel P. Bailey (Grand Rapids, MI: Eerdmans, 2004)

Kabak, Aharon Avraham, *Narrow Path: The Man of Nazareth*, trans. Julian Louis Meltzer (Tel Aviv: Institute of Translation of Hebrew Literature, 1968) (Hebrew 1936)

Kee, H. C., *Who Are the People of God? Early Christian Models of Community* (New Haven: Yale University Press, 1995)

Kessler, E., *Bound by the Bible: Jews, Christians and the Sacrifice of Isaac* (Cambridge: Cambridge University Press, 2004)

Kim, Johann D., *God, Israel, and the Gentiles: Rhetoric and Situation in Romans 9–11* (Atlanta: Scholars Press, 2000)

Klassen, William, *Judas, Betrayer or Friend of Jesus?* (Minneapolis: Fortress/SCM Press, 1996)

Knowles, Melody D., Menn, Esther, Pawlikowski, John T. and Sandoval, Timothy J. (eds.), *Contesting Texts: Jews and Christians in Conversation about the Bible* (Minneapolis: Fortress Press, 2007)

Kugel, James L., *The Bible as It Was* (Cambridge, MA and London: Belknap (Harvard University Press), 1997)

Kuschel, Karl-Joseph, *Abraham: Sign of Hope for Jews, Christians, and Muslims* (New York: Continuum, 1995)

Lachs, Samuel, *A Rabbinic Commentary on the New Testament: The gospels of Matthew, Mark and Luke* (New York: Ktav, 1987)

Lapide, P. and Rahner, K., *Encountering Jesus – Encountering Judaism* (New York: Crossroad, 1987)

Larsson, Goran, *Bound for Freedom: The Book of Exodus in Jewish and Christian Traditions* (Peabody, MA: Hendrickson, 1998)

Levenson, J. D., *The Death and Resurrection of the Beloved Son: The Transformation of Child Sacrifice in Judaism and Christianity* (New Haven: Yale University Press 1993)

The Hebrew Bible, the Old Testament, and Historical Criticism: Jews and Christians in Biblical Studies (Louisville: Westminster John Knox Press, 1993)

Levine, Amy-Jill, *The Misunderstood Jew: The Church and the Scandal of the Jewish Jesus* (San Francisco: HarperSanFrancisco, 2006)

McAuliffe, J. D., Walfish, B. D. and Goering, J. W. (eds.), *With Reverence for the Word: Medieval Scriptural Exegesis in Judaism, Christianity, and Islam* (Oxford: Oxford University Press, 2002)

Meier, John P., *A Marginal Jew: Rethinking the Historical Jesus: Mentor, Message and Miracles*, vol. II (New York: Doubleday, 1994)

Motyer, Stephen, *Your Father the Devil: A New Approach to John and 'the Jews'* (Carlisle: Paternoster Press, 1997)

Mulder, M. J. and Sysling, H. (eds.), *Mikra: Text, Translation, Reading, and Interpretation Of The Hebrew Bible In Ancient Judaism and Early Christianity* (Philadelphia: Fortress Press, 1988)

Ochs, Peter, *The Return to Scripture in Judaism and Christianity* (New York and Mahwah, NJ: Paulist Press 1993)

Peters, F. E., *Judaism, Christianity, Islam: The Classical Texts and their Interpretation* (Princeton: Princeton University Press, 1990)

Petuchowski, Jacob and Brocke, Michael, *The Lord's Prayer and Jewish Liturgy* (New York: Seabury, 1978)

Reinhartz, Adele, *Befriending the Beloved Disciple: A Jewish Reading of the Gospel of John* (New York and London: Continuum, 2001)

Reuling, H., *After Eden: Church Fathers and Rabbis on Genesis 3:16–21* (Leiden: Brill, 2006)

Rivkin, Ellis, *What Crucified Jesus?* (London: SCM Press, 1984)

Rubenstein, Richard, *My Brother Paul* (New York: Harper, 1972)

Ruether, Rosemary Radford, *Faith and Fratricide: The Theological Roots of Anti-Semitism* (Minneapolis: Seabury, 1974; New York: Search Press, 1975)

Saebo, Magne (ed.), *Hebrew Bible/Old Testament* (Göttingen: Vandenhoeck and Ruprecht, 2000)

Saldarini, Anthony J., *Matthew's Christian–Jewish Community* (Chicago: University of Chicago Press, 1994)

Sanders, E. P., *Jesus and Judaism* (London: SCM Press, 1985)
Paul and Palestinian Judaism (London: SCM Press, 1977)

Sawyer, J. F. A., *The Fifth Gospel: Isaiah in the History of Christianity* (Cambridge: Cambridge University Press, 1996)

Segal, Alan, *Paul the Convert* (New Haven: Yale University Press, 1990)

Sim, David, *The Gospel of Matthew and Christian Judaism: The History and Social Setting of the Matthean Community* (Edinburgh: T. & T. Clark, 1998)

Spiegel, Shalom, *The Last Trial: On the Legends and Lore of the Command to Abraham to Offer Isaac as a Sacrifice: The Akedah* (New York: Schocken, 1967)

Spurling, Helen and Grypeou, Emmanouela, *The Exegetical Encounter between Jews and Christians in Late Antiquity*, Jewish and Christian Perspectives (Leiden and Boston, MA: Brill, 2009)

Stemberger, Günter, *Jewish Contemporaries of Jesus: Pharisees, Sadducees, Essenes* (Minneapolis: Fortress Press, 1995)

Stendahl, Krister, *A Final Account* (Philadelphia: Fortress Press, 1996)
Paul among Jews and Gentiles, and Other Essays (London: SCM Press, 1977)

Tyson, Joseph, *Images of Judaism in Luke-Acts* (Columbia: University of South Carolina Press, 1992)

van Buren, Paul M., *According to the Scriptures: The Origins of the Gospel and of the Church's Old Testament* (Grand Rapids, MI: Eerdmans, 1998)

Vermes, G., *The Changing Faces of Jesus* (New York: Viking, 2000)
Jesus the Jew (London: SCM Press, 1973)

Williamson, Clark M. and Allen, Ronald J., *Interpreting Difficult Texts: Anti-Judaism and Christian Preaching* (London: SCM Press, 1989)

Winter, Paul, *On the Trial of Jesus* (Berlin: de Gruyter, 2nd rev. edn, 1974)

THEOLOGY

Aitken, J. K. and Kessler, E. (eds.), *Challenges in Jewish–Christian Relations* (New York: Paulist Press, 2006)

Ateek, Naim, *Justice and Only Justice: A Palestinian Theology of Liberation* (Maryknoll, NY: Orbis, 1989)

Banki, Judith H. and Pawlikowski, John T. (eds.), *Ethics in the Shadow of the Holocaust: Christian and Jewish Perspectives* (Franklin, WI and Chicago: Sheed & Ward, 2002)

Baum, Gregory, *Christian Theology after Auschwitz* (London: Council of Christians and Jews, 1976)

Bemporad, Jack, Pawlikowski, John T. and Sievers, Joseph (eds.), *Good and Evil after Auschwitz: Ethical Implications for Today* (Hoboken, NJ: KTAV, 2001)

Berger, David, *The Rebbe, the Messiah and the Scandal of Orthodox Indifference*, The Littman Library of Jewish Civilization (London and Portland: Oxford University Press, 2001)

Berger, David and Wyschogrod, Michael, *Jews and 'Jewish Christianity'* (New York: Ktav, 1978)

Berkovits, Eliezer, *Faith after the Holocaust* (New York: Ktav, 1973)

Borowitz, E. B., *Contemporary Christologies: A Jewish Perspective* (New York: Paulist Press, 1980)

Boyarin, Daniel, *Dying for God: Martyrdom and the Making of Christianity and Judaism* (Stanford, CA: Stanford University Press, 1999)

Boys, Mary C., *Has God Only One Blessing? Judaism as a Source of Christian Self-Understanding* (New York: Paulist Press, 2000)

Jewish–Christian Dialogue: One Woman's Experience (New York: Paulist Press, 1997)

Bradshaw, Paul and Hoffman, Lawrence (eds.), *Passover and Easter: Origin and History to Modern Times* (Notre Dame, IN: University of Notre Dame Press, 1999)

Passover and Easter: The Symbolic Structuring of Sacred Seasons (Notre Dame, IN: University of Notre Dame Press, 1999)

Braybrooke, Marcus, *Christian–Jewish Relations: The Next Steps* (London: SCM Press, 2000)

Brueggemann, Walter, *The Land* (Philadelphia: Fortress Press, 1977)

Buber, Martin, *I and Thou* (New York, Charles Scribner's Sons, 2nd edn 1958)

Carroll, James, *Constantine's Sword: The Church and the Jews* (Boston and New York: Houghton Mifflin, 2001)

Christ, Carol and Plaskow, Judith (eds.), *Womanspirit Rising: A Feminist Reader in Religion* (San Francisco, HarperCollins, 1979)

Cohen, Jeremy, *Christ Killers: The Jews and the Passion from the Bible to the Big Screen* (New York: Oxford University Press, 2007)

Cohen, Martin and Croner, Helga (eds.), *Christian Mission – Jewish Mission* (New York: Paulist Press, 1982)

Cohn-Sherbok, Dan, *Messianic Judaism* (London: Cassell, 2000)

Cunningham, Philip A., *Proclaiming Shalom: Lectionary Introductions to Foster the Catholic and Jewish Relationship* (Collegeville, MN: Liturgical Press, 1995)

A Story of Shalom: Religion Textbooks and the Enhancement of the Catholic and Jewish Relationship (Collegeville, MN: Liturgical Press, 1995)

Davies, W. D., *The Gospel and the Land* (Berkeley: University of California Press, 1974)

Eckardt, A. Roy, *Elder and Younger Brothers: The Encounter of Jews and Christians* (New York, Scribner's, 1967; repr. Schocken, 1973)

Eckardt, A. Roy and Eckardt, Alice L., *Encounter with Israel: A Challenge to Conscience* (New York: Association Press, 1970)

Long Night's Journey into Day: A Revised Retrospective on the Holocaust (Detroit: Wayne State University Press and London: Pergamon Press, 1988)

Fackenheim, E. L., *The Jewish Bible after the Holocaust* (Manchester: Manchester University Press, 1988)

To Mend the World: Foundations of Future Jewish Thought (Bloomington and Indianapolis: Indiana University Press, 1994)

Fisher, Eugene J., *Faith Without Prejudice: Rebuilding Christian Attitudes Toward Judaism* (New York and Ramsey: Paulist Press, 1977)

The Jewish Roots of Christian Liturgy (New York: Paulist Press, 1990)

Flannery, Edward H., *The Anguish of the Jews: Twenty-Three Centuries of Anti-Semitism* (New York: Macmillan, 1965; Mahwah, NJ: Paulist Press, 1985)

Flusser, David, Pelikan, Jaroslav and Lang, Justin (eds.), *Mary: Images of the Mother of Jesus in Jewish and Christian Perspective* (Philadelphia: Fortress Press, 1986)

Fry, H. P. (ed.), *Christian–Jewish Dialogue: A Reader* (Exeter: University of Exeter Press, 1996)

Fry, Helen, Montagu, Rachel and Scholefield, Lynne, (eds.), *Women's Voices: New Perspectives for the Christian–Jewish Dialogue* (London: SCM Press, 2005)

Frymer-Kensky, Tikva *et al.* (eds.), *Christianity in Jewish Terms* (Boulder, CO: Westview Press, 2000)

Gerhards, Albert and Leonhard, Clemens (eds.), *Jewish and Christian Liturgy and Worship: New Insights into its History and Interaction*, Jewish and Christian Perspectives, 15 (Leiden and Boston, MA: Brill, 2007)

Harries, Richard, *After the Evil: Christianity and Judaism in the Shadow of the Holocaust* (Oxford: Oxford University Press, 2003)

Harrington, Daniel, Avery-Peck, Alan J. and Neusner, Jacob (eds.), *When Judaism and Christianity Began: Essays in Memory of Anthony J. Saldarini* (Leiden and Boston, MA: Brill, 2004)

Hartman, D., *A Living Covenant: The Innovative Spirit in Traditional Judaism* (New York: Free Press; London: Collier Macmillan, 1985)

Hauerwas, S., *Sanctify Them in the Truth: Holiness Exemplified* (Edinburgh: T. & T. Clark, 1998)

Heschel, Abraham Joshua, *God in Search of Man: A Philosophy of Judaism* (New York: Noonday Press, 1976)

Hilton, Michael, *The Christian Effect on Jewish Life* (London: SCM Press, 1994)

Holwerda, David E., *Jesus and Israel: One Covenant or Two?* (Grand Rapids, MI: Eerdmans, 1995)

Isaac, Jules, *The Teaching of Contempt* (New York: Holt, Rinehart & Winston, 1964)

Jacobs, Louis, *A Tree of Life: Diversity, Flexibility, and Creativity in Jewish Law*, The Littman Library of Jewish Civilization (London: Oxford University Press, 2nd edn, 2000)

Kinzig, Wolfram and Kück, Cornelia (eds.), *Judentum und Christentum zwischen Konfrontation und Faszination: Ansätze zu einer neuen Beschreibung jüdisch-christlicher Beziehungen*, Judentum und Christentum 11 (Stuttgart: Kohlhammer, 2002)

Klein, Chalotte, *Anti-Judaism in Christian Theology*, trans. Edward Quinn (London: SPCK, 1978)

Klenicki, L. (ed.), *Toward a Theological Encounter: Jewish Understandings of Christianity* (Mahwah, NJ: Paulist Press, 1991)

Kung, Hans and Kasper, Walter, *Christians and Jews* (New York: Seabury Press, 1974)

Lapide, P. and Moltmann, J., *Jewish Monotheism and Christian Trinitarian Doctrine*, trans. Leonard Swidler (Philadelphia: Fortress Press, 1981)

Levinas, Emmanuel, *Entre nous: On thinking-of-the-other*, trans. from the French by Michael B. Smith and Barbara Harshav (New York: Columbia University Press, c. 1998)

Levine, L. (ed.), *Jerusalem: Its Sanctity and Centrality to Judaism, Christianity and Islam* (New York: Continuum, 1999)

Locke, Hubert G., *The Black Anti-Semitism Controversy: Protestant Views and Perspectives* (Selingsgrove, PA: Susquehanna University Press, 1994)

  Searching for God in Godforsaken Times and Places: Reflections on the Holocaust, Racism, and Death (Grand Rapids, MI: Eerdmans, 2003)

Madigan, Kevin and Levenson, Jon, *Resurrection: The Power of God for Christians and Jews* (New Haven: Yale University Press, 2007)

Magonet, Jonathan, *Talking to the Other: A Jewish Interfaith Dialogue with Christians and Muslims* (London: I. B. Taurus, 2003)

Marquardt, F.-W., *Von Elend und Heimsuchung der Theologie* (Munich Prologomena zur Dogmatik, 1988)

Merkle, John C. (ed.), *Faith Transformed: Christian Encounters with Jews and Judaism* (Collegeville, MN: Liturgical Press, 2003)

Metz, J.-B. and Moltmann, J., *Faith in the Future: Essays on Theology, Solidarity, and Modernity*, Concilium Series (Maryknoll, NY: Orbis, 1995)

Mittleman, Alan, Johnson, Byron and Isserman, Nancy (eds.), *Uneasy Allies?: Evangelical and Jewish Relations* (New York, Toronto and Plymouth, UK: Lexington, 2007)

Moltmann, J., *The Crucified God: The Cross of Christ as the Foundation and Criticism of Christian Theology* (London: SCM Press, 1974)

Mussner, Franz, *Tractate on the Jews: The Significance of Judaism for Christian Faith* (Philadephia: Fortress Press, 1984)

Novak, D., *The Image of the Non-Jew in Judaism: A Constructive Study of the Noahide Laws* (New York: Edwin Mellen Press, 1983)

  Jewish–Christian Dialogue: A Jewish Justification (Oxford: Oxford University Press, 1989)

  Talking with Christians: Musings of a Jewish theologian (London: SCM Press, 2006)

O'Hare, Padraic, *The Enduring Covenant: The Education of Christians and the End of Antisemitism* (Valley Forge, PA: Trinity Press International, 1997)

Papademetriou, George C., *Essays on Orthodox Christian–Jewish Relations* (Bristol, IN: Wyndham Hall Press, 1990)

Pawlikowski, John, *Christ in Light of the Christian–Jewish Dialogue* (New York: Wipf & Stock, 1982)

  Jesus and the Theology of Israel (Collegeville, MN: Liturgical Press, 1989)

Plaskow, Judith and Christ, Carol, *Weaving the Visions: New Patterns in Feminist Spirituality* (San Francisco: HarperCollins, 1989)

Pollefeyt, Didier, *Jews and Christians: Rivals or Partners for the Kingdom of God?* (Louvain: Eerdmans, 1997)

Poorthuis, Marcel and Schwartz, Joshua (eds.), *Saints and Role Models in Judaism and Christianity* (Leiden: Brill, 2004)

Race, Alan, *Christians and Religious Pluralism: Patterns in the Christian Theology of Religions* (New York: Orbis, 1982)

Rengstorf, K. H. and Kortzfleisch, S. von (eds.), *Kirche und Synagoge: Handbuch zur Geschichte von Christen und Juden I* (Stuttgart: Ernst Klett, 1968)

Rosenzweig, Franz, *The Star of Redemption*, trans. William Hallo (Notre Dame, IN: University of Notre Dame Press, 1985)

Roth, John K. (ed.), *Ethics after the Holocaust: Perspectives, Critique, and Responses* (St. Paul, MN: Paragon House, 1999)

Rottenberg, Isaac C., *Christian–Jewish Dialogue: Exploring Our Commonalities and Our Differences* (Atlanta: Hebraic Heritage Press, 2005)

Rubenstein, Richard L., *After Auschwitz: History, Theology, and Contemporary Judaism* (Baltimore: Johns Hopkins University Press, 2nd edn 1992)

Sacks, J., *The Dignity of Difference: How to Avoid the Clash of Civilisations* (London: Continuum, 2002)

Sandmel, David, Catalano, Rosann M. and Leighton, Christopher M., *Irreconcilable Differences?: A learning resource for Jews and Christians* (Boulder, CO: Westview, 2001)

Signer, Michael A. (ed.), *Memory and History in Christianity and Judaism* (Notre Dame, IN: University of Notre Dame Press, 2001)

Signer, Michael A. and Heinz, Hans-Peter (eds.), *Coming Together for the Sake of God: Contributions to Jewish–Christian dialogue from post-Holocaust Germany* (Collegeville, MN: Liturgical Press, 2007)

Soulen, R. Kendall, *The God of Israel and Christian Theology* (Minneapolis: Fortress Press, 1996)

Spicer, Kevin P. (ed.), *Antisemitism, Christian Ambivalence and the Holocaust* (Bloomington: Indiana University Press, 2007)

Stendahl, Krister, *Holy Week Preaching* (Minneapolis: Fortress Press, 1985)

Tanenbaum, Marc, Marvin, Wilson and Rudin, Jim, *Evangelicals and Jews in Conversation* (Grand Rapids, MI: Eerdmans, 1978)

Thoma, C., *A Christian Theology of Judaism* (New York: Paulist Press, 1980)

van Buren, P., *A Theology of the Jewish–Christian Reality, Part I: Discerning the Way* (New York: Seabury Press, 1980)

A Theology of the Jewish–Christian Reality, Part II: A Christian Theology of the People of Israel (San Francisco: Harper & Row, 1983)

A Theology of the Jewish–Christian Reality, Part III: Christ in Context (San Francisco: Harper & Row, 1987)

Von Kellenbach, Katharina, *Anti-Judaism in Feminist Christian Writings* (Atlanta: Scholars Press, 1994)

Wiese, Christian, *Challenging Colonial Discourse: Jewish Studies and Protestant Theology in Wilhelmine Germany* (Leiden: Brill, 2005)

Willebrands, Johannes, *Church and Jewish People: New Considerations* (Mahwah, NJ: Paulist Press, 1992)

Williamson, Clark, *A Guest in the House of Israel* (Louisville: Westminster John Knox Press, 1993)

A Mutual Witness: Towards critical solidarity between Jews and Christians (St Louis: Chalice Press, 1992)

Wyschogrod, Michael, *Abraham's Promise: Judaism and Jewish–Christian Relations*, ed. and intro. R. Kendall Soulen (Grand Rapids, MI: Eerdmans, 2004)

Yoder, John Howard, *The Jewish–Christian Schism Revisited* (London: SCM Press, 2002)

HISTORY

THE FORMATIVE PERIOD OF JUDAISM AND CHRISTIANITY – THE FIRST 500 YEARS

Barclay, John and Sweet, John (eds.), *Early Christian Thought in Its Jewish Context* (Cambridge: Cambridge University Press, 1996)

Boyarin, Daniel, *Border Lines: The Partition of Judaeo-Christianity* (Philadelphia: University of Philadelphia Press, 2004)

Brockmuehl, Markus, *Jewish Law in Gentile Churches: Halakhah and the Beginning of Christian Public Ethics* (Edinburgh: T. & T. Clark, 2000)

Cohen, J., *Living Letters of the Law: Ideas of the Jew in Medieval Christianity* (Berkeley and Los Angeles: University of California Press, 1999)

Davies, Alan (ed.), *Antisemitism and the Foundations of Christianity* (New York: Paulist Press, 1979)

De Lange, N. R. M., *Origen and the Jews: Studies in Jewish–Christian Relations in Third-Century Palestine* (Cambridge: Cambridge University Press, 1976)

Dugmore, C. W., *The Influence of the Synagogue upon the Divine Office* (Oxford: Clarendon Press, 1944)

Dunn, J. D. G., *Jews and Christians: The Partings of the Ways between Christianity and Judaism, and their Significance for the Character of Christianity* (London: SCM Press, 1992)

Dunn, James D. G., (ed.), *Jews and Christians: A Parting of the Ways A.D. 70 to 135* (Grand Rapids, MI: Eerdmans, 1989)

Feldman, Louis, *Jew and Gentile in the Ancient World* (Princeton: Princeton University Press, 1993)

Fine, Steven, ed., *Jews, Christians, and Polytheists in the Ancient Synagogue* (London: Routledge, 1999)

Fredriksen, Paula, *Augustine and the Jews* (New York: Doubleday, 2008)

Gager, John G., *The Origins of Anti-Semitism: Attitudes Toward Judaism in Pagan and Christian Antiquity* (New York and Oxford, Oxford University Press, 1983)

Goodman, Martin, *Mission and Conversion* (Oxford: Clarendon Press, 1994)

Hall, Stuart G., *Melito of Sardis On Pascha and fragments* (Oxford: Clarendon Press, 1979)

Hayward, C. T. R., *Saint Jerome's Hebrew Questions on Genesis*, Oxford Early Christian Studies (Oxford: Clarendon Press, 1995)

Hirshman, M., *A Rivalry of Genius: Jewish and Christian biblical interpretation in late antiquity* (New York: SUNY Press, 1996)

Horbury, William, *Jews and Christians in Contact and Controversy* (Edinburgh: T. & T. Clark, 1998)

Kamesar, A., *Jerome, Greek Scholarship, and the Hebrew Bible: A Study of the Quaestiones Hebraicae in Genesim*, Oxford Classical Monographs (New York: Clarendon Press, 1993)

Krauss, S. and Horbury, W., *The Jewish–Christian Controversy from the Earliest Times to 1789. Volume 1: History* (Tübingen: C. B. Mohr (Paul Siebeck), 1996)

Kugel, James and Greer, Rowen, *Early Biblical Interpretation* (Philadelphia: Westminster, 1986)

Lichtenberger, H., Lange, A. and Römheld, K. F. D. (eds.), *Die Dämonen/Demons: Die Dämonologie der israelitisch-jüdischen und frühchristlichen Literatur im Kontext ihrer Umwelt/The Demonology of Israelite-Jewish and Early Christian Literature in Context of their Environment* (Tübingen: C. B. Mohr (Paul Siebeck), 2003)

Lieu, J., *Image and Reality: The Jews and the World of Christianity in the Second Century* (Edinburgh: T. & T. Clark, 1996)

Lieu, J., North, J. and Rajak, T. (eds.), *The Jews Among Pagans and Christians in the Roman Empire* (London and New York: Routledge, 1992)

Limor, Ora and Stroumsa, Guy G., *Contra Iudaeos: Ancient and Medieval Polemics between Christians and Jews*, Texts and Studies in Medieval and Early Modern Judaism 10 (Tübingen: Mohr, 1996)

Meeks, R. A. and Wilken, R. L., *Jews and Christians in Antioch in the First Four Centuries of the Common Era* (Missoula: Scholars Press, 1978)

Neusner, J., *Aphrahat and Judaism: The Christian–Jewish Argument in Fourth-Century Iran*, Studia Post-Biblica 19 (Leiden: Brill, 1971)

Judaism and Christianity in the Age of Constantine (Chicago: University of Chicago Press, 1987)

Parkes, James W., *The Conflict of the Church and Synagogue* (New York: Hermon Press, 1934; repr. 1974)

Schäfer, Peter, *Jesus in the Talmud* (Princeton: Princeton University Press, 2007)

Judeophobia: Attitudes toward the Jews in the Ancient World (Cambridge, MA and London: Harvard University Press, 1997)

Schreckenberg, Heinz and Schubert, Kurt, *Jewish Historiography and Iconography in Early and Medieval Christianity* (Minneapolis: Fortress Press, 1992)

Segal, Alan, *Rebecca's Children: Judaism and Christianity in the Roman World* (Cambridge, MA: Harvard University Press, 1986)

Setzer, Claudia, *Jewish Responses to Early Christians* (Minneapolis: Fortress Press, 1994)

Shanks, H. (ed.), *Christianity and Rabbinic Judaism: A Parallel History of Their Origins and Early Development* (London: SPCK, 1993)

Simon, M., *Verus Israel: A Study of the Relations between Christians and Jews in the Roman Empire (AD 135–425)* (The Littman Library of Jewish Civilization, Oxford: Oxford University Press, 1986)

Stanton, Graham N. and Stroumsa, Guy G. (eds.), *Tolerance and Intolerance in Early Judaism and Christianity* (Cambridge: Cambridge University Press, 1998)

Stemberger, Günter, *Jews and Christians in the Holy Land: Palestine in the Fourth Century* (Edinburgh: T. & T. Clark, 2000)

Stökl Ben Ezra, D., *The Impact of Yom Kippur on Early Christianity* (Tübingen: Mohr Siebeck, 2003)

Taylor, Miriam, *Anti-Judaism and Early Christian Identity: A Critique of the Scholarly Consensus* (Leiden: Brill, 1995)

Wilken, Robert L., *John Chrysostom and the Jews: Rhetoric and Reality in the Late Fourth Century* (Berkeley: University of California Press, 1983)

Judaism and the Early Christian Mind (New Haven, Yale University Press, 1971)

Wilson, Stephen G., *Related Strangers: Jews and Christians 70–170 CE* (Minneapolis, Fortress Press, 1995)

MEDIEVAL, EARLY MODERN AND ENLIGHTENMENT

Abulafia, Anna Sapir, *Jews and Christians in the Twelfth-Century Renaissance* (London: Routledge, 1995)

Blumenkranz, B., *Juifs et chrétiens dans le monde occidental, 430–1096* (Paris: Mouton, 1960)

Chazan, Robert, *In the Year 1096: The First Crusade and the Jews* (Philadelphia: Jewish Publication Society, 1997)

Cohen, Jeremy, *The Friars and the Jews: The Evolution of Medieval Anti-Judaism* (Ithaca and London: Cornell University Press, 1982)

Cohen, Jeremy (ed.), *Essential Papers on Judaism and Christianity in Conflict: From Late Antiquity to the Reformation* (New York and London: New York University Press, 1991)

Dahan, Gilbert, *The Christian Polemic against the Jews in the Middle Ages* (Notre Dame, IN: University of Notre Dame Press, 1998)

Dan, Joseph (ed.), *The Christian Kabbalah: Jewish Mystical Books and Their Christian Interpreters* (Cambridge, MA: Harvard College Library, 1997)

Elukin, Jonathan, *Living Together, Living Apart: Rethinking Jewish–Christian Relations in the Middle Ages* (Princeton: Princeton University Press, 2007)

Hertzberg, Arthur, *The French Enlightenment and the Jews* (New York: Columbia University Press, 1990)

Hood, John Y. B., *Aquinas and the Jews* (Philadelphia: University of Philadelphia Press, 1995)

Horowitz, Elliot, *Reckless Rites: Purim and the Legacy of Jewish Violence* (Princeton and Oxford: Princeton University Press, 2006)

Katz, J., *Exclusiveness and Tolerance: Studies in Jewish–Gentile Relations in Medieval and Modern Times* (London: Oxford University Press, 1961)

    Out of the Ghetto (Cambridge, MA: Harvard University Press, 1973)

Maccoby, Hyam (ed.), *Judaism on Trial: Jewish–Christian Disputations in the Middle Ages*, The Littman Library of Jewish Civilization (London: Oxford University Press, 1993)

Marcus, Jacob R., *The Jew in the Medieval World: A Source Book 315–1791* (New York: Atheneum, 1981)

Popkin, R. H. and Weiner, G. M. (eds.), *Jewish Christians and Christian Jews* (Dordrecht: Kluwer, 1994)

Robinson, Jack Hughes, *John Calvin and the Jews* (Ann Arbor: University Microfilms International, 1991)

Rubin, Miri, *Gentile Tales: The Narrative Assault on Late Medieval Jews* (London and New Haven: Yale University Press, 1999)

Schreckenberg, Heinz, *Die christlichen Adversus-Judaeos-Texte und ihr literarisches und historisches Umfeld (1.-11. Jh.)*, Europäische Hochschulschriften 23/172 (Frankfurt/M.: Peter Land, 4th edn, 1999)

    The Jews in Christian Art: An Illustrated History (New York: Continuum, 1996)

Shapiro, James, *Oberammergau: The Troubling Story of the World's Most Famous Passion Play* (New York: Pantheon, 2000)

    Shakespeare and the Jews (Columbia: Columbia University Press, 1996)

Sherman, Franklin, *Luther and the Jews: A Fateful Legacy* (Allentown, PA: IJCU, and Baltimore: ICJS, 1995)

Signer, Michael and Van Engen, John, *Jews and Christians in 12th Century Europe* (Notre Dame, IN: University of Notre Dame Press), pp. 123–70

Stow, Kenneth R., *Alienated Minority: The Jews of Medieval Latin Europe* (Cambridge, MA: Harvard University Press, 1992)

    Jewish Dogs, an Image and Its Interpreters: Continuity in the Jewish–Catholic Encounter (Stanford: Stanford University Press, 2006)

Talmage, Frank (ed.), *From Disputation to Dialogue* (New York: Ktav, 1975)

MODERN

Bauman, Zygmunt, *Modernity and the Holocaust* (Cambridge: Polity Press, 1991)

Bea, Augustin, *The Church and the Jewish People: A Commentary on the Second Vatican Council's Declaration on the Relation of the Church to Non-Christian Religions* (London: Geoffrey Chapman, 1966)

Bialer, Uri, *Cross on the Star of David: The Christian World in Israel's Foreign Policy, 1948–1967* (Bloomington: Indiana University Press, 2005)

Braybrooke, M., *Children of One God: A History of the Council of Christians and Jews* (London: Vallentine, Mitchell, 1991)

Brockway, Allan, van Buren, Paul, Rendtorff, Rolf and Schoon, Simon, *The Theology of the Churches and the Jewish People: Statements by the World Council of Churches and Its Member Churches* (Geneva: WCC, 1988)

Cornwell, John, *Hitler's Pope: The Secret History of Pius XII* (London: Viking, 1999)

Croner, Helga (ed.), *More Stepping Stones to Jewish–Christian Relations: An Unabridged Collection of Christian Documents 1975–1983* (Mahwah, NJ: Paulist Press, 1985)

Stepping Stones to Further Jewish–Christian Relations: An Unabridged Collection of Christian Documents [1948–1975] (London and New York: Stimulus, 1977)

Dalin, David G. and Levering, Matthew (eds.), *John Paul II and the Jewish People: A Jewish–Christian Dialogue* (New York, Toronto, Plymouth: Rowman & Littlefield and Sheed & Ward, 2008)

Ellis, Marc H., *Unholy Alliance: Religion and Atrocity in Our Time* (London: SCM Press, 1997)

Everett, R. A., *Christianity without Antisemitism: James Parkes and the Jewish–Christian Encounter* (Oxford: Pergamon Press, 1993)

Fisch, Harold, *The Dual Image: A Study of the Jew in English Literature* (London: World Jewish Library, 1959)

Fisher, Eugene and Klenicki, Leon (eds.), *In Our Time: The Flowering of Catholic–Jewish Dialogue* (Mahwah, NJ: Paulist Press and Stimulus, 1990)

Gopin, Marc, *Holy War, Holy Peace: How Religion Can Bring Peace to the Middle East* (New York: Oxford University Press, 2002)

Greenberg, I., *For the Sake of Heaven and Earth: The New Encounter between Judaism and Christianity* (Philadelphia: Jewish Publication Society, 2004)

Halevi, Yossi Klein, *At the Entrance to the Garden of Eden* (New York: Harper-Collins, 2001)

Haynes, Stephen B., *Reluctant Witnesses: Jews and the Christian Imagination* (Louisville: Westminster John Knox Press, 1995)

Henrix, Hans Hermann and Kraus, Wolfgang (eds.), *Die Kirchen und das Judentum, vol. II: Dokumente von 1986–2000* (Paderborn and Gütersloh: Bonifatius Verlag and Gütersloher Verlagshaus, 2001)

Herberg, Will, *Protestant–Catholic–Jew* (New York: Anchor, 1960)

Heschel, Susannah, *Abraham Geiger and the Jewish Jesus* (Chicago: University of Chicago Press, 1998)

Jacob, Walter, *Christianity through Jewish Eyes: The Quest for Common Ground* (New York: HUC Press 1974)

Kessler, E. and Wright, M. (eds.), *Themes in Jewish–Christian Relations* (Cambridge: Orchard Academic Press, 2004)

Klappert, B., *Israel und die Kirche: Erwägungen zur Israellehre Karl Barths*, Theologische Existenz Heute 207 (Munich: Kaiser, 1980)

Krajewski, Stanislaw, *Poland and the Jews* (Krakow: Wydawnictwo Austeria, 2005)

Krondorfer, B., *Remembrance and Reconciliation: Encounters between Young Jews and Germans* (New Haven: Yale University Press, 1995)

Levine, Deborah J., *Teaching Christian Children about Judaism* (Chicago: Liturgy Training Publications, 1995)

Lipstadt, Deborah, *Denying the Holocaust: The Growing Assault on Truth and Memory* (New York: The Free Press, 1993)

Littell, F. H., *The Crucifixion of the Jews: The Failure of Christians to Understand the Jewish Experience* (Macon: Mercer University Press, 1986)

Littell, F. H. and Locke, H. G. (eds.), *The German Church Struggle and the Holocaust* (Detroit: Wayne State University Press, 1974)

Littell, Marcia Sachs and Gutman, Sharon Weissman (eds.), *Liturgies on the Holocaust: An Interfaith Anthology* (Valley Forge, PA: Trinity Press International, new and rev. edn, 1996)

Mendes-Flohr, Paul and Reinharz, Jehuda (eds.), *The Jew in the Modern World: A documentary history* (New York: Oxford University Press, 2nd edn 1995)

Merkley, Paul C., *The Politics of Christian Zionism 1891–1948* (London: Frank Cass, 1998)

Oesterreicher, John M., *The Unfinished Dialogue: Martin Buber and the Christian Way* (New York: Philosophical Library, 1986)

Rendtorff, Rolf and Henrix, Hans Hermann (eds.), *Die Kirchen und das Judentum, vol. 1: Dokumente von 1945–1985* (Paderborn and Gütersloh: Bonifatius Verlag and Gütersloher Verlagshaus, 2001)

Rittner, C., Smith, S. and Steinfeldt, I., *The Holocaust and the Christian World* (London: Kuperard, 2000)

Rittner, Carol and Roth, J. K. (eds.), *Pope Pius XII and the Holocaust* (Continuum, 2002)

Rosenstock-Huessy, Eugen (ed.), *Judaism Despite Christianity: The "Letters on Christianity and Judaism" between Eugen Rosenstock-Huessy and Franz Rosenzweig* (University, AL: University of Alabama Press, 1969)

Rothschild, F. (ed.), *Jewish Perspectives on Christianity* (New York: Crossroad, 1990)

Rudin, A. James, *Israel for Christians: Understanding Modern Israel* (Philadelphia: Fortress Press, 1983)

Ruether, Rosemary Radford and Ruether, Herman, *The Wrath of Jonah: The Crisis of Religious Nationalism in the Israeli–Palestinian Conflict* (Minneapolis: Fortress Press: 2002)

Saperstein, Marc, *Jewish Preaching in Times of War, 1800–2001*, The Littman Library of Jewish Civilization (Oxford: Oxford University Press, 2007)

Sonderegger, K., *That Jesus Christ Was Born a Jew: Karl Barth's 'Doctrine of Israel'* (University Park, PA: Pennsylvania State University Press, 1992)

Ucko, Hans, *People of God, Peoples of God: A Jewish–Christian Conversation in Asia* (Geneva: WCC, 1996)

Wigoder, Geoffrey, *Jewish–Christian Relations since the Second World War*, Sherman Studies of Judaism in Modern Times (Manchester: Manchester University Press, 1988)

JEWISH–CHRISTIAN RELATIONS: REFERENCE
WORKS AND WEBSITES

DICTIONARY

Kessler, E. and Wenborn, N. (eds.), *A Dictionary of Jewish–Christian Relations* (Cambridge: Cambridge University Press, 2005)

JOURNALS

Christian Jewish Relations (London, Institute of Jewish Affairs, 1980–91).
Service International de Documentation Judéo-Chrétienne (SIDIC) www.sidic.org/en/default.asp
Studies in Christian–Jewish Relations, http://escholarship.bc.edu/scjr/

MAJOR WEBSITES

www.bc.edu/research/cjl/
www.ccjr.us/
www.csc.huji.ac.il/
www.icjs.org/
www.jcrelations.net
www.unigre.it/JudaicStudies/default_en.asp
www.woolfinstitute.cam.ac.uk/cjcr/

Glossary

***Adversus Iudaeos* literature**   Lit. 'Anti-Jewish' writings, refers to a body of Christian polemical texts specifically directed against Jews and Judaism, written from the first to the eighteenth century. This literature appears in the form of systematically arranged tracts, or an account of a dialogue or public debate.

Allegory   Gk, *allegoria*, a mode of interpretation of a text widely used in antiquity, meaning 'speaking one thing and signifying something other than what is said'.

Anti-Judaism   Although 'anti-Judaism' and 'antisemitism' are sometimes deemed equivalent, 'anti-Judaism' describes religious and theological defamation of Jews and Judaism, which might not always translate into personal hatred. However, it is used by some to soften the impact of actual antisemitism.

Antisemitism   A post-Enlightenment phenomenon, following earlier forms of anti-Judaism, it refers to denigration of Jews associated with the emergence of modernity in Europe. Antisemitism involves a deep-seated disdain for Jews and Judaism, much of which is based on Christian theology.

Apostasy   Gk, *apostasia*, means to separate or to rebel. In Judaism, apostasy entails the deliberate forsaking of God and/or his commandments. In the New Testament apostasy denotes the deliberate rejection of God and the renunciation of Christianity.

Arab Christianity   Christian Arabs constitute minorities in numerous Arab countries and in Israel. Until 1948, they shared this minority status with Jews in the Arab world. Today, relations between Arab Christians and Jews are difficult because of the Arab–Israeli conflict.

Assimilation   The absorption of a person or group into a surrounding culture. Assimilation has long been viewed as a dangerous consequence of modernity.

Atonement   Lit. 'becoming at one with another', refers to reconciliation between one person and another or between a person and God. For Jews, *Teshuvah* repentance (a 're-turning' from bad ways) is required. Christians believe that Jesus' death becomes a vicarious atonement on behalf of all those who believe in him.

Balfour Declaration   Letter dated 2/11/1917 and addressed to Lord Rothschild, a prominent English Jewish Zionist, in which the British Foreign Secretary Arthur Balfour publicly declared the support of the British government for the Jewish claim to Palestine.

Birkat Ha-Minim   Lit. 'malediction of the heretics', established in late first-century Rabbinic Judaism as an addition to the *Amidah*. Most scholars understand it as a polemic response to Christianity.

Catechesis   An education in Christian faith, especially the teaching of Christian doctrine. The 1992 *Catechism of the Catholic Church* draws upon Vatican II's new approach to Judaism.

Christ and Christology   The term 'Christ' refers to Jesus' divinely constituted role as Messiah, Lord and Saviour of humankind. The process of rethinking Christology in the light of Jewish–Christian dialogue is taking place as Jews are now seen as integral to the ongoing divine covenant.

Christian Hebraists   Refers to proficient Hebrew scholars, primarily from the sixteenth to the eighteenth century. Protestants used the Hebrew Bible and rabbinic commentaries to support their case for scriptural over ecclesiastical authority, persuading Christians to return to the original Hebrew text of the Bible and also use Jewish exegetical tradition.

Church fathers   The fathers (Lat. *patres*) are early Christian teachers, from the end of the first century to the early Middle Ages. The patristic literature is the main body of Christian texts from these years and provides knowledge of Judaism and Jewish–Christian relations.

Conversion   Refers to the adoption of a new religious identity, or a change from one religious identity to another. Unlike Judaism where there has been a reluctance to seek converts, conversion is central to Christianity and has been and remains a controversial subject in Jewish–Christian relations.

Crucifixion   Refers to the nailing of an individual to a wooden cross and normally refers to the crucifixion of Jesus. Crucifixion was common in the ancient world and two issues are important in Jewish–Christian relations: the identity of those responsible and the paradox of a crucified Messiah.

Crusades   Holy wars (eleventh to sixteenth centuries) preached by the papacy against those deemed to be the enemies of Christ, which resulted in the violent deaths of thousands of Jews, primarily in France and Germany. Many were forcibly baptised and others died as martyrs, sanctifying God's name (*Kiddush ha-Shem*) rather than undergoing baptism.

Dabru Emet   'Speak Truth', a Jewish statement on Christians and Christianity issued in 2000. It is the first cross-denominational Jewish statement in modern times about Christianity and reflects on the place of Christianity in contemporary Jewish thought.

Deicide   Refers to the accusation that Jews killed God and is a major theme of *Adversus Iudaeos* writings. Although the accusation that Jews had killed Christ appears in the New Testament, the first charge of deicide occurred in the second century with Melito, who accused the Jews of Jesus' generation and of all subsequent generations of deicide.

Diaspora   Gk for 'dispersion', describes religious communities living outside their ancestral homeland. The Heb. *galut* means 'exile', demonstrating a tension between the views that Jews outside of Israel live in a Diaspora (a voluntary situation desirable to the individual) or in *galut* (an undesirable situation).

Disputation   A form of discourse where one party refutes the validity of the other in order to invalidate the foundation of the other's faith. The thirteenth century witnessed public disputations (e.g., Barcelona, 1263) which took the form of a trial in front of an audience of king, nobility, clergy and laity.

Dreyfus Affair   1894 trial for treason of the French Jewish captain Alfred Dreyfus, found guilty by antisemitic army officers on the basis of forged documents and sent to life imprisonment. The Affair caused civil unrest in France and, although Dreyfus was pardoned, it profoundly influenced Theodore Herzl and the political Zionist movement.

Easter   Pre-eminent annual Christian festival which celebrates the resurrection of Jesus. Its date is calculated by the same method used for determining the date of the Jewish festival of Passover.

Ecumenism   Lit. 'the inhabited world', from Gk *oikoumene*, refers to initiatives aimed at greater religious unity among diverse Christian denominations. Jewish–Christian relations are sometimes understood as a sub-section of the ecumenical movement.

Emancipation   Refers to the legal processes by which Jews acquired civil and political rights in their countries of residence. This was regarded by some Jews as a welcome end to hardship and exclusion, and by others as a harbinger of assimilation.

Enlightenment   The eighteenth-century European Age of Enlightenment, or Age of Reason, challenged traditional religion and the political role of the Church. The Enlightenment led to increased contact between Jews and Christians and to a more balanced dialogue.

Eucharist   Gk, *eucharistia*, lit. 'thanksgiving', originally applied by Jews to grace before and after meals. The Eucharist, also called 'the Lord's Supper', was applied to a religious shared meal and later became a self-standing bread and wine rite.

Evangelism   Lit. telling the 'good news' (the Gospel) of God's saving love and forgiveness of sin in Jesus Christ. This 'good news' is the Church's mission and evangelism aims at conversion, although a broader understanding is held by many Christians today, which does not aim at converting non-Christians generally or Jews in particular.

Exegesis   Refers to the interpretation of Scripture and has always been central to Jewish–Christian relations. Most polemic between Jews and Christians has been rooted in scriptural exegesis, despite methods of rabbinic and patristic exegesis having much in common.

Expulsions   Expulsions of Jews from Christian lands have occurred since antiquity, but most significant are the two which took place at the end of the thirteenth century (England) and the end of the fifteenth century (Spain).

Feminism and feminist writings   An ideology grounded in women's experience of gender-based subjugation, emphasising that women have the same rights as men. Jewish and Christian feminists seek to recover women's voices and formulate new patterns of relationships. Anti-Judaism has marred Christian feminist theology but some contemporary scholars are attempting to heal this rift.

Forgiveness   Forgiving sin is a divine attribute. In Judaism, forgiveness is dependent upon individual repentance but in Christianity it is primarily a gift mediated through Christ.

Fundamentalism   Jewish and Christian fundamentalists reject modern scriptural criticism and human evolution, as well as abortion and euthanasia. Jewish fundamentalists focus on Israel and seek, with Christian fundamentalist support, the building of a Third Temple. The latter believe the creation of the Jewish state and the Third Temple are prerequisites for the second coming of Jesus. Some also actively seek the conversion of Jews.

Gaonim   This term refers to the rabbis of the major Babylonian academies, headed by the Gaon ('Excellence'), who from the eighth century CE developed the study and interpretation of the Talmud and midrashic literature. The gaonim also arranged the Jewish liturgy, created new prayers and hymns and fixed the traditional order of service.

Ghetto   The first ghetto was decreed in 1516 in Venice when Jews were ordered to live apart from the majority Christian population. Jews saw the Ghetto as 'sacred space', to be self-governed. The term is also applied to places like the Warsaw Ghetto established by the Nazis prior to transporting Jews to Auschwitz.

Gnosticism   A modern term coined from the Gk for knowledge, *gnosis*. It influenced Christianity and Paul's tendency to distinguish sharply between the 'spirit of the law' and the 'letter of the law' lent itself to Gnostic interpretation. Marcion, a Christian Gnostic, rejected much of the Bible, accepting only some of Paul's letters.

Good Friday Prayer for the Perfidious Jews   A prayer for the conversion of Jews, the *perfideles* ('unfaithful' or 'half-believers'). Pope John XXIII ordered the term *perfidiis* be dropped in 1959 and the 1970 revision of the Roman Missal completely changed the prayer, asking God to strengthen the Jewish People in their faith. The approval of a newly revised Latin Tridentine Rite in 2008 calling for Jewish conversion caused great controversy.

Halakhah Heb. 'to walk', refers to Jewish law developed over two millennia. There also exists a strand of Christian *halakhah*, in addition to the fact that Jesus, as an observant Jew, would have followed Jewish law by, for example, attending synagogue on Sabbath and wearing fringed garments.

Hoi Ioudaioi Lit. 'the Jews', mostly used negatively in the New Testament, especially in the Gospel of John, where the expression is used extensively, with frequently changing referents but often with a pejorative meaning in the context of fierce conflict (with a climax in John 8:31–59). This raises the question whether anti-Judaism exists in the New Testament.

Holocaust Refers to the murder between 1933 and 1945 of nearly 6 million Jews under the Nazis, and millions of others including Roma, Poles, Soviet POWs, homosexuals, Jehovah's Witnesses and communists. The Holocaust is a central preoccupation of post-war Jewish–Christian relations and three areas dominate discussion: anti-Judaism/antisemitism; Christian responses, 1933–45; and post-Holocaust responses.

Host desecration An accusation against the Jews of Europe, which developed in the thirteenth century, that Jews sought to desecrate a eucharistic wafer as re-enactment of the crucifixion.

Idolatry The worship of different gods, particularly through the use of tangible images. In controversy Jews, alongside Muslims, associated Christianity with idol worship because of Christian use of images of the crucified Jesus, of Mary and of the saints.

Inquisition The 'Holy Office of the Inquisition' began in the thirteenth century against Christian heretical groups and lasted until the nineteenth. It was not primarily concerned with Jews *per se*, but Judaism was a major factor as was concern about the Talmud. The Inquisition contributed to expulsions of Jewish communities (e.g., Spain, 1492).

Intermarriage Marriage between members of different faiths, each of whom maintains their own religious identity, has long been a contentious issue for both Judaism and Christianity. It has become even more pronounced in recent decades with the decline of social and cultural barriers that previously reinforced the religious division.

International Christian Embassy Established in 1980, the International Christian Embassy Jerusalem is one of the foremost organisations of advocates of Christian Zionism.

Judaising Christians Refers to Christians who have gone beyond an appreciation of Judaism to be actually observing aspects of religious ritual. The term 'Judaiser' was used polemically for those who were judged to be abandoning Christianity for Judaism.

Khazars A national group and powerful state in Eastern Europe between the seventh and the tenth century CE, the rulers of which were converted to Judaism in the eighth or ninth century.

Kiddush ha-Shem Heb., 'sanctification of God's name' and associated specifically with martyrdom by Jews in medieval Christendom.

Kingdom of God Refers to God's sovereignty and rule over Israel and, by extension, over the nations. Jesus proclaimed that the kingdom of God had come near.

Law (see also Torah) Often used (incorrectly) to translate 'Torah', the word reflects the Gk and Lat. translations (*nomos* and *lex*), giving rise to the misapprehension that Judaism is based entirely on legalism. While Torah does contain much law, its more important characteristic is 'instruction' or 'revelation'.

Liberation theology Combines Marxist social criticism with (primarily) Christian belief and argues that Christians should take an active role in eradicating exploitation and oppression. Liberation theology is notable for its support of Palestinian Christians and its criticism of the state of Israel. Proponents include Naim Ateek and Marc Ellis.

Logos Gk 'word', 'reason', used as a theological designation of Jesus in the fourth Gospel. Jewish philosopher Philo drew together Scripture and Greek philosophy, speaking of the *Logos* both as 'boundary figure' between God and the universe and as an active principle of order in the cosmos.

The Lord's Prayer Also called the Paternoster and found in Matthew 6:9–13 and Luke 11:2–4. The prayer provides insight into the origins of Christianity within Judaism and its formulations have antecedents in Hebrew Scriptures and in synagogue liturgy.

Marranos Lit. 'swine' or one who 'mars' Christian faith; a derogatory term, originating in fifteenth-century Spain and referring to Jews who converted to Christianity and continued to observe Judaism. Another term is 'Crypto-Judaism', because of the covert nature of the practice of Judaism by Marranos living among Christians.

Messiah Heb., *mashiach*, 'anointed', translated into Septuagint by Gk *christos*, which in the New Testament is the title of Jesus, rendered into English by 'Christ'. The difference of messianic beliefs is the main distinction between Judaism and Christianity, yet the Roman Catholic Church stated in 2001 that 'the Jewish messianic expectation is not in vain', a huge shift in traditional Christian thinking about the Jewish messianic hope.

Midrash Heb. for searching, inquiring and interpreting, generally referring to a genre of rabbinic literature, although there also exists a Christian form of midrash in the New Testament. In Judaism, midrash consists of an anthology of homilies, a commentary on a particular book of the Bible, and is a religious activity.

Mission   Refers to the sending out of someone to fulfil a particular task, and is a contentious subject. For Jews, it conjures up images of centuries of Christian persecution. Christian mission has traditionally been understood as converting non-Christians to belief in Christ, and that has included Jews. Jews have not understood their mission as converting others to Judaism but as faithfulness to Torah.

Mysticism   The attitudes and practices employed to attain immediate and transformative contact with God. The most important link between Jewish and Christian mysticism is in their common background in Second Temple Judaism, especially its apocalyptic strands.

Noachide laws   Jews traditionally view Noah as a prototype of simple religiosity who was given a set of principles by which to live, the 'Noachide laws'; non-Jews are defined as monotheists if they adhere to them. The concept was widely applied to Muslims and, after some early doubts about the Trinity, also to Christians.

Nostra Aetate   Promulgated in 1965, achieved a reversal of the Church's 'teaching of contempt' against Jews and Judaism and is the most significant Christian document concerning Jewish–Christian relations since Paul in Romans 9–11. It rejected anti-Jewish theological polemic, condemned antisemitism, and replaced them with a renewed vision of the continuing role of the Jewish people in God's plan of salvation.

Passion narratives   Accounts of the suffering, death and burial of Jesus described in the Gospels and in other non-biblical literature. These accounts tend to exaggerate Jewish responsibility for the death of Jesus and to downplay Roman responsibility. They have been problematic and harmful through the centuries in Jewish–Christian relations.

Pharisees   One of several Jewish groups from the late Hellenistic and early Roman periods. The caricature of the Pharisees as equating with hypocritical and legalistic behaviour has resulted in much misunderstanding. In the New Testament they are the main rivals of Jesus although the level of overlap and coherence between the teachings of Jesus and the Pharisees probably outweighs the areas of difference of opinion.

Pogrom   A Russian word meaning 'devastation', denoting attacks on Jews, particularly in the late nineteenth and early twentieth centuries. Pogroms directly foreshadowed the Holocaust, the worst being in Russia in 1881, 1903 and 1905 and in Ukraine during the Russian Civil War (1918–20), leading to millions of Jews emigrating to the West and to Palestine.

Proof-text   An exegetical practice that uses biblical passages to draw conclusions without regard to historical context. A proof-text would be lifted from its location both in time and in the narrative and pressed into the service of solving an unrelated theological or exegetical problem. Used by both Jewish and Christian interpreters.

Redemption   Lat., *redemptio*, Heb., *g'ulah*, describes personal and collective efforts to gain divine deliverance from sin and oppression. Christianity asserts that because humans are born 'in sin', they achieve redemption through belief in the saving power of Jesus. Jews believe redemption requires the observance of God's commandments (*mitzvoth*).

Religio licita   Lit. 'permitted religion', refers to Roman tolerance of Judaism because of respect for its antiquity. The Romans recognised Christianity as a new sect that was not subject to legal protection because it was not an *ethnos* and lacked ancestral pedigree. This changed with the conversion of the Emperor Constantine to Christianity in 312.

Remnant theology   Proposes the continuity between the Hebrew Scriptures and the New Testament, notably the ongoing election of the Jewish people. Based on Romans 9–11, its origins can be traced back to the desire of seventeenth-century English Puritans to study the Scriptures in their original languages.

Renaissance   Denotes a revival of culture in the fourteenth and fifteenth centuries and a renewed Christian interest in Hebrew. The Renaissance enabled Christians to appreciate Jewish mystical and exegetical traditions.

Replacement theology   Refers to the traditional Christian teaching that with the coming of Jesus Christ the Church has taken the place of the Jewish people as God's elect community. Equivalent to supersessionism, it implies the abrogation of God's covenant with Jews.

Rhineland Synod (1980)   The statement of the Synod of the Evangelical Church in the Rhineland was the first of a German Protestant church to recognise the theological importance of relations with Jews. It assumes that Christians are dependent on Jews for the development of Christian faith and need Jewish partners.

Salvation   Heb., *yeshuah*, meaning 'divine deliverance', associated with the need for deliverance from sickness, captivity and exile. Christians modified the term to describe the work of God in Christ, made possible by the life, death and resurrection of Jesus.

Sanhedrin   A Hebraicised form of the Gk *sunēdrion* (lit., 'sitting together'), Second Temple Judaism's legislative and judicial council in Jerusalem is vilified by the early Church as complicit in the death of Jesus and persecution of his followers; the Rabbis praised it; Josephus mentions it in connection with the death of James, the brother of Jesus.

Septuagint (LXX)   Applied to the whole of the Old Testament in Gk, including the Apocryphal books, it holds a special place in the Church as the version of the Bible quoted in the New Testament and used by many church fathers.

Shekhinah   The Shekhinah, Hebrew for 'divine presence', originated with God's glory 'dwelling' over the tabernacle (Exod. 40:35) and came to be associated with the feminine aspect of God and continuity.

Shittuf Heb. meaning 'partnership' or 'association' of an additional power with God and used in Orthodox Judaism to describe non-Jewish religions, especially Christianity and Islam. It is applied to religions not considered idolatrous but viewed as combining elements of Judaism and paganism, resulting in the watering-down of monotheism.

Shoah Heb. meaning 'total destruction', biblical in origin, and used to describe the Holocaust. In English, it is used as an alternative to 'Holocaust' which, also biblical in origin, is the Gk translation of the Heb. *olah*, meaning 'whole burnt offering'.

Sicut Judeis Latin name of a Papal Bull, first promulgated by Pope Callixtus II in the twelfth century and aimed to protect Jews in response to the increasing Christian violence that characterised the First Crusade.

Son of God In Judaism, 'son of God' is used to refer to either the people of Israel or the king and is associated with election and obedience, often with a commission to accomplish a task. In Christianity, 'Son of God' is a title for Jesus, expressing his divinity and special relationship with God.

'Suffering servant' Figure appearing in Isaiah, esp. 52:13–53:12, and subject to debate regarding its identity. The servant has been identified as the prophet himself; a contemporary of the prophet; the people of Israel; or the Messiah. For Christians, it applies to Jesus as the Christ while most Jewish commentators insist that the servant is the people of Israel.

Talmud Heb., lit. 'Teaching', refers to the most important rabbinic works. The Jerusalem Talmud (sometimes also called the Palestinian Talmud) dates from late fourth century and the Babylonian from the fifth. It has long been at the centre of controversy and its references to Christianity, although sparse, are polemical. In the Middle Ages, Christian accusations against the Talmud resulted in hundreds of copies being burnt (e.g., Paris, 1240).

Targum Jewish translation of the Hebrew Bible into Aramaic, dating from the first to the eighth centuries.

Testimonia Refers to collections of primarily biblical quotations, organised around common themes. They were used in Judaism and in the early Church as proof-texts in order to support certain theological viewpoints.

Toledot Yeshu Heb., lit. 'family history of Jesus', the first extant Jewish polemical anti-Christian tract, dated from the sixth to the tenth century.

Torah Heb., lit. 'teaching', 'instruction', often translated as 'law'. Traditionally misunderstood by Christian scholars as solely a collection of laws, it is a common link between Judaism and Christianity. Torah can be used to describe the Five Books of Moses (Written Torah) or in its broadest sense is equated with the whole body of Jewish teaching and law (Oral Torah).

Trial of Jesus   The events that led to Jesus' death have fuelled hostility against Jews as 'Christ-killers'. In general, the Gospels tend to exaggerate the responsibility of the Jewish leaders in Jesus' death and to exculpate Pilate and the Romans. They record contradictory traditions about different 'trials' convened to judge Jesus, one Jewish and another Roman.

Typology   Like its cousin allegory, typology is a form of non-literal or figurative reading of the Bible, used by Christian and Jewish commentators in the light of either Christian faith in Jesus or the new reality facing Judaism after the destruction of the Temple (70 CE).

Usury   Refers to the taking of interest beyond the principal of the loan, prohibited by the early Church. Jews were excluded from many occupations and encouraged to engage in financial services. Although moneylending at interest was a necessary economic reality, it became a byword for Jewish evil. The image of the Jew as usurer was used in the antisemitic publications of the Nazis and Soviets.

Vatican II   The Second Vatican Council (1962–5) marked a turning point in the history of Jewish–Christian relations, particularly with the promulgation of *Nostra Aetate* (October 1965), the council's declaration on interfaith relations.

Virgin birth   The Christian belief that Christ was born of a virgin became central to Christian theology, underpinning the belief that Jesus was both God and Man. This was also a claim that met the most visceral rejection from Jews.

Vulgate   Jerome's translation of the Bible into Latin, known as the Vulgate, owing to its 'common' (i.e., widespread) use in the Latin church. Jerome sought to return to the *hebraica veritas* ('the Hebrew truth') by translating the Old Testament from the Hebrew rather than from the Greek Septuagint.

Yellow badge   From medieval times Jews were often required to wear badges to distinguish them from Christians, articulated at Lateran Council IV in 1215. During the Holocaust the Nazis enforced the wearing of a yellow star of David.

Zionism   Biblical in origin, modern political Zionism began in the nineteenth century, seeking to return Jews to Zion (Jerusalem) and establish a national home in Palestine. After the Holocaust, Zionism became a pre-eminent part of Jewish identity, even though Jews argue over its place in history and its future course. Christians are also divided, some deeply critical, others supporting Israel, sometimes known as 'Christian Zionists'.

Index